INSIGHT SALES

(RETAIL)

GET SMARTER.

GET THE S.P.I.C.E³

GARY R. FORD MBA, PhD

IN CONSULTATION WITH BERNIE SPAK

Insight Sales (retail)

Get Smarter. Get The S.P.I.C.E³

Published by Insight Publishers

Address: Thorsby, Alberta, Canada

Website: www.garyrford.ca/insight

Edited, designed and typeset by the Author

Printed in the United States of America or Canada

ISBN: 978-0-9939737-1-0

Cover Image by Kelly Vanderbeek
beginningsbykelly.com

DEDICATION

Dedicated to all salespeople who want to achieve greater sales performance by selling with integrity and pursuing the goal of enhancing customer success.

TABLE OF CONTENTS

PREFACE

Have you ever wondered why in every sales team a few sales people are so much more successful – selling two, three and even four times as much as their peers? Well I have, and that sent me on a mission to discover what it was that high performers were doing that less successful sales people weren't doing.

- I interviewed sales people that would answer my two key questions – "How do you sell?" and "How is what you do different from your peers who aren't doing as well?"

- I avidly read books by recognized sales experts on persuasion sales, relationship selling, information selling, consultative sales, SPIN selling, customer centric sales, collaborative selling, exceptional sales, and challenger sales.

- I videotaped sales people in sales role-plays and examined the structure of what they were doing, noted the communication skills they were using, and questioned them to determine the underlying values, beliefs and attitudes that were shaping their behavior.

- I asked customers of our best sales people what they noticed and these customers told me they had gained new insights and truly felt that what these sales people did with them was outstandingly different from what they experienced with any other salesperson they encountered.

- Bernie Spak, a professional sales person with many years of experience in different sales and sales management roles, offered his thoughts and ideas during our conversations, plus demonstrated effective sales behavior in video taped role-plays.

What I discovered about effective selling converged exceedingly well with what I had previously learned in my post-graduate studies in business administration and educational psychology where I focused on learning how to be an effective change agent. Change agents help people and organizations to undergo change.

What I discovered concurred with my own practical experiences as a salesperson, psychologist, sales manager, business owner, and adult educator. Many of the principles, structural approaches, values and skills appropriate for effective change agents are the principles, structural approaches, values and skills appropriate for effective selling. Buying is about change.

This book presents what emerged from this convergence – an organized sequence of sales steps, and a clear delineation of the skills to use at each step. We tested this "GET SMARTER" sales approach by training others. Newly trained salespeople experienced strong performance improvement when they put these ideas, skills, and processes into practice with their own customers.

This is your opportunity to discover what emerged.

INTRODUCTION

In our experience, too many retail salespeople are hired by managers desperate to fill a position and then immediately placed on the sales floor with too little preparation and training. As a result customers have lost faith in retail salespeople. This book was written with the goal of bringing skill and professionalism back into retail sales.

If you are a retail salesperson, a salesperson working in any sales environment where customers come to you, or if you are about to become one, then this book is for you. If you are a retail sales manager that needs a sales process to teach to sales team members, this book is also for you. This guide shows the sales approach and skills used by the best salespeople in today's market place, those who succeed and excel whether the economy is hot or cold.

What you are about to read will challenge the assumptions and thoughts you have about selling. You will be confronted with a new approach to selling that deepens your responsibilities as a salesperson while taking you to new heights in sales performance. Ironically, taking on this additional responsibility will make your sales easier once you master this approach. You'll experience more, bigger, and easier sales to increasingly satisfied customers.

Salespeople who rise to the top are those that intuitively challenge their customers to new insights. This is a book addressing the strategy and tactics of Insight Sales where the salesperson uses a listening process that deepens the customer's understanding and delivers new insights about his or her own needs and wants, facilitates willingness to change, and leads to complete solutions not previously considered by the customer.

The material in this book is derived from observing the behavior of a collection of high performance individuals. The best of the best salespeople have something going for them that their more average peers do not. Yet what they do is quite learnable.

Whether you sell cosmetics, cars, clothing, packaged goods or complex technology, this approach works. Whether you sell inexpensive items or luxury products, this approach works. This approach works because it takes the customer to new levels of understanding of what he or she needs, and delivers solutions that reduce the customer's costs and increase his or her benefits.

This approach is not magic but real world selling. You will be presented with a practical step-by-step approach with full explanations for why you would choose to sell in this manner. This approach and the accompanying skills will make you a better salesperson, achieving better sales results by helping your customers to better understand and meet their needs.

WHY PEOPLE BUY

The best salespeople understand how and why people choose to buy, and use a sales approach that best fits the buying process.

We've had an opportunity to observe many sales teams and most have had one or two salespeople that significantly outperformed their peers. A few exceptional salespeople achieve results well above the rest. This seems to be true whether the economy is functioning at a high level or low.

Our economy is just now creeping out of a prolonged economic slow down. Worrying about the economy, customers held on to their money and delayed purchases. They chose the safety of living with their status quo as opposed to spending their dollars with little hope of a positive return on their investment. Many salespeople saw significant declines in their sales results. Many companies floundered as their sales teams failed to produce. In addition, the market place has undergone severe alteration.

- The Internet has become a powerful tool for putting information in the hands of the customer who is now able to access extensive information about products and services ranging from features and specifications to customer reviews.

- Business practices have arisen to take advantage of online selling thereby driving costs out of the acquisition process.

- Price has become a much more significant factor influencing the customer's buying decisions.

- More and more competition has turned most products into commodities with only minor differentiations between them.

- Retail consumers have turned either to the big box wholesalers with no salespeople and guaranteed lowest prices, or to online suppliers where purchases can be made with the click of a mouse.

- It's now possible to buy virtually anything without talking to a salesperson.

Paradoxically, in such an environment, the role of the successful salesperson is even more paramount. The customer's needs have become more complex. The producer needs a knowledgeable and skilled salesperson to help the customer discover how these complex needs can be resolved at levels higher than the customer expects. A salesperson is needed to deliver complex solutions to real problems to willing customers who have higher expectations.

Often however, salespeople are unwelcome. In general, many customers have come to believe that most salespeople add little to no value to the buying process. Having encountered salespeople who failed to really attend to our needs, who made outrageous claims about the superiority of the products and services being sold, and who moved on to the next customer without another thought given to whether or not our purchases contributed to our personal success, we've become jaded consumers.

Most particularly, old sales models such as persuasion, information and relationship selling no longer work as they once did:

PERSUASION SELLING

The salesperson's focus is on getting immediate sales. First contact with a customer involves "qualifying" that customer as someone who is ready to buy now. The salesperson wants the customer to buy his or her products now so that the salesperson can move on to sell to the next consumer.

The salesperson persuades the customer to buy what the salesperson has to sell without a real focus on customer needs. Often, deals are offered or prices and terms are negotiated so the customer feels an urgency to buy. The salesperson does most of the talking, arguing the benefits and advantages of his or her products.

When the customer talks, it is often to express resistance to the persuasion offered by the salesperson. The salesperson typically uses manipulative sales techniques in an attempt to overcome the objections. However, in this economy, customers are increasingly immune to the pressure the persuasive salesperson tries to create. Customers have so much choice as to where to buy.

INFORMATION SELLING

In this approach, the focus is on what the salesperson believes is the customer's need for accurate information about products and their features. The salesperson focuses on products and services, with an emphasis on explaining features and benefits.

The salesperson expends little effort getting to know the customer. The urgency the salesperson feels is to give the information clearly and quickly so the customer can make an informed decision. The salesperson educates the customer about products by sharing his or her product expertise. The customer is frequently given information to take out of the store to facilitate later decision-making.

However, the informed customer may be no more motivated to buy than before gaining the product knowledge, particularly because there is no anticipation of relevant gain. The salesperson typically does not make any effort to specifically relate the products and services to the unique problems and needs of the customer. However, the newly informed customer is now better prepared to shop around in search of the best price.

RELATIONSHIP SELLING

The focus is on the salesperson's need to get into a relationship with the customer. The salesperson frequently visits with his or her customers, engages in friendly conversations, makes the customer feel special, and sometimes provides gifts. This is all done with the goal of building customer loyalty. This is justified as low pressure selling.

Talking in such a sales interaction tends to be equally shared, social in nature, and too seldom about the customer's problems and needs. The salesperson wants to win sales but believes that he or she must first build a good relationship with the customer. The salesperson doesn't focus all that much on the unique problems and customer needs that could be resolved with solutions provided by the salesperson.

Even though relationships exist, customers either don't buy or turn to the lowest priced provider just to save money or to sustain their own ability to compete.

This general inadequacy of most sales approaches even extends to what has been the recommended selling model for the past thirty years.

CONSULTATIVE SELLING

The focus is on discovery of the customer's current needs then providing what the salesperson has to sell as a solution to satisfy those needs. The salesperson asks questions of the customer about the problems he or she is experiencing and makes recommendations that solve those problems. The salesperson may ask the customer to consider the known costs, then show the customer how the solution can remove those costs.

Too often, this approach depends upon the customer having a prior understanding of his or her problems and the costs of those problems. Typically, the salesperson assumes the customer knows he or she needs to find a solution. The salesperson then presents solutions that address the customer's known problems.

In today's economy where the customer has broad access to expertise and information, there is little need to look for a consultant who is a salesperson with a fixed agenda to sell his or her solutions to known problems. Knowing his or her own needs, the customer can identify the solutions on his or her own and find the lowest cost supplier.

Customers need something more from salespeople than known solutions to known problems. They need help discovering what they really need, how important it is to solve their problems, and what could ultimately be achieved.

Working from one of these or a hybrid of these traditional sales methods, poor and average salespeople generally floundered in the stagnant market place. Unable to persuade customers to buy if they couldn't offer the lowest price, being insignificant as an information source in comparison to information offered on-line, offering less than relevant relationships, and trying to offer solutions and expertise to clients who have their own knowledge of problems and solutions, most salespeople experienced diminished results.

However, in every industry there have been a few exceptional salespeople for whom sales did not falter, and for whom results even increased as they helped their customers to discover new ways to achieve success. We wondered what this difference in performance was about and set out to interview, observe and work with high performers to learn their secrets.

We've discovered that these salespeople make themselves indispensable to their clients by delivering something more than products and services. Positive sales results have been achieved by salespeople who skillfully practice an approach that helps their customers to uncover and better understand their real problems and to find the complex solutions that truly make a difference to customer success. We call this Insight Selling.

INSIGHT SELLING

This approach is also consultative in nature. However, the focus is on a deeper discovery of the customer's real and full set of needs. The salesperson helps the customer to achieve deeper insights about the nature of how he or she falls short of what could be achieved.

The salesperson's conversation with each customer challenges and reframes the customer's understanding of his or her own situation, problems, costs, constraints, and opportunities. Before any product, service or solution is offered, the salesperson creates value by delivering new insights.

The salesperson then provides a complete solution to satisfy those needs. Such solutions reduce costs the customer might not even have realized he or she had, increase benefits beyond what was expected, and make entirely new outcomes possible. The salesperson expands understanding and makes recommendations that increase customer success.

This insight approach leads to a sale because the customer realizes it is better to make the purchase, apply the new solution, and achieve previously unanticipated but better results, than it is to do nothing. The salesperson presents a solution that has clear value to the customer.

The insight process is part of that value. The customer gains insight about his or her own needs and opportunities, only by working with that salesperson. These customers have new insights, set higher goals, make larger purchases, and achieve greater success.

Buying something new is about making a change. The best salespeople appear to have an intuitive, if not conscious understanding of what it takes to inspire a person to make a significant change in behavior. The best salespeople understand how and why people choose to buy, and use a sales approach that best fits the buying process.

This knowledge gives the salesperson the ability to lead his or her clients to deeper understanding, and to insights that elevate the customer's expectations. These insights increase the salesperson's value.

This knowledge of what it takes to lead another person to change is quite learnable. Our economy depends on more and more salespeople developing a better understanding of the psychology of change and the process of creating readiness to buy.

READINESS FOR CHANGE

Buying is about making a change. Customers, whether individuals, couples, families or small businesses, appear in retail stores to buy something they hope will achieve some new result and change their status quo for the better. However, being ready to buy requires a willingness to give up the status quo.

Readiness For Change

		State	Common Emotions	Intentions
GREEN	GO Zone	Ready for Change	Eagerness, Excitement, Expectations,	We know what we can do, so let's do it.
YELLOW	WAIT Zone	Accepting Status Quo	Calm, Comfortable, Accepting	Let's just stay the same.
RED	STOP Zone	Stuck and Pained	Loss, Frustration, Irritation, Anxiousness	We really need to do something but can't.

Our status quo is the existing state or condition, the way things are now. Within our status quo, there are reasons for change but we tend to ignore or deny them. For the most part, we tend to be programmed to keep things the same, predictable, safe. So how do people get ready for change?

Readiness for change is based on three different emotional states. A person can be in a state of high readiness for change (*the green "GO" zone*), or in a state that is simple acceptance of his or her current situation (*the yellow "WAIT" zone*), or in a state where he or she feels stuck and pained in some particular way (*the red "STOP" zone*). This is true for individuals, couples, families and organizations.

It's safe to say there are always problems within a given status quo – most are small, but potentially some are big. However, to maintain a state of comfort (*the "WAIT" zone*), we have the capacity to subconsciously deny either the existence or consequence of the problems. It's as if our brain functions to keep us in a state of equilibrium by denying or covering over any reasons to change. It's as if we unconsciously think to ourselves, "This is just the way things are."

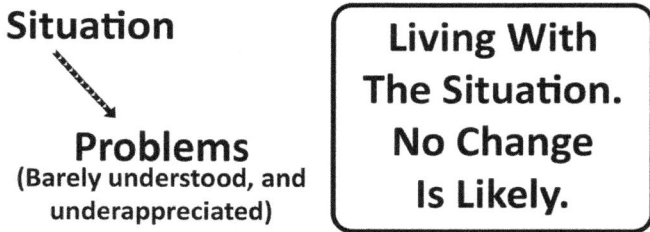

Situation
↘
Problems
(Barely understood, and underappreciated)

Living With The Situation. No Change Is Likely.

Problems have symptoms, many of which we ignore. In some cases, we might acknowledge some minor symptoms while ignoring major ones. It's as if the minor symptoms distract us, and we give ourselves permission to think they're acceptable so we have no reason to change.

This ability is so inherent that we can accept serious dysfunctional symptoms as just normal. In paying attention to only some of our symptoms, we often fail to interpret what our problems really are. Too often, we think we have one problem when we actually have another.

If we allow awareness of the real problem to surface, it's likely we will downplay the significance of the problem – "Yes, it can be frustrating when that happens, but it's no big deal." To minimize the significance of our problems, we ignore the consequences of those problems, or treat the costs of the problems as inconsequential. By doing so, we minimize our motivation to make any sort of change.

If directed to explore the implications of those problems, we confront the costs and the lost benefits – both tangible and intangible.

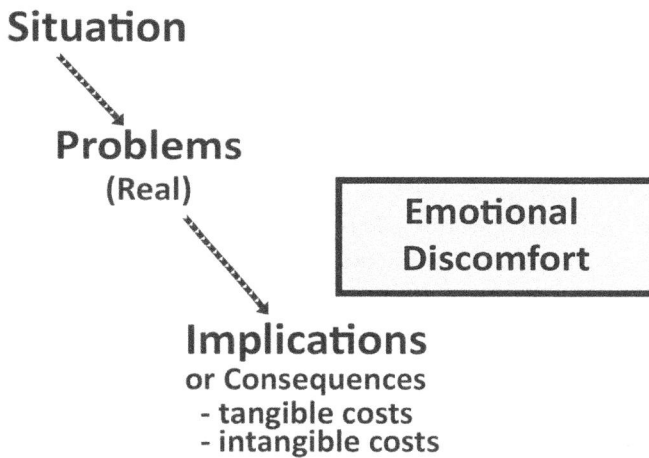

Situation

Problems
(Real)

Emotional Discomfort

Implications
or Consequences
- tangible costs
- intangible costs

Tangible costs include what we currently pay to do what we do. For an individual, tangible costs could be monthly or repetitive expenses, costs of repairs, rent, supplies or whatever the person pays now. In a business setting, this might be extra costs because our business processes aren't efficient, maintenance costs, actual business lost to competitors, costs of delayed work if we don't have high performance solutions in place, and business lost because we don't have the ability to do what customers want.

Intangible Costs are those costs that may be more emotional than dollar based, or dollar based costs where it is hard to accurately measure the financial implications. For an individual, this could be a lingering want for something better, recognizing that one isn't as successful as he or she wants, living in a demotivated or depressed state, alienation from loved ones, a sense some meaning in life is missing, or feelings of loneliness, sadness, pent up anger, etc. In a business setting, these might include lower morale, a competitive disadvantage, personal discomforts for the business owners or their personnel, alienation of workers, lower reputation, or lost business opportunities that hadn't even been considered as residing within the company's business model.

Looking from another perspective, when we live within our status quo, intangible benefits that could be present may instead be absent. For an individual, intangible benefits might include a heightened sense of purpose, new opportunities, a greater feeling of satisfaction, or an excitement about what can be achieved. In a business environment, personnel might be more enthusiastic about their work if the problems were no longer getting in the way. The business might be better prepared to respond to new demands from clients. The company's clients might better perceive the business as a leader in their field.

If the problem persists, such a person or business would miss out on these benefits. The simple insight that things could be better precipitates awareness of the costs of not changing, of doing nothing new.

If people don't acknowledge and truly experience these tangible and intangible costs, they're likely to prefer the status quo over change. However, when a person focuses on the implications or consequences of the problems, he or she begins to realize there is an irritation or some form of negative feeling.

Realizing how much the status quo actually costs can induce some degree of emotional discomfort, becoming a catalyst for change. This could be experienced as disappointment, irritation, frustration, exasperation, even the more intense emotional pain of loss, regret, and grief; or just simply a state of wanting better results.

Change is an emotional process, often involving some degree of discomfort. This is why people generally avoid change. However, once these emotions are triggered by insight as to how serious the problems really are, how much they actually cost, people want to change. When the person can't ignore the costs any longer, they itch for change. He or she likely won't change yet, but will begin to think seriously about needing something different.

Even though people know they have problems with significant consequences, they often don't change because they feel constrained, prevented in some way from making things better. They become aware of the constraints that block their ability to make that change.

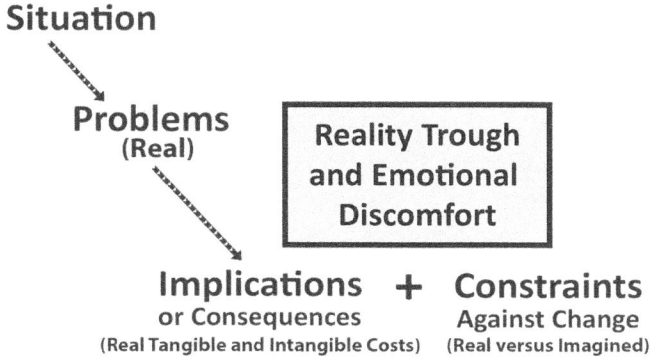

Situation

Problems
(Real)

Reality Trough and Emotional Discomfort

Implications **+** **Constraints**
or Consequences   Against Change
(Real Tangible and Intangible Costs)   (Real versus Imagined)

This results in discouragement, frustrations, perhaps hopelessness and despair if the costs are high and the roadblocks are seen as insurmountable (*being in the "STOP" or stuck zone*). We call this awareness of the costs and constraints, the "Reality Trough" – the place where a person realizes the low point of his or her current situation.

Some of these constraints will be real. As such, change is only possible if a solution overcomes or removes the constraint. However, we also tend to imagine constraints. For example, these imaginary roadblocks could be a perceived lack of resources, even though we may have what it will take to make the change. Or the imagined roadblocks could be arbitrary rules we somehow impose on ourselves, even though there is no other person or force putting these rules in place. Alternatively, we might feel blocked because we have a belief we aren't physically or emotionally capable of effectively making the change despite evidence to the contrary.

Once perceived constraints are really explored, people become more aware of which are real and which are imagined. Sometimes, just thinking about their excuses, while facing the real costs of not changing, will cause people to realize the reasons aren't limiting after all. Upon this realization, the imagined constraints can be set aside.

Once a person does this, the solution only has to overcome the real constraints.

Instead of denial, the person confronts the reality of his or her own situation and experiences the related emotions. In this state, a person is likely to be on the lookout for how things could be made better. Once a person actually wonders how things can get better, new expectations begin to emerge.

He or she starts to form minimal expectations as to what change would have to deliver. These minimal expectations are seldom much of a reach beyond what he or she already has and seldom involve any significant form of perceptual shift. In its simplest form, the person may wonder if a small change would accomplish enough gain to be worth undergoing. This person sets his or her goals relatively low.

However, if this person dwells on what he or she would **really** like to achieve and manages to reframe his or her thinking around new higher-order wants and desires then excitement grows. With new insights about the additional results that could be achieved, the person becomes eager for change.

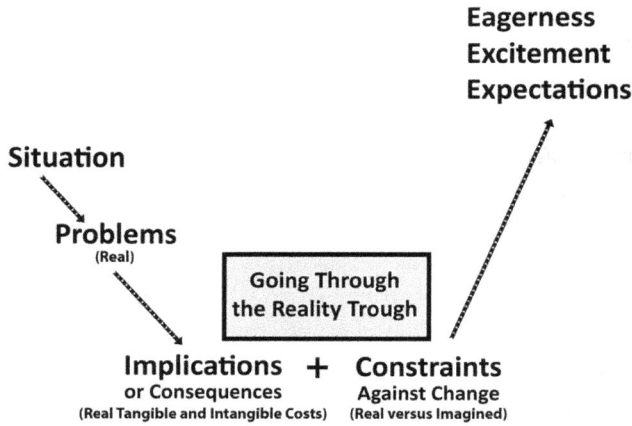

Eagerness
Excitement
Expectations

Situation

Problems
(Real)

Going Through the Reality Trough

Implications **+** **Constraints**
or Consequences   Against Change
(Real Tangible and Intangible Costs)   (Real versus Imagined)

It's imperative that the much better results appear achievable. The person may initially be hesitant to reframe his or her thinking into a desire for greater results, believing the better results aren't achievable. He or she may even second-guess his or her right to hold such desires. But if an individual can come to think the higher order goal is achievable, he or she will make a dramatic paradigm shift accompanied by growing excitement. He or she will no longer want to settle for what he or she has.

From this excitement, the person moves to an eagerness to find a way to make things better. Having defined what he or she really hopes to have, versus what he or she has, readiness for change has been achieved. In thinking about the gain to be experienced by solving the problem, attention shifts and the person will search for a true and powerful solution. Instead of wanting to stay the same, this person really wants to achieve a different and better outcome.

At this point, the person is much more likely to go after what he or she really wants. He or she may do this in small ways, like just listening to whatever relevant information comes into his or her world, or in big ways such as initiating a search for a truly valuable solution.

This exploration of the real costs of the problems, the discovery of the real constraints, and consideration of what could ideally be achieved, involves going through the Reality Trough to reach an eager, excited state of readiness for change. We call this insight process, the S.P.I.C.E^3 Sequence:

- **S**ituation or status quo,

- **P**roblems,

- **I**mplications of those problems,

- **C**onstraints, and

- **E**xpectations, **E**xcitement and **E**agerness.

When people gain insight as they explore their own S.P.I.C.E^3, they're increasingly ready to undergo change. They have a clear hope things can get better, and a desire to achieve that outcome.

READINESS TO BUY

When we blend the Readiness to Change model with the S.P.I.C.E^3 Sequence, we can better understand what it takes for people to get ready to buy.

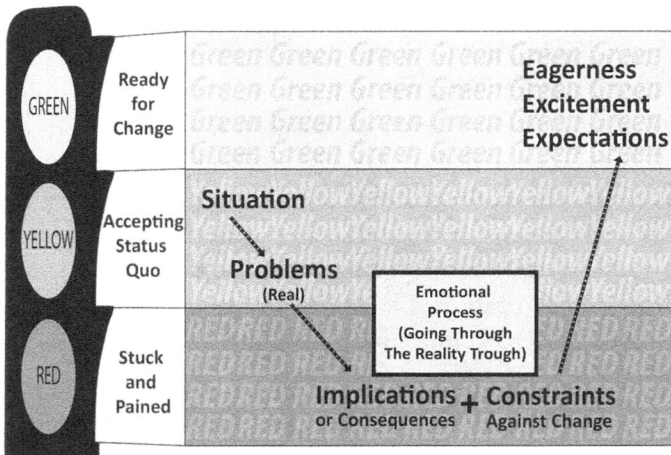

An individual has to move from the comfort of his or her status quo, travel through the Reality Trough to confront the implications of staying the same, bump up against what he or she believes to be roadblocks, and then consider what could be gained if a change is made. Buying occurs once the person or organization clearly sees a solution to his or her real problems. People buy when in the green "GO" zone.

Selling is all about helping the customer move into the green "GO" zone. Because of a natural tendency to deny problems and their costs, the salesperson must help the customer to bring the Reality Trough into full awareness. This is an insight-oriented approach.

As a salesperson, you help the customer discover an urgency to give up the old to acquire something new. Giving up the familiar for something new has tangible costs as well as emotional costs. The person experiencing these costs and emotions must come to believe the new state, and the gain to be had, is worth the price to be paid.

If an insight-oriented salesperson helps a customer to move through these emotional change processes, then that salesperson becomes someone the customer wants to work with again. This truly differentiates the salesperson from his or her competitors.

THE SALESPERSON'S ROLE

By asking the right questions and leading the conversation with active listening skills, you steer the customer's attention to readiness for change. You want to hear the customer go from,

"Things are okay the way they are."

to

"Well, I'm frustrated by… but I can live with it."

through

"I guess the costs are bigger than I thought."

and

"I can't do anything because…."

to

"You mean things really could be better?

to

"Wow! The benefits would be….".

and finally to

"How do I do this?"

If you can do this with every customer, you're a highly skilled salesperson. If not, you want to learn how.

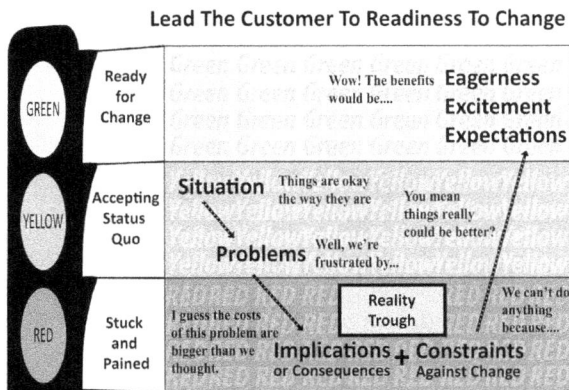

Learn Your Customer's S.P.I.C.E[3]

If you have a solution to provide, this conversation will result in the sale of a complete solution. The customer will know what you've done and will value your participation. The customer will want to do this again in the future, particularly once he or she has realized all of the benefits derived from implementing your new solution. Over time, this will lead to a new status quo, one that has new problems for you to solve.

CUSTOMER TYPES

On the retail sales floor, you will likely encounter customers in different states of readiness for change, and you will need to feel comfortable exploring the S.P.I.C.E^3 with each of them.

EAGER CUSTOMERS

Some customers will be in your store, eager to find something they think they need to buy. This type of customer is looking to buy something during this visit. However, you have to be careful when helping this customer that you don't get seduced into believing that he or she has a clear and full awareness of his or her own S.P.I.C.E^3.

First off, don't assume this eager customer knows he or she has a problem and knows what that problem really is. On the other hand, this customer may know exactly what problems he or she is trying to solve, but may not yet fully appreciate what a solution has to deliver in terms of improved results. There may not be sufficient understanding of the potential benefits he or she wants to achieve.

In turn, the customer may not have felt the full extent of the implications of his or her problems and not yet appreciate how bad things are. This will mean a lower incentive to buy an optimum solution. Break free of any assumption that you don't have to take time to learn this eager customer's S.P.I.C.E^3. You still need to help this customer fully appreciate the full extent of his or her needs.

CURIOUS CUSTOMERS

Some customers will be in your store just because they want to see what's new. This doesn't mean that they are motivated to buy now, or that they even recognize that problems exist within their status quo. Being curious doesn't mean readiness to change. You will need to move this customer type through the Reality Trough within his or her S.P.I.C.E^3 to bring about a shift from being a window shopper to a ready buyer.

DISINTERESTED CUSTOMERS

Given that customers come to you, you may not expect to encounter disinterested customers, but it is likely that you will. Somehow, they find their way into stores just to look. These customers strongly hold a belief things are okay the way they are. A person in this state may agree he or she has problems within the status quo, but doesn't consciously experience much pain. If a customer doesn't experience any pain or see how to derive any benefits from change, he or she will prefer to stay the same and not change. Many salespeople find these customers hard to sell to because there is no perceived need for what the salesperson is selling.

There's just not enough excitement for change. The value of change is believed to be too small. This customer chooses to live by the axiom, "The devil you know." However, below their level of awareness, such customers do have real problems and needs, and could potentially benefit from your solutions. It may be their unconscious mind that gets them into your store. The real needs must be brought into conscious awareness.

Customer That Prefers The Status Quo

It takes a skilled salesperson to get this disinterested customer to fully examine his or her S.P.I.C.E^3, to uncover the true problems and the real consequences of staying the same, of not changing, of not buying a solution. You must facilitate insight within the disinterested customer and help him or her to develop a heightened awareness of the real costs and degree of actual pain.

DISCOURAGED CUSTOMERS – WITH LOW HOPE FOR GAIN

In some cases, a customer will engage in shopping because he or she knows the real costs and feels the true degree of pain within his or her status quo. Likely, he or she has some thoughts about fixing the problem but does not yet believe he or she could make the situation any better. This customer likely sees certain constraints in his or her way and doesn't have a clear sense of how things could get any better.

Lacking any knowledge of what better results could be achieved, there is no vision of a better way to be. This person is likely going to feel very frustrated and lack hope things can get better. He or she will feel stuck in the painful "STOP" zone.

Wants Change Badly But Doesn't Yet See Any
Potential Gain From A Change

The customer may even be bitchy and angry, and may even direct that at you with a refusal to accept your help. This person wants change badly, but doesn't yet see the possibility of change. In this place, the customer is stuck in his or her current way of looking at the world. This customer has unconscious blinders on thereby preventing a new perception of the better way things could be.

As the salesperson, it would be your job to lead the customer to new ways of thinking about what could be achieved. It is up to you to get past any barriers the customer might put in your way, and induce an insight in the customer about what could really be achieved if the right solution was applied. You must elevate the customer's expectations.

Instead of telling the customer what could be achieved, it is the insight-oriented salesperson's job to help the customer ponder what benefits could be experienced if the problem(s) could be solved. Steer the customer's attention to wondering what he or she could accomplish if an ideal solution exists.

If you do this, a shift in perception is brought about. Instead of dwelling on what can't be achieved, the customer is inspired to consider new results. Instead of hopeless thinking, the customer shifts to hopeful thoughts.

From there, the customer can imagine what would be gained if he or she could find the right solution. The customer becomes excited about those benefits, and eager to make a change. By elevating the customer's expectations, and excitement about potential benefits, the salesperson will have a customer eagerly anticipating the salesperson's recommendation.

RESISTANT CUSTOMERS

It's less likely that resistant customers will appear in your stores but it can happen. A customer might know he or she needs something but drop into your store only to compare what you have before going to buy at one of your competitors. This customer might talk to you only to get information that he or she can use to shop elsewhere. For some reason, such a customer might have a prejudice against your store.

A skilled salesperson will engage this customer, answer questions and at the same time, trigger a deeper conversation that allows mutual exploration of the customer's S.P.I.C.E[3]. This discussion could deliver new insights for the customer and lead to a modification of his or her prejudice against doing business with this salesperson. This process has value to the customer and might displace any loyalty he or she has to the competitor. As you will encounter such resistant customers, you need to build the skills for bringing about such conversations.

* * *

To be effective, you need to be able to get into S.P.I.C.E^3 conversations with each of these customer types. When you do, you will ultimately be selling to customers eager to buy the solutions you sell. You must be the catalyst that shifts each customer type to a readiness to buy.

THE REALITY TROUGH

To bring about changes in customers who are prematurely eager to buy; those who are just curious; disinterested, or resistant customers; or those with low hope for anything being better than what they currently experience; take the customer into and through his or her Reality Trough.

As a salesperson, you actually have to work to deepen the trough. If a customer doesn't experience the emotional discomfort because of his or her denial, you must help the customer rise out of denial into a greater awareness of his or her needs.

When discussing the implications of the customer's problems, there can be what most people consider to be negative feelings. These feelings are a consequence of expanded awareness and just a natural element of realizing the full costs of the status quo. You should not avoid the surfacing of these feelings. The more intensely the customer examines these costs, and the more extensive they are, the higher the customer's motivation will be to find a solution to those problems.

Getting the sale will be so much easier when the customer has moved through a deep Reality Trough. He or she will be much more excited about buying when new insights emerge – insights about the true nature of his or her situation, about the real problems, the full extent of the costs of not making a change, what really stops progress, and what better results could be achieved instead. The customer will be ready because he or she now acknowledges the need for a solution, and sooner rather than later.

If you think surfacing customer feelings isn't the job of a salesperson, you'll miss opportunities to help your customers. If you avoid the Reality Trough, you will also miss opportunities to sell complex solutions for complex problems. You will lose sales, customers will lose opportunities for greater success, and your employer will suffer your lower performance.

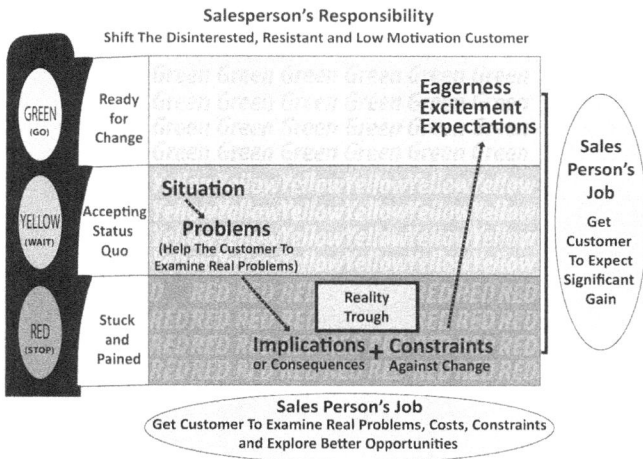

Salesperson's Responsibility
Shift The Disinterested, Resistant and Low Motivation Customer

GREEN (GO)	Ready for Change		**Eagerness Excitement Expectations**
YELLOW (WAIT)	Accepting Status Quo	**Situation** **Problems** (Help The Customer To Examine Real Problems)	
RED (STOP)	Stuck and Pained	Reality Trough **Implications + Constraints** or Consequences Against Change	

Sales Person's Job — Get Customer To Expect Significant Gain

Sales Person's Job
Get Customer To Examine Real Problems, Costs, Constraints and Explore Better Opportunities

We're not suggesting your purpose is to induce tears, deep sadness, or pain. Just use the skills known to make it easier for the customer to truly explore and experience the consequences of his or her status quo. For most problems, the feeling will mostly be surprise at what the customer's situation actually costs. For some, the realization might be more dramatic as he or she discovers that substantial costs have been ignored.

Be willing to let whatever feelings are there rise to the surface of the customer's awareness. Through this insight, the customer will be more aware of his or her need to solve the problem and be much more motivated to change.

For those salespeople who just don't accept the need to explore the Reality Trough with their customers, or where the solution is simple and less costly, or when the customer is already in the Reality Trough and ready to change, we do admit such customers may buy when the conversation just explores their S.E.E. (*situation, expectations, and exciting benefits*). They may buy when they more clearly see what they want to achieve.

However, we think the resulting motivation is not as high as it could be, and may lead the customer to purchase only part of a complete solution or to further shop around. In addition, the salesperson does not fully understand the problems, implications

23

and constraints, and may not recommend the right and complete solution.

The same could be said about the salesperson that is only comfortable exploring the customer's P.E.E. (*problems, expectations, and exciting benefits*). Some exploration of the customer's problems would help the salesperson to identify a workable solution, but the customer's motivation to buy from this particular salesperson will not be all that high. In addition, not understanding the customer's constraints, the salesperson may recommend a solution that will not work.

Little emotional investment is made as both parties continue to deny the Reality Trough. In doing so, they both fail to fully understand the real costs, the real constraints, and the true emotions of the customer's status quo. The customer's readiness to buy specifically what this salesperson recommends, and only from this salesperson, will not be as great as it would be if both participants explored the customer's full S.P.I.C.E^3.

Later in this book, we address the skills for opening up the conversation so the full extent of the Reality Trough can be discovered and discussed. Using such skills, you will be able to help your customers achieve high motivation to change. Your customers will want to buy and implement the best possible solution – one you will provide.

VALUE VERSUS PRICE

A lot of traditional selling revolves around negotiation of price. This is usually because, along with the customer, the salesperson has focused only on product and price. Both the salesperson and the customer are thinking about the products as commodities rather than uniquely configured solutions to real problems. Instead of focusing on the customer's needs (*his or her S.P.I.C.E^3*), the conversation tends to be about products.

The customer knows there are alternative suppliers of similar products and is all too willing to seek out the best-priced provider. This is because the salesperson has not established any particular value in the mind of the buyer for him or herself, the solutions he or she sells, or the company he or she works for.

Buyers, when surveyed, indicate value is actually of higher priority than finding the best price when making their buying decision. They don't just want to buy. They want what they buy to lead to their own improved results. However, when the customer doesn't perceive any difference in value between products and services offered by different competitors, he or she will make the decision based on price.

If the salesperson can establish that he or she is able to provide true value differentiated from what the competitor is offering, the customer will choose value.

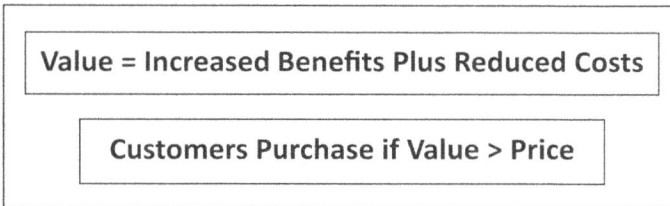

Value = Increased Benefits Plus Reduced Costs

Customers Purchase if Value > Price

Value is the combination of the higher benefits of a new solution plus any reductions in costs when compared to the old way of doing things. When the salesperson uses an insight-oriented sales approach and helps the customer to fully realize his or her S.P.I.C.E[3], the value is more clearly understood.

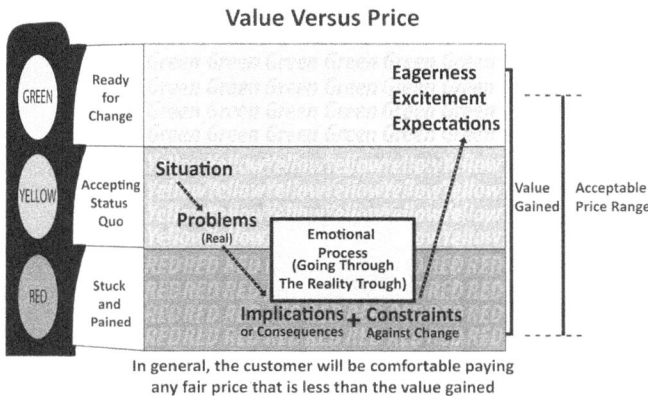

Value Versus Price

In general, the customer will be comfortable paying any fair price that is less than the value gained

If the customer realizes he or she needs a solution, understands his or her current tangible and intangible costs, and is aware a solution exists that will reduce costs and give additional benefits, the customer will pay almost up to the measurable value to be derived from the solution. This is especially true when even more value is added by intangible benefits. The more the total value exceeds the price, the more willing the customer will be to purchase. However, the difference does not have to be high. The customer only needs to be able to see a positive return on his or her investment.

For example, if within the status quo, the tangible and known costs are $500 per month, and a solution will wipe out those costs, plus give the additional benefit of helping the customer to make an extra $300 per month, the customer would conceivably pay anything less than $800 per month for the solution. If paying less, they feel the value is worth the price.

BUYER'S REMORSE

Buyer's remorse occurs when customers regret their purchases and wish to return them. The customer may have felt pressured by a persuasion-oriented salesperson to buy something he or she didn't really want. Alternatively, the customer may have no real need for the item but may have been induced to buy when a skilled information salesperson mesmerized him or her with a razzle-dazzle product demonstration. Or guilt may have induced the customer to buy from the salesperson focused on creating a friendly relationship.

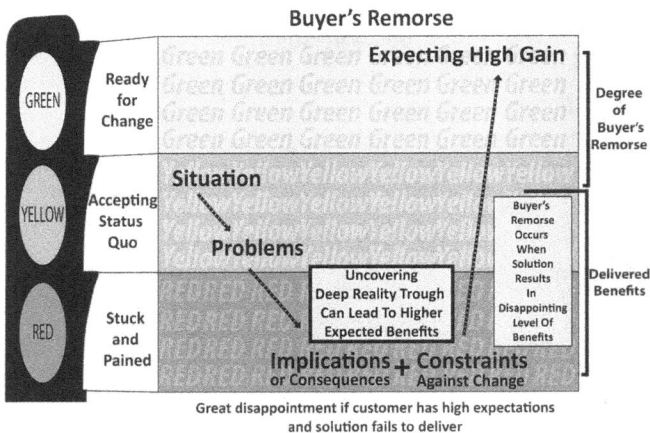

Great disappointment if customer has high expectations and solution fails to deliver

Customers seldom return goods, or have buyer's remorse, when they purchase from a skilled insight-oriented salesperson that takes them through their S.P.I.C.E[3]. The customer is equally involved in the insight process and knows what he or she could gain from a new solution. Having learned the customer's S.P.I.C.E[3], the salesperson can provide the right solution.

However, even if the salesperson learns the customer's full S.P.I.C.E[3], buyer's remorse will happen if the solution doesn't meet all of the customer's expectations, doesn't deliver the benefits that were promised, or fails to produce the anticipated gains.

Once the salesperson has learned the customer's private information and taken the customer through his or her Reality Trough, it is the salesperson's responsibility to only offer a complete solution capable of bringing about the results the customer is expecting. If the salesperson can't do so, then he or she should advise the client that the solution is not yet available; or if the solution does exist and the salesperson is unable to provide that solution, refer the customer to another supplier who has what the customer needs.

If the solution is truly not yet available from either the salesperson or a competitor, the salesperson would make a promise to do everything in his or her power to find the solution. The customer will wait if he or she knows this salesperson will be vigilant about meeting the specific needs and will deliver when the right solution is available. The salesperson should not recommend that the customer buy a less than adequate solution.

For example, there are stories about a real estate agent in California who was very successful in her marketplace. Unlike most real estate salespeople who would take their customers from house to house showing everything in the client's price range, this exceptional salesperson would only show the customer the house that was totally right for him or her. If such a house was not yet on the market, then the agent would say this to the customer, promise to find the right house, search for that house, and once the right house had been located, call the customer to say, "I've found your new home." Based on her reputation, the way she learned about her customer's full set of needs, and the insights achieved during their conversations, customers would wait as long as it took. Her customers didn't want to settle for anything less.

SUMMARY

People are more willing to undergo change, and are more enthusiastic about making buying decisions when helped to mentally organize what they discover about their own S.P.I.C.E³. The customer is more motivated to buy when he or she achieves greater clarity about:

- his or her current <u>situation,</u>

- the <u>problem(s)</u> he or she has in the current situation,

- the <u>implications</u> of those problems – what the problems cost the customer, how much frustration he or she has, and what is the <u>pain</u> of the status quo,

- the <u>constraints</u> or reasons keeping him or her from doing something about this before now, and

- his or her <u>expectations</u> about what a solution would have to achieve, his or her <u>excitements</u> about the extra benefits that could be gained by finding the right solution, and his or her <u>eagerness</u> to get the problem solved.

Understand this process. See it as your responsibility to take your customers through this S.P.I.C.E³ cycle, bring about new insights, and help your customers to get ready for change. Then find the proper solutions for your customers' needs.

YOUR OWN S.P.I.C.E³?

Take a moment and think about yourself. What is your own S.P.I.C.E³ with regard to your sales results?

- What is your current **situation**?

  o Are you selling products or solutions?

  o Are you fully aware of your situation and the resources available to you?

- What **problems or difficulties** do you have when trying to reach your sales and life goals?

  o Are you a peak, average or low performer in your organization?

- Are you able to get all of your customers into conversations where you discover their real problems, the costs of those problems, what is inhibiting their change, and what opportunities they truly want to realize?
- Are you experiencing any of the following:
  - ✔ general frustration with your results,
  - ✔ time spent with customers without getting a sale,
  - ✔ being brushed off by potential customers when you approach them,
  - ✔ surprises when a customer doesn't buy from you when you thought he or she would,
  - ✔ a feeling you work too hard for too little gain,
  - ✔ lost sales to competitors,
  - ✔ customers buying only products at the lowest price,
  - ✔ sales falling short of your quota or assigned targets,
  - ✔ few sales of complex and large solutions, or
  - ✔ uncertainty as to how to proceed with some customers.
- What do your selling problems **cost** you?
  - Are you experiencing any of the following:
    - ✔ lesser income than you aspire to,
    - ✔ a lower reputation as a salesperson than you would like,
    - ✔ lost customers and wasted time,
    - ✔ confrontations by your boss about your performance,
    - ✔ disappointment at home because you aren't producing enough income,
    - ✔ unfulfilled desires for vacations or enhancements to your lifestyle, etc.?

- o If you multiply your average sale by the number of customers that you approached but didn't buy from you, what is the real dollar amount of lost business?
- What **stops you** from improving your own performance?
  - o What constraints do you believe limit your ability to improve your current results?
  - o Which of these roadblocks are real or imagined?
  - o What is truly holding you back?

Are you feeling your own Reality Trough as you consider these questions? If not, why not? Are you involved in denial, or is your success level so high that your status quo has no room for change? Or have we not yet asked the question that takes your attention to your own frustrations? If so, what question should you ask yourself?

- What would you **expect to gain** if you could sell more complex solutions to more clients?
  - o What financial gains could you realize?
  - o How many more customers could you help achieve greater success if you were able to inspire all of them to examine their S.P.I.C.E^3?
  - o What growth in personal satisfaction would you experience if you could help more clients achieve greater success through the solutions you provide?
  - o What benefits would your family realize if you were an even more successful performer in your sales role?
  - o What would happen to your value to your employer if you increased your mastery at selling in both tough and good economic conditions?
  - o What would your world be like if you could double, triple, quadruple your sales by working smarter, not harder?

Are you feeling any increased sense of what is possible for you as a salesperson, any increase in the fire in your belly, any eagerness to develop more sales skills as you consider these questions? If not, what highly desirable benefits have we failed to ask about?

By addressing your own reality, you have the opportunity to seek out ways to improve your own results. We think there is a lot to gain by applying what the best salespeople are doing in your own retail sales work.

GET SMARTER

Use a sales approach that best fits with how and why customers become inspired to buy new solutions.

The insight-oriented salesperson helps the customer find solutions that offer unexpected new opportunities for the customer to succeed. The goal is to regularly solve new customer problems with complete solutions while earning trust, respect, and an ongoing relationship.

The interaction between salesperson and customer is so different from traditional methods of selling, that the insight-oriented salesperson becomes a differentiated aspect of the solution to the customer's problems. We've noticed that in insight-oriented interactions, customers open up and share a lot more information about themselves, their problems and their expectations. More rapport is established and the customer feels more comfortable with the salesperson.

The sales process involves two-way communication emphasizing both information giving and open negotiation, but the customer will be encouraged to do about 70% of the talking. The customer's story is usually much larger than anything seen in persuasion, relationship, information or simple consultative selling approaches, and as a result, sales are usually larger. These sales typically involve complex solutions for complex problems.

As problems are clarified with the salesperson, the customer may initially express surprise by what he or she learns about real needs. However, the customer typically buys what the salesperson recommends. Frequently, the customer will express appreciation because the salesperson has considered all of his or her needs. The salesperson is appreciated for the learning the customer achieves through their shared conversation. Price is seldom brought up as an issue because the customer sees the true value of the solution being proposed.

The best salespeople approach customers with a great deal of confidence they will make a difference in the level of success experienced by their customers. Such salespeople derive confidence from knowing what they are doing. Although the best salespeople have skills that allow them to adapt their own behavior in response to each customer, they also have an organized agenda they use with each client to move through the sales process. As Bernie says, "this agenda allows you to be comfortable in your own skin when meeting with highly successful people."

Specifically, smart salespeople use an approach that includes processes to learn the customer's S.P.I.C.E^3 and specific skills proven to increase sales effectiveness. To help you keep track of where you are in the sales process, we use the acronym "GET SMARTER" for the ten steps in this insight-oriented approach.

	STEP	ACTIVITY
G	Greet	A greeting and approach by the salesperson showing interest in the customer and beginning a conversation.
E	Engage	Continued engagement in conversation allowing relationship building to occur.
T	Take Time To Learn The Customer's Needs (Get the S.P.I.C.E^3)	Getting the customer's S.P.I.C.E^3 during an open discussion of the customer's needs, taking time to actively listen to the customer such that the customer does most of the talking and the salesperson clarifies for understanding (*reaching for deeper insight*).
	Half Time	*Determining the best possible solution, preparing to make the recommendation, and if necessary, rehearsing a summary of the customer's S.P.I.C.E^3 to show full understanding before a recommendation is made.*
S	Show Full Understanding – Summarize The Customer's S.P.I.C.E^3	Before trying to sell anything, showing full understanding by summarizing what has been learned about the customer's needs and expectations, and then asking if you fully understand. Summarizing in the order of the customer's S.P.I.C.E^3, stirring up the feelings of the customer's Reality Trough, so the customer arrives at eagerness to hear/see the solution.

M	Make Your Recommendation	Recommending the complete solution by referring to the benefits the customer is hoping to achieve.
A	Ask How To Proceed	Asking for a decision and initiating a call-to-action by simply asking the customer what he or she thinks should happen next.
R	Reinforce The Customer's Decision	Reinforcing the benefits of the customer's decision and letting the customer know he or she has made a wise choice for specific reasons, re-iterating the specific benefits that matter to the customer.
T	Thank You And After Sale Support, Service and Follow-Up	Thanking the customer for the opportunity to earn his or her business, helping the customer through the purchase transaction, and staying in contact with the customer as part of the on-going relationship.

Use the "GET SMART" steps daily with each of your customers and then on a regular frequency, stop and engage in the following two steps:

E	Evaluate	Assessing the salesperson's performance in three ways - through customer feedback, self-analysis, and measurement of the results clients have realized with the solutions the salesperson provided.
R	Repeat	Returning to the beginning and repeating the insight-oriented selling process with both new and existing clients.

Each of the steps in the "GET SMARTER" approach calls for specific skills addressed in subsequent chapters. Learn the specific skills that facilitate effective insight-oriented selling. We're fairly confident this material will challenge you to make changes in how you approach and deal with your customers.

We invite you to use this list of steps and the related skills because we strongly believe that the value of implementing this model will far exceed the price you have to pay in learning something new. Each sale will be larger because you will be selling complete solutions. Sales will get easier as you gain skill, and as your customers realize the value you deliver.

If you sell cosmetics, cell phones, clothing, jewelry, hardware supplies, drapes, or electronics in a retail store, you might wonder if this applies to you. But it doesn't matter what you sell in the retail environment. These principles, this approach and these skills can all enhance your success as a salesperson. Your customers have needs – problems they would like to solve by buying the things you sell. You can use the Insight Sales approach to be a more successful salesperson and to help your customers achieve more success in their own situations.

Other approaches may get a one-time sale but this approach can bring about substantial on-going sales. This is how you achieve "customers for a lifetime". These lifetime customers will comfortably refer family, friends and colleagues because they know you add value. Because a referred customer expects to buy from you, your customers will become easier customers.

Insight Sales is the most effective and most satisfying approach because it involves working with customers instead of doing something to them, or just giving away your expertise and letting them go away to buy elsewhere. This approach is used with the goal of achieving sales that are profitable both for the client, the selling organization, and the salesperson.

So let's dig into the steps and the skills. Get out your yellow marker and make these ideas your own.

THE FIRST HALF OF THE SELLING PROCESS

Your first task isn't to pitch your product, or to sell something, but to get to know the real needs of your potential client. Half of your selling time should be spent on this first task. This is a radical shift from traditional selling.

STEP ONE – GREET YOUR CUSTOMERS

> You can't sell without getting into conversations with potential buyers – and lots of them.

In retail sales, you have to be able to both approach and greet your customers to get them to converse with you. The way in which you greet will significantly determine whether or not you even have a chance to sell. Show the customer he or she is valuable to both you and your organization, and help the customer to feel comfortable talking with you. Begin with the intention of building a long-term relationship. Forming that relationship starts as soon as you and the customer meet.

THE GOALS OF THE GREETING STEP

In the Insight Sales approach, you're a solution provider. If a customer is shopping in your store, it's safe to assume he or she has a problem to be solved. You need to start a relationship in which the customer is comfortable enough with you to talk about these problems. Your primary goals at this stage are to:

- create a positive first impression for you and your store,

- help the customer to feel comfortable and welcome,

- make your presence known to each customer that comes into your store or store section,

- establish your credibility as someone that can help,

- begin a conversation where you learn about the customer, and

- get as many customers as you can to accept that conversation with you.

You really have to greet and approach a great number of people to get the sales you need. This is particularly true if nine out of every ten customers blow you off with "No thanks, I'm just looking." On the other hand, if you get more customers to accept you and to engage with you in an open sales conversation, you have a greater chance to make more sales.

The ultimate goal of this step is to begin a conversation where you and the customer can find out what the real problems are, and then help the customer to find a complete solution to those problems.

FIRST IMPRESSIONS

First impressions have a significant impact. You want yours to clearly show each customer you are someone who has value to offer. Be seen as someone who the customer can trust to look after his or her needs. Your task is to find out what the customer's problem is, and then sell a complete solution. However, to do so, you need to establish a very positive first impression.

Your first impression is influenced by many things, some of which are:

- how you dress and your personal grooming,

- your activities at the time you first encounter the customer,

- your underlying attitudes,

- your demeanor and how you carry yourself (*which is heavily influenced by your attitudes*),

- the expectations you have about the customer's possible reaction, and

- your initial greeting behavior (*what you say and what you do*).

You want this first impression to attract the customer to you, or make him or her receptive to your approach.

Bernie Spak says, "Building rapport and trust with a customer through a positive first impression takes a conscious effort. This is an important part of building your personal brand as a salesperson. Ultimately what the customer experiences with you in the sales process will define your brand, but that initial impression is like a well thought out logo or book cover."

Consider your personal appearance, your hygiene, your tone of voice, and your body language. Is it appealing enough, fresh enough, eager enough, and relevant enough in the environment in which you sell to get people engaged? Or does it turn people away and create immediate resistance that will take additional time to overcome?

To form a positive first impression, your interaction with the customer requires:

- a warm and sincere smile,

- good eye contact, especially when the customer talks to you,

- a non-threatening position relative to the customer's personal space,

- a firm but gentle and humbly offered handshake if circumstances seem appropriate,

- an erect and open body posture, preferably with your right heel turned slightly toward your left instep, and your hands visible and in front of you,

- a sincere, enthusiastic, and "welcoming" attitude, plus

- a warm, humble, attentive expression of interest in working with the customer.

There has to be a connection and you must do everything you can to connect. As you reflect on this very critical part of the selling process, is there anything about your own first impression that may be getting in the way of your selling success?

DRESS AND GROOMING

Many people working in retail are young, and at a stage of life when being seductively attractive is very important to them. Too often, this shows in their dress and behavior at work. However, work is not a place to show off one's physical endowments, or to engage in flirtatious behavior.

Be at your retail position "dressed for business". The dress should parallel the dress code specified by your company, and if none exists, dress the way your customers generally expect of people in a retail establishment like your own. A retail sales clerk in a t-shirt shop could legitimately wear a t-shirt at work, but this would not be typical dress for most other retail establishments. Dress like the majority of your customers, likely in casual business attire.

Cleanliness and grooming also say a lot about you. We've had retail salespeople show up at work smelling so bad that customer's spoke to us about how unpleasant it was to encounter them. We've had salespeople, who were out partying late the night before, appear at work in unclean, wrinkled clothing and disheveled hair. Too many younger employees engaged in social activities late into the prior evenings and showed up at work looking very tired.

If you want to be a successful retail salesperson, pay attention to the details your customer will see when he or she first encounters you. Be professional and you will reap the rewards of greater sales.

ACTIVITIES WHEN ENCOUNTERING CUSTOMERS

Customers are generally wary when they enter a store, see a group of salespeople behind a desk or counter, and one of the salespeople is immediately dispatched to speak to the customer. The customer feels like he or she has just swum into a pool of bigger fish waiting to prey on the one little fish that is the customer. Instead of looking like someone who is coming to give service, it can look like the salesperson is attacking because it's his or her turn.

Customers are seldom wary when they see a person who is busy and working hard. They aren't threatened when they see someone carrying stock to the retail floor, arranging product so it is more accessible on the shelves, placing new outfits on mannequins, improving product demonstrations, cleaning or dusting. Such salespeople look conscientious and like they know what they're doing. Such people do not look like they're waiting to pounce on the customer. They look harmless and helpful.

Our advice is to do helpful housekeeping work on the retail floor, even when using an "up system". An "up system" involves salespeople taking organized turns dealing with customers who enter the store. If busy merchandising and it's not your turn when the customer approaches you, then greet the customer effectively to show him or her your retail establishment is a good place to be. Let the customer tell you why he or she approached you, then introduce the salesperson that is up next.

When making the introduction, give encouraging comments to the customer about how knowledgeable this salesperson is about what the customer is looking for, and give the salesperson a summary of what you've learned about the customer's needs. Both parties will appreciate what you've done. If you don't work in an "up system" environment, be busy and help every customer who asks for assistance.

If you do work with an "up system" and tend to sit or stand behind a counter taking or making phone calls when there are no customers needing service, make sure that you look up frequently and make eye contact with anyone who is waiting. Do not ignore potential customers. Be attentive.

UNDERLYING ATTITUDES AND YOUR PERSONAL DEMEANOR

We've noticed the best salespeople think of every person who walks through the door as someone who will buy, <u>but</u> first they must get to know this customer. They expect the customer to buy from them, if not today, then tomorrow or the next day. They intend to sell the customer true solutions that reduce costs, increase benefits, and add to customer success. For each customer, such salespeople hold the attitude this person is worth knowing, and the salesperson believes he or she has value to add to this customer's well being.

The best salespeople know their own success depends on helping each customer to succeed. Their goal is to help the customer achieve better results. The best salespeople know they can only do this by establishing rapport and winning some trust. With this basic premise, they approach in order to get to know the customer and his or her needs, not to get a quick sale.

The best salespeople have a personal demeanor of confidence, mixed with humility and compassion for their fellow beings. This confidence does not come across as arrogance. Their wish to connect with the customer does not come across as a desire to just get a sale. These salespeople are seen as caring about the customer because they do.

They do not approach feeling any pressure to get a sale. There is no pressure because the salesperson knows he or she will get the sale the right way.

This can't be faked with any reliability. Some less than ethical salespeople think of their potential customers as prospects who must be convinced to buy now, often using sales tricks and manipulative closes. These thoughts underlie their approach and greeting. But most people aren't fools and have the ability to detect a lack of authenticity. The best salespeople know this. Only integrity and authenticity get the best results.

Your demeanor comes from your beliefs and attitudes, your goals and motivations. To be effective using the insight sales approach, hold beliefs, attitudes, goals and motivations that favor the customer's success. Any sign of arrogance, zealousness to get the customer's money, or treating the customer as just someone to be sold to, will have a particularly unwelcome smell to the customer.

YOUR EXPECTATIONS

The expectations you have about the customer's possible reaction to your approach will also show. If you are inherently shy and avoid contact because you fear rejection, this will show as a slight hesitation when you approach. Your discomfort will transfer to the customer and generate some awkwardness for the both of you.

If you expect to be rebuffed, you may already be rehearsing your separation comment. Too many salespeople encounter a hesitant response, or even a simple non-response and conclude that they have lost their opportunity to make a sale. Regrettably, we've even seen retail situations where a less than confident salesperson approached, offered assistance and started to turn away even as the customer was saying "I need a XXXXX. Can you help me?"

The best retail salespeople tend to approach without any expectation as to how the customer will react to their greeting. They have an open mind, assume anything is possible, and give the customer the chance to react in his or her own way. They watch, listen, and feel the customer's reaction. Their next response would vary with every person they engage because each relationship is unique and they are starting a new relationship, not just trying to make a sale.

YOUR INITIAL GREETING BEHAVIOR

What you say and what you do can make a difference. The salesperson who rushes up, steps close to the customer with a large smile on his or her face and reaches into the customer's personal space to offer a hearty handshake, can come across as TOO friendly. For most customers, this type of assault is usually unwelcome. Such glad-handing fits the stereotype of the salesperson with a persuasion orientation. This does not fit the insight-oriented sales approach, which is much gentler, respectful, much more sensitive, and empathic.

Equally awkward is the salesperson that stands too far back, speaks hesitantly or too quietly, fails to make eye contact, and mechanically says, "Can I help you?". The salesperson needs to be close enough to be seen as actually interested, and needs to show that interest.

People have a personal space and a salesperson needs to be sensitive to what that spatial zone is for each customer. Be close enough but not too close. In our culture, this space is usually just under three feet of distance – an arms length. Figure out what each customer needs and give the person room to adjust to your presence.

GREETING AND APPROACH

In the retail setting, there are two different forms of first contact with customers – a Greeting and an Approach. They are somewhat different. A greeting typically occurs when you speak to the customer as he or she walks past you, or approaches you. A greeting involves a welcome message, acknowledging the customer's presence, and letting him or her know you're available to serve if any assistance is wanted. In an approach, you move toward the customer first then greet and initiate a conversation. Both are valid ways to initiate contact. Be able to effectively employ both methods.

THE GREETING

John Lawhon, an expert on retail selling, states in *Selling Retail* (J. Franklin Publisher, 1986) that your greeting should be from a position where you stand at least 20 to 30 feet inside the store. He says it's best to stand ninety degrees to the side of the walkway and speak as the customer passes by, saying something like,

> "Good morning, welcome to (*the name of your store*). May I direct you to what you're looking for?"

This is a non-threatening placement. Speak to the customer as he or she walks by. Do not move forward, as this will be an approach. An approach at this early stage may be felt as threatening because the customer likely isn't yet ready to welcome your assistance. Retail operations like Walmart and Canadian Tire know the power of a friendly greeting and have one person at the front entrance of their very large stores specifically working as a greeter who can provide directions. That person responds when approached by customers with questions.

In the greeting, you welcome the customer and offer to provide directions. You are not offering to sell the customer something at this moment. If the customer asks for your directions, this will then give you a chance to engage in conversation.

According to Lawhon, although this is a greeting without threat, it may still not lead to a conversation. The customer may say "Thanks but I'm just looking." John suggests you turn the customer's reaction to your greeting into a conversation by saying something like,

> "Great. We have a lot of stuff to browse. If you tell me what you're looking for, I'll gladly show you where it's located."

If the customer insists he or she is okay and would prefer to be left alone, Lawhon suggests you say something like,

> "Enjoy your visit. Likely, one of us will check in with you periodically to see if you have any questions."

As this is a greeting, and not an approach, you're making these comments while staying in place, to the side of the walkway. You are **not yet** moving toward the customer.

Always greet customers, particularly when you are not already engaged with another customer. Because you aren't encroaching into the customer's space, John Lawhon says you can't greet too much. Even if busy stocking the shelves, when any customer passes you by, offer a greeting.

> "Good afternoon, thank you for coming to (*the name of your store*). Do you need any assistance?"

It's okay to walk by a customer, and just offer a greeting, "**Hello and welcome to (*the name of your store*).**" Then keep walking, unless the customer looks like he or she wants to talk with you. If so, acknowledge that indication and approach.

THE APPROACH

An approach is what you do when you go toward a customer. Be sensitive to the timing of your approach. Watch the customer's behavior and see when he or she is ready for you to move closer.

Customers generally don't want to be approached by a salesperson as soon as they enter a store unless they are looking for a particular item and in a hurry. In most instances, we prefer to get oriented to the whole store before we want to talk about our needs with a salesperson.

If you intend to approach the customer to begin the sales process, it's best to give the person time to come in, orient him or herself, and settle down. Give enough time for the customer to get comfortable and feel ready to talk.

The clues the customer is ready will typically be visible once he or she is at least 30 feet inside your store, or in the middle of the store if you work in a smaller location. If you see the customer looking about as if looking for a salesperson, or standing and looking at specific products, it's probably safe to approach.

If you pay attention to people who visit your store, you will learn to recognize the clues they're ready to be approached. Time your approach to the customer's readiness, and you will increase the number of times you get involved in a sales conversation.

There are several different types of greetings to use when you approach. Learn them so you have some flexibility in how you open a sales conversation:

THE "WELCOME" APPROACH

The "Welcome to (*the name of your store*)" approach involves a specific statement of welcome. You walk up to the customer, welcome the person to the store, and get him or her to talk with you. Approach, stop just about an arm's length away, and say,

> "Welcome to (*the name of your store*)! My name is (*your name*), and how may I be of assistance?

If you recognize the customer has been in the store before, you could say,

"Welcome back to (*the name of your store*). I've noticed you here before. My name is (*your name*). What brings you in today?"

If you don't feel comfortable offering your name at this stage, Harry Friedman, retail sales guru, recommends you could simply say,

"Thanks for coming to (*the name of your store*). What's the special occasion that brings you in today?"

THE MERCHANDISE APPROACH

The Merchandise approach is different. In this approach, you speak to the customer when he or she is looking at specific items of merchandise. Walk up, stand to the side just over an arm's length away, and say something like,

"Hello. My name is (*your name*). It looks like you're in the market for a new XXXXXXX? (pause)"

Refer to the type of product the customer is looking at. This should be offered as a question inviting the customer to speak to you about what he or she is shopping for. Alternatively, you could say,

"I see you looking at XXXXX. Are you planning on doing some (*what the XXXXX does*)?"

and fill in the blank with a description of what the product will do.

You could comment on the fact the item is well accepted in the market place by saying something like,

"That's a very popular product. Is it something you have a use for?"

Your goal is to get customers telling you about their interest in the products they have in their hands or they're looking at on the shelves.

THE "I HAVE SOMETHING FOR YOU" APPROACH

Your third option is the "I have something for you" approach. Using this approach, you offer the customer a gift to start the relationship off. Your goal is to approach the customer, give something of value, and get into a conversation. You could say something like,

"Our flyer this week offers some really compelling savings that might be valuable to you. Here's a copy for you to examine. Was there anything in particular you were shopping for today?"

or

"We have a page of coupons exclusive to (*the name of your store*) to save you money. I wanted to make sure you have one. (*As he or she reaches out to take it from you*) What brings you in today?"

You'll see this approach in action at retail cosmetic counters. The retail salesperson stands in front of his or her counter, and offers a sample spritz to anyone who approaches. If the customer accepts the spritz, the salesperson will then ask about the customer's reaction to the scent, and lead into the question about what brought the customer to the salesperson's counter today.

THE FRIENDLY NON-BUSINESS APPROACH

Many retail sales professionals argue the best approach is the friendly, non-business approach simply saying,

"Hi. How are you doing today?"

Or the salesperson could notice something unique about the person, and use this to start a conversation.

"I notice you're wearing a Colts team jacket. I have an interest in the team, and I'm curious about your involvement with them?"

or

"I see you're wearing a blood donors badge. My brother was just in an accident and needed blood, so thank you for your contribution. Is this something you do regularly?"

If you think about it, this is how you meet people in social circumstances, so use these natural skills to start this relationship. Your goal is to start a conversation to build rapport.

THE FRIEDMAN 180° PASS-BY NON-BUSINESS APPROACH

Harry Friedman, an expert on retail selling, teaches the "180 degree pass-by" method. The phrase means you actually walk as if you're just passing by, get just past the customer, turn and ask a question, preferably something personal about the customer. You might pass, turn and say...

"Gosh, you look like you're in a hurry to find what you came to buy. May I help?"

or

"Excuse me, but I have to say that is a fantastic shirt."

or

"Wow. What a terrific outfit. You look like a million bucks. Good to have you here. May I be of assistance?"

or

"I just noticed the lapel pin for (*name of a local charitable organization*). I'm a supporter. What's your involvement with them?"

or

"I'm sorry, that was rude of me, how are you doing today?"

Because you've passed by, you're not a threat to the customer. He or she is likely to respond positively and engage you in conversation. This approach should be used with integrity – you say what you truly think, feel, believe and not just use a "pick-up line" that smells phony.

THE "HOW'S THE WEATHER?" APPROACH

Some salespeople fall into the rut of using a "How's the weather?" greeting. This may work because it is frequently used socially. However, as it is too typically used, it doesn't immediately differentiate you from other retail sales personnel. It also increases your chances of getting a "No Thanks. Just Browsing." response. Be different and say something more specific to the customer and you'll get his or her attention.

"Great tan. I'm guessing it's quite sunny out today?"

or

"If you're in here today, does that mean it's freezing outside and you just came in to get warm?"

or

"The way you're dressed, spring must have sprung out there. What brings you in today?"

or

"Wow, you're quite wet. It's raining heavily out there?" (*clearly expressed as a question*)

Again, what you say should be sincere and not just a smarmy pick-up line.

THE "CAN I HELP YOU?" APPROACH

Again, this short phrase springs easily off the tongue and is used by many salespeople. The intention is to be helpful, but customers all too often experience the approaching salesperson as an intrusion, and want to brush the salesperson away.

Although most sales teachers say don't use the "Can I help You?" approach, Bernie says you can deliberately use it to turn the customer's reflexive brush off response into humor. Have a solid response that brings a smile to the customer's face and a conversation will start.

"That's great. Browsing can be fun... but it can be dangerous as well. You might be seduced by some impulse to buy. Be careful out there."

Use humor, and playfulness. Get the customer smiling, chuckling, laughing with you, and continue the conversation. When we meet people in social situations, there is often an element of play or having fun. Don't be afraid to use humor to make first contact with a customer. Get this other person smiling and into a conversation with you.

DEALING WITH THE BRUSH OFF

Customers learn the habit of saying they're just browsing in order to brush off the retail salesperson. It's best to use the more conversational approaches so this brush off is less likely to happen. However, if you do get the brush off, use a comeback to remain engaged with the customer.

After all, your goal is to get the customer to talk to you about his or her needs. The customer's reply might just be a reflexive response, or it may be a sincere request for privacy. Get past the reflexive response. We recommend you say something like,

> "That's great, we want you to enjoy your visit to (*the name of your store*). However, we don't want to ignore you. So if you need any assistance, please don't hesitate to ask either myself or one of my colleagues."

As you say this, make good eye contact and watch for him or her to immediately ask for help. In our own experience, customers most typically interrupt before this statement is even finished, and ask for assistance. There are many responses one could make to the brush off.

> "That's great. We want to make sure you get the attention you need, so if you need assistance, please don't hesitate to ask."

or

> "Fantastic. What are you looking for that got you to come all the way over to our store?"

or

> "You're welcome to browse. Have you been here before?"

If the customer answers "yes"...

> "Great, you know our salespeople are wearing (*whatever the sales uniform is if your company has one*) and we're here to help you. Please just ask for assistance when you need it."

If the customer answers, "No"…

> "I can point out the different areas of the store to help you find what you're looking for, if you like?"

NON-VERBAL "GO AWAY" CLUES

The customer may give you non-verbal clues showing he or she wants to be left alone, or wants to distance him or herself from you. The customer might do any of the following:

- step back,

- look away,

- give you briefer answers to your queries, or

- focus his or her attention on product and try to ignore you.

If the customer does this, say something like,

> "It seems you want some space to shop on your own for a few minutes. That's okay. We want you to enjoy your visit to (*the name of your store*). However, we don't want to ignore you. If you need any assistance, please don't hesitate to ask either myself or one of my colleagues."

If the customer wants to be left alone, do so, but stay alert and watch for new clues the customer wants assistance.

(Regrettably, you also want to be watchful that the customer who refuses help isn't just there to shoplift.)

WHEN TO MOVE TO THE NEXT STEP

Recognize the right time to shift from Step One where you make first contact into Step Two where you get conversational. You know it's time to transition when:

- the customer smiles at you,

- he or she maintains eye contact with you,

- you feel like you've initiated some small degree of rapport with the customer,

- the customer makes a conversational reply,

- the customer begins to share information about his or her needs,

- the customer starts talking about your products, or

- the customer tells you what he or she is looking for.

It should take only a few seconds from the point at which you initiate your greeting to the transition to Step Two where you more fully engage in conversation.

THE TRANSITION TO ENGAGING

Your Greeting or Approach should take you to engaging in conversation. One option is to establish rapport by personalizing the conversation. React to something you notice about the customer. This might be derived from how he or she greets you, something about his or her clothing, or perhaps something you know about the customer as a result of his or her social standing in the community. Alternatively, you might focus the conversation on his or her reason for coming to your store. Be curious about this person just as you would with any other person you first meet.

There are several ways to transition to the next step:

1. Engage in whatever social chit-chat the customer offers up.

   "Yes, the Oilers were very impressive last night. I really enjoyed that game. I watched on TV. Did you go to the game itself?"

2. Share something of yourself that might be of interest to the customer. For example, you might mention you use the product the customer is looking at or that you have had special training in its use.

   "That's a great XXXXXX. I use that myself."

3. Paraphrase whatever response he or she gives to your greeting.

   "Sounds like you've come to get some printer supplies?"

   or

   "You want to know where we keep the XXXXXX ?"

54

or

"If I understand correctly, you're just out looking at the new models today?"

4. Answer any questions the customer asks you. Be helpful and positively responsive. Be enthusiastic.

"Yes that XXXXXX will do a wonderful job at (*desired result*)."

or

5. Ask your own transitional question to move the focus on to what the customer is shopping for.

"So what's the special occasion that brings you to (*the name of your store*) today?"

or

"How can I be of assistance?"

or

"You seem to be looking for a XXXXXX today?"

or

"Did you have any questions about what you're looking for that I can answer for you?"

or

"What got you to make the effort to come to our store today?"

You want to meet the customer in his or her moment, socializing if that is what he or she offers; or use a transitional question to remind the customer he or she had a purpose, something that motivated him or her to come out shopping.

Step Two – Engaging

It's not enough to simply introduce yourself and your company to the customer. Cause an open conversation to occur and a working relationship to begin.

To be successful using the "GET SMARTER" sales approach, truly master the second step for engaging customers in conversation. Engaging will allow you to transition from the greeting to learning about the customer's needs.

THE GOALS OF THE ENGAGING STEP

In the Engaging Step, you have three main goals that should guide your behavior with the customer:

- get the customer into a conversation with you, most typically by talking about what is of interest to the customer,

- build trust and rapport with this customer so he or he is comfortable talking with you, and

- set the stage to begin a focus on the customer's needs.

In this step, we engage the customer in an expanding conversation. First, "meet the customer in his or her moment" and then steer the interaction to a conversation about his or her needs. Some customers need more engagement after the greeting and before you get to the business of learning their needs. Others may be quite willing to discuss their needs, and open up right away. The ultimate goal isn't just conversation but a conversation where you're able to fully learn the customer's S.P.I.C.E[3].

Unfortunately, consumers have learned from many of their other retail shopping experiences that too many retail salespeople aren't very helpful. Many customers have come to prefer to look at the goods and make their own decisions based on their own understanding of the products.

However, many products do not easily lend themselves to self-help shopping. Unless the customer is already extremely knowledgeable about product features and benefits and about the location of the products in your store, he or she could leave without buying, or buy the wrong thing. Only a very small group of customers will do the homework to be knowledgeable enough to shop effectively on their own.

Some people will obtain a bit of knowledge before visiting your store but wind up less informed than they think they are. They may resist assistance because they think they know what they need to know. However, most customers would be better off receiving the help of an ethical and knowledgeable insight-oriented consultant who discovers their needs, deepens the customer's insight and recommends the right solution to those needs.

ENGAGING EFFECTIVELY

You have to be able to engage customers of all types and all shopping inclinations and get them into a conversation. This transition step is very important to your success. Get people talking with you, even when at first they don't want to. Establish trust and rapport early in the conversation so the customer will open up to you.

In some cases, this step might occur right away as you greet or approach the customer. On the other hand, the customer might try to take charge by:

- asking product and pricing questions as soon as you approach,

- demanding a negotiation of your price, as a first assault when you approach, or

- rebuffing your greeting with the typical blow-off comment of "No Thanks. I'm just looking."

You are the sales professional and must gain control of the interaction as quickly as possible.

It's your job to meet the customer in his or her moment and use what is relevant to the customer to get your conversation going. Don't treat all customers the same way. Pay attention to how he or she acts when you greet and adjust your behavior accordingly.

If the customer has questions of you, answer the questions, then ask a question of your own. If he or she wants to negotiate about price, engage the customer in negotiation without giving anything away, and then ask what he or she will be using the discussed solution for. If the customer wants to socialize first then engage in social talk. Start from what appears to be important to the customer and then steer the conversation to a more open discussion of his or her needs.

According to Roy Williams in his book *Wizard of Ads: Turning Words into Magic and Dreamers into Millionaires* (Bard Press, July 1998), there are two general types of customers, the transactional customer and the relational customer. Engage with and sell to both types. To do so, it helps to understand how they differ.

THE TRANSACTIONAL BUYER

- This customer is very price conscious and wants the best possible deal.

- He or she likes the process of shopping and comparing recommendations and quotations.

- This customer will visit many retail locations to find the best price on a specific item.

- For the transactional customer, time spent shopping is <u>not</u> as important as the deal. Time has less value to the transactional buyer than saving money and getting the best deal possible.

- This customer researches and learns about the products and services in order to build his or her own expertise. He or she wants to be totally informed about the features and capabilities of the products and services.

- In turn, the transactional customer wants to be recognized as an expert in these products or services.

- The transactional customer will often challenge the salesperson's knowledge, and offer assistance to other customers shopping in the store.

THE RELATIONAL CUSTOMER

- This customer can be anxious when buying because he or she worries about making a mistake.

- Relational customers dislike the process of shopping and comparing. In many cases, they hate it. They just want to find one supplier, and get everything they need.

- The relational customer's time is worth more than the savings he or she might get by hunting around for a deal.

- The relational customer looks to the expertise of others to influence his or her decision-making. He or she wants someone else to do the research and find the right solution, then recommend where and what to buy.

- The relational customer doesn't want to become an expert in the products. He or she wants to be an expert in his or her own business and wants that expertise to be respected.

- These customers want to buy from someone they can trust. Alternatively, they will get advice from a trusted friend or colleague and then ask for a specific product.

As we think about these two types of customers and the buying experience, it's important to acknowledge the current economic environment is generally designed to appeal to the transactional buyer. This presents a challenge to the insight-oriented salesperson, but one that must be successfully addressed.

Williams asserts that research shows that at any one time, when shopping for a product, 52% of customers are transactional and 48% are relational. However, a person is not always a transactional or a relational buyer. This is influenced by product type, shopping environment, the nature of the problems the customer is dealing with, and the priority the customer places on time at any given moment.

We believe people would rather be relational buyers but have to shop in a transactional world. A very large portion of transactional buyers can be turned into relational customers.

This happens when a salesperson meets the customer in his or her own moment and engages the customer in a conversation that builds a relationship where problems can be openly discussed. Customers become relational in orientation when the salesperson brings them to new levels of insight.

Learn to recognize whether the customer is being transactional or relationship oriented when you first meet. Be transactional when you encounter a transactional buyer and then make a transition to a relational interaction when you have rapport. Be relationship focused when you meet the relational buyer.

DEALING WITH TRANSACTIONAL BUYERS

Transactional buyers prefer self-help buying and looking for the best prices for the products they decide they need. If a transactional buyer encounters a salesperson, he or she is likely to commence the interaction with either feature-specific or price-oriented questions. Answer the customer's questions directly and immediately. Make sure the customer knows he or she is seen as a significant customer.

If the transactional buyer tells you a competitor has a lower price, welcome the competitive information. To show the customer you want his or her business, you could assure such customers your price matching policy means price will not be a reason to shop or buy elsewhere. Thank these customers for helping you to be more aware of the marketplace.

Respect the transactional customer's expertise. Invite him or her to share his or her knowledge with you. Listen carefully to what the customer tells you. Show that you appreciate what he or she shares. Learn from the customer.

Then, when the customer feels like you hold his or her knowledge level in esteem, offer your own expertise so it enhances the customer's. Do this without being competitive about who knows more. Help the transactional customer to build even more expertise. This adds value to conversing with you. Build the customer up and he or she will reward you with a more open conversation, and over time with more business and referrals.

Build a relationship on the exchange of expertise and information. Once engagement has taken place, you'll be able to transition to learning the customer's S.P.I.C.E[3].

In 1983, when we opened our software-only store, many new customers presented questions we couldn't answer. Some of our existing customers were very knowledgeable and we learned a lot by listening to them. When confronted by a question we couldn't answer and if one of these other "experts" was in the store, we would turn and ask if he or she knew the answer. The "expert" would often join in our conversation with the customer, give helpful information to the two of us, and feel appreciated in the process. Because we showed this respect, these "experts" became loyal customers and frequently influenced their friends to buy from us.

DEALING WITH RELATIONAL CUSTOMERS

Relational customers would prefer to buy from someone with whom they have a relationship. Unfortunately, the relational shopper, which is the easiest shopper to work with, becomes a transactional customer if the relationship isn't offered.

A skilled salesperson knows to meet this relational customer in his or her moment by initiating a conversation, and ultimately a relationship. If the customer's moment is one of wanting help from a knowledgeable and insight-oriented salesperson, be that salesperson. "GET SMARTER" is the perfect sales approach for the relational customer. The key is how you handle the engagement step. Go from a greeting to a conversation, offering an insightful relationship.

When meeting the relational customer, ask him or her about his or her own business. Get the customer talking about him or herself. Get your customer talking about what he or she hopes to do with the products he or she is shopping for. Learn about the customer's personal interests. Then build a relationship through listening to what the customer is telling you. Use active listening skills to draw the customer out.

We recommend you treat most customers as relational. Even the transactional customer doesn't have all the knowledge, and may not yet fully appreciate what he or she could accomplish with the right solution. If you meet your potential customers in their own personal moment and then offer a relationship, you'll find more people choose to be relational customers.

ENGAGEMENT STRATEGIES

Engage the customer in the conversation he or she wants to have, and then steer the conversation toward disclosure of the customer's S.P.I.C.E.^{3}. This is your responsibility as a salesperson. Be able to get into a conversation with anyone. Your livelihood and the wellbeing of your company depend on you being able to do this.

GETTING PAST THE FOCUS ON PRODUCT

Your customer may ask you about a product or specific service. Use a way to deal with the question that allows you to move into a deeper conversation. First paraphrase the question to make sure you understand what the customer is really asking. Once you know you understand, and the customer knows, answer the question. Then, re-direct the customer's attention to his or her full set of needs, and ask questions that deepen insight and understanding of those needs.

Unfortunately, most salespeople ask too few questions to learn about their customers. Answer the customer's inquiry, and then respond with a question of your own to encourage the customer to consider some element of his or her S.P.I.C.E[3].

S: Welcome to our store. You appear to be looking for something specific?

C: How much is this one? (holding it in his or her hand)

S: $499 for that model. Sounds like you're looking for an XXXXXX to do YYYY, is this correct?

C: Yes. Mine broke down this morning and I need a new one.

S: Seems like you were inconvenienced by the failure of your old one. What happened?

C: I spilled my orange juice on it, and it went up in a puff of smoke.

S: Wow. I'm guessing that was pretty frustrating? Probably means costly delays in your work. What do you do with your XXXXXX? (*and so on to get a conversation going.*)

Hopefully, this conversation can be continued so the focus shifts from the product to the customer's situation.

Instead of either interrogating the customer or simply relinquishing control over the sales process, there are better approaches for re-direction and getting to a discussion of needs. In the easiest re-direction approach, answer the customer's question to meet in his or her particular moment, show you have expertise, and establish credibility. Then, explain you would like to ask a question in turn.

Explain why you would like to know more about the customer's needs. Do this in such a way that you induce the customer to wonder if there is more to what he or she needs than the customer first thought. This could include telling the customer any of the following:

- You don't want to recommend the wrong solution. You simply need to know more in order to make the right recommendation.

- It's your intention to fully understand his or her needs in order to recommend the right solution.

- Your company has a huge selection of different versions of the product he or she is shopping for, and you want to supply the best choice.

- You want to determine if your company has the best solution for the customer's needs or if he or she would be better talking to some other supplier.

Then, ask permission to explore what the customer will be using the item for or what the customer is trying to accomplish and isn't yet able to satisfactorily achieve.

The simple approach works and you could use it as your preferred style. However, we think there is a way to be even more effective using a sophisticated re-direction. You can respond to customer questions using this process:

- agree with the importance of the question,

- clarify the underlying meaning of the question (*paraphrase*),

- answer the question,

- explain your intention to understand his or her needs, and

- ask a situation or expectation question.

First, you would agree with the customer's concern and the importance of the question. Then clarify to achieve an understanding of the customer's underlying meaning. You would do this because people don't always say what they mean. If a customer asks, "Is that expensive?", you could say something like,

"That's an important concern. You need a cost effective way to (*what the customer wants to do*), correct?"

Answer the real question you uncover, which might actually be what the customer asked or could be something he or she wants to know but is too hesitant to ask directly. It's possible the customer could have asked a roundabout question. Following your clarification, give your answer.

"We do have solutions that will do that and our prices range from $$ to $$$."

Then explain your intention to understand all of the customer's needs.

"I'd like to know more about what you're doing because I want to make sure you get the best choice from what is available."

Finally, ask a question about his or her current situation or about the results he or she expects to get. For example, you could say:

"It will help if I understand more about what you will be using this for and what you are trying to accomplish?"

or

"What results would you be looking to achieve?"

You come across as a more impressive insight-oriented consultant when you agree, clarify, answer, explain and then ask. You meet the customer right in his or her moment, and then take control of the conversation to lead it into Step Three – Take the Time to Learn The Customer's Needs (Get the customer's S.P.I.C.E[3]).

S: (**Approach**) "Welcome to Body Smart. How may I be of assistance."

C: "Is this particular cream a good moisturizer?"

S: (**Validate question**) "Given our dry winters and how the central heating in our homes dries out our skin, that's a good question. *(Clarify the meaning of the question)*

I'm guessing that you're experiencing the symptoms of itching and dry skin?"

C: "My shins in particular are driving me crazy and I need some relief."

S: (**Answer The Question**) "Yes, this cream is a vitamin E moisturizing cream. (**Explain Your Need To Know More**) It would help me to recommend the right products for you if you could tell me more about your circumstances. (**Ask About The Customer's Situation and Problem**) Please tell me when the itching started, how bad it is, and what you've already been using to try to get that relief?"

C: "Well it started about three weeks ago...?

TOUGH CUSTOMERS

Many salespeople say, "It isn't that easy. Some customers are really tough." Such salespeople struggle to get conversational with:

- gruff and belligerent individuals,
- individuals who just don't want consultative help,
- arrogant people who speak "rudely",
- people who are private and don't talk much,
- people who just want to talk about anything but their needs,
- people who just want their questions answered, not to be asked questions, or
- people who just want the best price on a particular item.

Well such salespeople are right – some customers are a real challenge. However, your success depends on being able to sell to these customers as well. The best salespeople find ways to get past these barriers. So the important question you have to confront is, "Are you going to develop the skills that make it easier to get past any roadblocks your customers put up?"

Each customer who manages to brush you off, or prevents you from learning his or her S.P.I.C.E³ is a lost opportunity. Depending on how many customers you encounter each day, this could be a significant percentage of your daily sales if you don't turn these interactions into open conversations about each customer's needs.

You lose when the customer doesn't buy, again later when he or she doesn't come back to your store, and even later when the customer doesn't refer others. Each person you encounter is a potential influencer. Instead of referring people to you, he or she will refer friends, family and colleagues to the salesperson that ultimately gets conversational and wins his or her business.

It's important to remember each customer who brushes you off is likely to buy something, either today or in the very near future, and if not from you, from your competitor. If your competitor wins the sale, the competitor gets stronger and you get weaker.

Remember, the customer also loses if you and your organization actually have the best solution for his or her needs. If a customer doesn't explore his or her S.P.I.C.E³ with you and buys something less than the proper solution, he or she won't achieve full success. It could be worse. If he or she buys the wrong solution from a competitor because that competitor was more persuasive, the customer may encounter failure to do what he or she wants to do.

It's your job to get past any roadblocks the customer puts in the way of engagement, and get into an effective conversation about his or her S.P.I.C.E³. Ask yourself, "What can I do to be the one who gets that sale?" And then, find the answer.

DEALING WITH GRUFF/BELLIGERENT CUSTOMERS

Some customers can be gruff in their responses to you – curt, offering non-verbal signals suggesting they won't be very cooperative, maybe even making statements to you that feel like criticism. In such cases, you probably need to use the powers of perseverance and patience. Use a comeback that catches the customer's attention.

C: "Look. I'm just browsing." (*said with a touch of irritation*)

S: "Well, that's okay. We have a lot to browse. What are you browsing for?" (*makes eye contact and smiles*)

C: "I want to look at your XXXXXX."

S: "Great. They're over here. What will you be doing with it?"

The customer tried the brush off in a gruff voice but warmed up to the eye contact, smile and the gently teasing response.

The salesperson did what it took to get the customer talking. The salesperson neither argued with the customer, nor did he quit. He hung in, made a response to capture the customer's attention, and began a deeper conversation.

If the customer isn't already walking away from you, persevere, use patience, stay calm, have a bit of a playful smile on your face and relish the challenge. Find some way to respond to any gruff or critical comments, a way to get the customer's attention without overtly disagreeing.

Perhaps you could explain your positive intent, and then agree this might not seem appropriate to the customer right now. Make sure you make solid eye contact when ever possible, to show confidence and respect for the customer. For example,

S: "Sounds like I hit a nerve, and this is a particularly bad time to talk with you about your concerns with XXXXXX?" (Pause to wait for an answer while making eye contact and holding a bit of a smile)

C: "Well, I guess it's not your fault. I've been tense lately because my XXXXXX keeps failing and I haven't worked out a solution."

If you think customers are tougher than these examples, we can look at situations where the customer is even more challenging to deal with. For example, what can a salesperson do to handle the customer who is critical about the salesperson's ability to be helpful, or challenges the salesperson's expertise?

S: "Welcome to our store. How can I help you today?"

C: "You probably can't. I'm pretty sure I know more about this stuff than you do."

S: "That might be true. I gather you use this technology all the time. However, we do have a broad selection of products and I want to help you get what you need. Tell me what kinds of products you're looking for and what you'll be doing with them."

C: "Well, we need a graphics workstation. I'm looking for a system with four 128bit octocore processors, fast video and lots of memory and storage. Do you have anyone who can help me with that?"

S: "I have some knowledge in that area. We have several options that could potentially fit. Tell me more about what this system will be doing? CAD, CAM, Graphic Design, Website development?"

C: "Okay, where can we sit down for a few minutes?"

Predominantly, the salesperson maintained his personal confidence, and appeared to agree with the customer ("**That might be true.**"). Instead of arguing with the customer, he invited the customer to show off her own technical knowledge. The salesperson only then asserted his own comfort in having a conversation about the needs the customer presented. This is just the start of a much larger conversation about the customer's S.P.I.C.E[3].

Customers can say things that might provoke a defensive response. Remain calm and simply meet whatever response the customer gives you with a persistent intention to make sure he or she buys the proper solutions.

The following example was a real encounter in one of our computer stores.

S: "How're you doing today?"

C: "I'm doing fine. I think I found what I'm looking for, so I'm all right. You guys have been all over me like leeches." (*holding an item in his hands*)

S: "Yeah... I noticed you've been approached a couple of times by different sales guys so I thought I'd just come over, and protect you from more of them."

C: "Yeah. All I wanted to do was just study the product. I want to see if it will do what I want."

S: "You definitely have that right. It might seem like we're leeches but we just want to make sure everyone gets the assistance they need. Sometimes we get so busy customers don't get any help at all, and that upsets our manager. But I noticed you were trying to concentrate, and got hit by a couple of our sales guys. So maybe I'll just stand here, and others will think you're being taken care of. Actually, I know quite a bit about this product."

C: "Yeah?"

S: "But I'm just going to stand here and maybe talk with you a little bit and maybe stop others from coming to interrupt you. Did you get a chance to look at this particular feature here?"

C: "Well. I was just looking at it, but I don't know what "pick a style" means. I gather there's some flexibility in the product."

S: "There's a lot of flexibility. Pick a style means many slideshow templates are included. I take it you're going to be doing some digital presentations?"

C: "Yeah. I'm trying to build some training tapes for my staff, and I was thinking I could add some video for extra pizzazz."

This salesperson used a non-business friendly approach, "How are you doing today?" Then he did something different in response to the customer's reaction. He became the customer's ally when he said, "I noticed you've been approached...". He showed empathy for the irritation the customer might have been feeling about being "bothered" by other salespeople. He provided a reason for this phenomenon when he explained the manager's expectation, **"When it's busy, some customers are ignored. That really upsets our manager."** but he then solidified his alliance with the customer when he said, **"I'll just talk with you to keep the others away."**

This was a creative and spontaneous response coming from the salesperson's commitment to stay in relationship with the customer. It came from his confidence that he had something to offer and the customer would be better off getting his assistance.

He did this within 80 seconds, and got a conversation going that ultimately allowed him to uncover this customer's S.P.I.C.E^3. By doing this, he made sure the customer got the proper solution to his needs – a complete solution – not just a software package.

If, on first contact, a customer responds with a gruff, curt or rejecting comment, hold your defensive reactions in check. Remember the customer's response isn't really about you. It came from assumptions about you as a salesperson, and those assumptions are incorrect if you intend to use the "GET SMARTER" sales approach.

Meet the customer in his or her moment, paraphrase to be sure you understand what he or she is saying to you, come back with both a form of agreement and a humorous reply while looking directly at the customer with a smile on your face. Give a playful response while making good eye contact. Maintain confidence that you can be helpful and offer real value. Explain your intentions. Hang in there.

DEALING WITH FEATURE SHOPPERS

Some customers just want to pepper the salesperson with questions about product features. This might seem like a good thing in that it gives an opportunity to sell the product the customer is asking about. However, if the salesperson doesn't learn about the customer and his or her specific needs, the salesperson can't know if this is the right product for the customer. And when the salesperson doesn't get the customer's S.P.I.C.E^3, products are typically bought only at the best price. In turn, only products are acquired – not complete solutions, so sales are smaller.

The salesperson would do better by turning these questions into an opportunity to engage in a conversation. The goal is to learn what is needed to make the most effective recommendation.

S: "Hi there. That's an excellent XXXXXX."

C: "Yeah. Do you know this XXXXXX? I want to know if it comes with (*desired feature 1*)?"

S: "It does. Do you already have an XXXXXX now that you're using?"

C: "No. I'm just getting into this. So, this XXXXXX, it also has (*desired feature 2*), right?"

S: "Yes. However, if you're going to be doing a lot of (*typical use of the product*), the (*desired feature 2*) for this product might not be enough for you. You may need a professional version. Alternatively, it might be more than you need. Can I ask, what you'll be using it for?"

C: "Well, I like this. It looks pretty good. I'm just interested in this product. So you're saying it does do (*desired use 1*) and I can (*desired use 2*)?"

S: "Yes, it has some ability to do that. But again, depending on what you're doing, it may not have all of the capacity to suit your needs, or too much capability and more complicated than what your needs call for, so I would like to learn more about your intended use."

C: "Well this one may be enough for me. How much is this one?"

S: "This one is regularly $2499 but on sale for $1999 – some terrific savings right now. However, all of our XXXXXX are on sale right now so let's make sure we get the right one that matches your needs. How will you be using it and how heavy will that use be?"

C: "I expect to use it every day for a couple of hours… (*and he continues on describing what he will be doing with what he intends to buy*)."

The salesperson approached the customer with the merchandise approach by referring to the product the customer was studying. The customer ignored that greeting and aggressively asked if the product had a feature he desired. The salesperson answered the question, **"It does."** and then asked a question in turn. The customer ignored the question and asked another feature question.

Again, the salesperson responded with an answer, and then a statement that raised a concern. In this case, the salesperson suggested the product either might not be enough or might be too much for the customer's needs. And then the salesperson once again asked a "needs" focused question, **"Can I ask what you'll be using it for?"** The salesperson is meeting the customer in his or her moment by answering the customer's specific questions, but the salesperson is also trying to steer the customer to a conversation about his or her needs.

Throughout this example, it's important you notice what the salesperson didn't do. She never said anything bad about the product. In fact she praised it, and said it was a good deal. She never said it was the wrong one for the customer. She just said she wanted to make sure she could learn enough about the customer's needs to recommend the right one.

And, she answered the customer's feature questions then created a bit of uncertainty in the mind of the customer by pointing out the risk the product might not be the right choice to best meet his needs. Only at this stage, about a minute and fifty seconds after the salesperson approached, did the customer shift and begin to engage in a conversation with the salesperson.

* * *

For the "GET SMARTER" sales model to work, engage each customer in a comfortable, open, and personal conversation where he or she will reveal his or her Situation, Problems, Implications, Constraints, and Expectations/Excitements/Eagerness. By doing this, you will help your customers to achieve new insights and deeper understanding of their needs.

Build your skills for doing this so you're especially able to do this with "tough" customers. These are customers with whom almost everyone else is probably failing. These customers have developed their skills for keeping the upper hand in their interactions with salespeople. They do buy, but on their own terms, wherever they find the best deal.

You have a problem. If you don't get these customers into a conversation, form relationships, and show extra value by helping them to understand their own needs, they won't have any loyalty to you or your company. They will go wherever they can find the best deal.

In addition, if the customer buys without using your expertise, he or she can make a mistake and buy the wrong products. This means he or she may bring back costly returns. If you use the right skills and turn this into an insightful consultation, you win, your employer wins, and the customer wins by getting the right solution.

We've looked at just a few examples of how this can be done. In these examples, we've seen the following strategies in action:

- **Persist** – hang in there, don't just back off when the customer tries to distance him or herself from you.

- **Align yourself with the customer** – validate and identify with the customer's feelings, thoughts and needs.

- **Meet the customer in his or her moment** – answer any direct questions asked by the customer, agree with his or her concerns, and react conversationally to anything the customer says or does.

- **Show empathy** – paraphrase what the customer says and reach for full understanding.

- **Use humor** – diffuse any tension between the customer and yourself with eye contact, a smile, and a humorous reply.

- **Establish expertise** – humbly but confidently say things to show you know your stuff and can address the customer's needs.

- **If necessary, cause some doubt** – suggest that there may be more to think about than just what the customer is presenting as questions or statements.

- **Explain your intentions** – indicate you would like to ask some questions, explain why, and ask permission to do so.

- **Ask S.P.I.C.E[3] questions** – ask a question to learn what the customer wants to do with the product, and then ask again if the customer doesn't freely volunteer information.

You have to have your own engagement strategies. Even if you didn't like any of the approaches shown in our examples, you have to appreciate that these salespeople came up with responses to remain in the game. Do you have what it takes to stay in the game yourself?

Greeting and then Engaging only take a few moments but they are very important moments. You need to achieve engagement with most of the people you encounter in your sales role. The best salespeople get more people talking about their needs. For you to be amongst the best, you need to develop your skills for effective engagement.

It can be done. It's up to you as the salesperson to get over, around and through customer roadblocks in such a way that the customer wins. Develop your ability to react effectively to the difficulties some customers put in the way of getting into a conversation.

If your best efforts to get engaged in an open conversation aren't working, improve your engagement strategies and skills. Don't blame the customer if you fail to do so. You've now seen strategies that work. You have some options to use when the going gets tough.

If you find yourself locked out of a high number of conversations and forced to either let the sale go or use persuasion selling to try to win the business, work on your engagement skills.

Talk to your sales manager and ask for help. Selling will become much easier and much more rewarding.

On the other hand, you're wasting time – yours and your customer's – if you engage in long non-business related conversations. You want the conversation to be more than socializing. Make these conversations relevant business conversations while inducing the customer to open up and tell you about his or her needs. Transition as soon as you reasonably can to the business of learning the customer's S.P.I.C.E[3].

TRANSITION TO LEARNING THE CUSTOMER'S NEEDS

Once the person is engaged in an open conversation with you, steer the conversation to a discussion of the customer's needs. To do so, ask a transition question to move the focus on to what the customer is shopping for.

"So please tell me more about what you'll be using this XXXXXX for?"

or

"What problems with your existing XXXXXX are causing you to look for a new one?"

or

"Why are you looking for a new XXXXXX?"

or

"Have you used an XXXXXX before?"

or with a small business customer that has come to your store

"I'd like to understand your business better, particularly any issues you might be having where our products could be of assistance. Can you tell me more about what your company does and how it does that work?"

You want your transitional question to remind the customer he or she had a purpose for coming in to your store. Your transition should lead right into that purpose.

STEP THREE – TAKE TIME TO LEARN THE NEEDS

(GET THE S.P.I.C.E³)

Before you ever recommend (*or pitch*) a product or service, know the customer's S.P.I.C.E³:

- his or her situation,

- his or her problems,

- the implications of those problems,

- the constraints that have prevented problem solving before now, and

- his or her expectations and excitements about what he or she could achieve if those problems were solved.

Otherwise, you could be selling the wrong things. And, if you know the S.P.I.C.E³, you won't be selling products. You'll be selling solutions.

Steer this conversation to an exploration of the customer's needs (his or her S.P.I.C.E^3). Endeavor to elevate your customer's insight about what has to change. In the second step, you were building an open relationship so that in the third step, you could readily learn about your customer and his or her needs.

G	Greet	Greet and approach showing interest in the customer and beginning a conversation.
E	Engage	Engage in conversation allowing trust and relationship building to occur.
T	Take Time to Learn The Customer's Needs (Get the S.P.I.C.E^3)	Initiate an open discussion of the customer's needs to get his or her S.P.I.C.E^3, taking time to actively listen as the customer does most of the talking while you clarify for understanding. Reach for deeper insight.

Steps One and Two can happen quickly (*in a matter of just a few seconds*) but this Step Three is not a fast or brief step. Take enough time to get key information. It definitely does **not** mean you ask only one or two questions, get a few answers then launch into selling your products. This step requires that the salesperson conduct an effective and extensive diagnosis of the customer's needs, most particularly when the problems and related solutions are complex. This step is the primary step in our "GET SMARTER" sales process.

GOALS FOR – LEARNING THE CUSTOMER'S NEEDS

When discussing the customer's needs, your goals are to accomplish all of the following:

- get the customer to trust you,

- get the customer to tell you important information, some of which he or she might not have expected to share with you, and even some of which he or she hadn't even considered as relevant to solving his or her problems,

- learn the customer's particular S.P.I.C.E^3,

- take the customer through his or her Reality Trough, opening up the customer's awareness to the emotions that reside within that trough,

- help the customer to achieve new insights,

- work with the customer so you both achieve full understanding of the customer's needs, and

- build the customer's eagerness to hear your recommendation.

Learn about the customer's needs and expectations. Only in part do you need to know what the customer is shopping for, or hopes to buy. Because what the customer is shopping for might not be the best solution for his or her needs, you want to learn all about the customer's S.P.I.C.E^3 and what motivated the customer to shop.

* * *

We invite you to take a moment and think about what you should know about any customer in order to be able to recommend the right solution, a complete solution, to meet his or her needs. Write your thoughts down. Think carefully about your answer. What do you need to know about your customer before you can recommend the right product, service or solution? Please do not read ahead until you have written your own thoughts down.

* * *

How easy was it for you to answer this very important question? Do not discount the significance of this exercise. A professional salesperson should know what it is he or she needs to discover about each customer before making any recommendation. Anything less may be experienced by the customer as irresponsible and unethical selling.

Before you encountered our question, did you already have a list of the key information you need to learn? If so, we congratulate you, as many salespeople do not. If you did not, we encourage you to make your list now. We intend to help you in this process.

Gather information in a **conversation** as opposed to an interrogation. You want this conversation to feel good to the customer. You want the customer to experience forming a new insight-oriented relationship with you.

The customer should feel comfortable confiding to his or her expert, and feel a willingness to listen to the expert's advice. You want a conversational interaction where the customer shares private and possibly personal information. To clarify what we think you should be after, consider an iceberg.

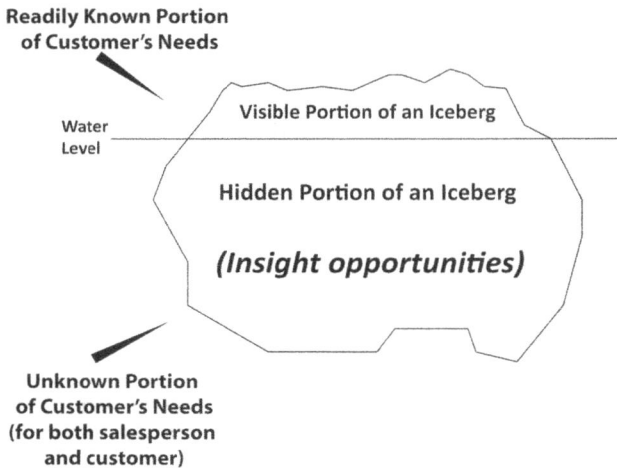

Readily Known Portion
of Customer's Needs

Water
Level

Visible Portion of an Iceberg

Hidden Portion of an Iceberg

(Insight opportunities)

Unknown Portion
of Customer's Needs
(for both salesperson
and customer)

Only about 30% of an iceberg is visible above water while the rest is hard to discern below the water line and almost invisible. Both the customer and the salesperson only know a small portion of the customer's needs. A much larger portion is certainly unknown to the salesperson before any meeting occurs, and a large portion is below the customer's conscious awareness. Much of the customer's real needs are unknown by the customer until a conversation brings the needs to light.

Many untrained salespeople fail to get a sale because they don't take the time to learn this less obvious information about their customers' needs. On the other hand, highly successful salespeople learn all they can about their customers at this stage in the sales process, and they appreciate that bringing this information out into the open is critically important.

The best salespeople want their customers to achieve new insights that give clarity about new opportunities for the customer to solve problems, reduce costs, and increase payoffs. The best salespeople know they must listen more than talk in the first part of the sales interaction.

Below, we present what we believe you need to learn. If you answered our earlier question about what you need to know about your customer, you developed your own list. So as you read our list, compare your list to what we suggest is critical information.

GETTING THE S.P.I.C.E³

Neil Rackham, a sales expert and author of *SPIN Selling* (McGraw Hill, 1988), originally developed the notion of asking SPIN questions to conduct a proper needs assessment. He made the significant observation that the best salespeople were able to regularly discover the customer's problems and the implications of those problems before offering what they had to sell.

This concept is brilliant and one we validated through observation of our own best salespeople. Great salespeople regularly take their customers through a realistic examination of problems and their implications so that both the salesperson and the customer achieve a conscious understanding of the costs of the status quo, and an emotional clarity that the customer has to do something about this.

As a result of our own observations, we have expanded on Rackham's ideas. We now think there are five main elements to discover about your customer, each of which contains subsets of important information.

You need to do this in a manner that helps the customer to expand his or her own understanding. You need to lead the customer's awareness to the information that might be buried in his or her unconscious mind, or otherwise ignored in the unconscious process of denial. Both of you need to learn five essential elements of the customer's needs and we call this the customer's S.P.I.C.E³.

Situation	The customer's current situation; what he or she does; what he or she uses now; how he or she does it; why the customer does it; who is the actual doer, if not the customer; and any under-utilized potential resources within the customer's situation.
Problems	The symptoms, difficulties, real problems, opportunities, and challenges the customer has when doing what he or she does; and what wishes he or she has to do it better.
Implications	What these problems cost the customer, both tangibly and intangibly; and what feelings the customer has about these costs, including feelings about lost opportunities.
Constraints	Why the customer hasn't fixed these problems or concerns before now; and what has blocked him or her from taking appropriate action.
E^3 xpectations, excitement, and eagerness	What the customer would minimally expect to gain; what results would really excite the customer (*reduced costs, improved performance, new opportunities, new results and benefits*); and how eager the customer is to get the problem solved.

So did your own list include all five of these main elements and all or most of the questions within each element? If not, what did your list fail to include? What did our list fail to include? Notice that none of our questions are about product. Products make up solutions and we don't want to focus on the solutions until we fully understand the customer's problems and desires.

We want to learn all that we can about the customers S.P.I.C.E^3 because that is what matters to the customer. This is the full definition of the problem the customer wants to solve. Too often, salespeople fail to learn this information about their customers because they don't think this information is important? We think it is critical for elite sales performance. You must strive to be an effective problem solver and help the customer to close the gap between where he or she is within the status quo and where he or she really wants to be.

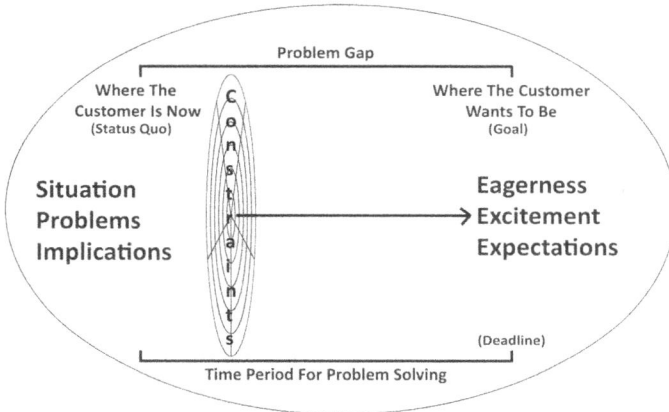

Problem Gap

Where The Customer Is Now (Status Quo)

Where The Customer Wants To Be (Goal)

Constraints

Situation
Problems
Implications

Eagerness
→ Excitement
Expectations

(Deadline)

Time Period For Problem Solving

* * *

As a further challenge, we invite you to pick a relatively new client with which you've recently had a face-to-face meeting. Pick a client you think you know something about, but preferably not one you've been serving for a long time. Pick one who hasn't yet made the decision to buy from you. Take a clean sheet of paper, and list what you <u>know</u> about this client within the five S.P.I.C.E[3] sections (*see the S.P.I.C.E[3] sheet Appendix 3*).

Please don't write what you assume about the client, only what you know. Notice how easy or difficult this exercise is for you to do. Notice if any sections are easier to fill out than others. Save this list because we will ask you to look at this list once again later in this chapter. Please do not read ahead until you have completed writing down what you know about your client.

* * *

As a solution provider, you are expected to have a deep appreciation for the actual problem or problems that your solutions solve. Be able recognize particular symptoms as clues to problems the customer might not yet fully appreciate. By asking about the existence of those symptoms, by searching out their origins, you may expand the customer's awareness as to the true nature of his or her problem(s).

Get the customer to address the implications of his or her problems so reality becomes clearer to him or her. This will surface the feelings of frustration the customer has with his or her situation. This takes the customer into the emotions of his or her Reality Trough, and from that place, the motivation to find a better solution will emerge.

It's also important to examine what reasons the customer thinks have kept him or her from solving the problems before now. We want to learn about these perceived roadblocks because these constraints become reasons not to buy. If the salesperson does not know the constraints and fails to offer a solution that removes the constraints, the customer would just object to the recommended solution.

Ask about constraints to induce the customer to consider whether or not these constraints are real or imagined. The salesperson must know the real constraints so that any recommended solution includes ways and means to overcome them. As well, it helps if the customer realizes some of the constraints are only imagined. This gives him or her greater permission to make a purchase.

In turn, it's very important to get the customer to share what he or she minimally expects, so the salesperson knows the minimum standards the solution must meet. The salesperson must learn the standards against which his or her recommended solution will be judged.

Beyond the minimal expectations, knowing what additional desirable results would generate greater customer excitement allows the salesperson to know the particular benefits upon which the customer will place the greatest value. If the customer is invited to think about what he or she would ideally like to achieve, a higher level of expectation is determined. By learning what benefits truly excite the customer, we have a better target for what our solution must deliver to be differentiated from any solution offered by a competitor.

It is equally valuable to know how eager the customer is to hear what you have to recommend. Are there important deadlines that you must know about before making your recommendation? Has the customer shifted from accepting the way things are to a real eagerness to discover a new solution with increased benefits? Does the customer want a solution right now?

If the customer isn't feeling eager, he or she is likely to resist. Before you make any recommendation, learn what the customer would really like to achieve and move him or her to expecting those better results now so the customer is full of anticipation. Instead of resistance, the customer would be in a state of desire.

Focus on the customer's expectations and potential for excitement so you know exactly what the recommended solution has to deliver. What the customer reveals as he or she discusses these expectations gives you the language with which to present a recommended solution. In addition, by learning how eager the customer is, you will know whether or not to proceed to the recommendation stage.

Discovering this S.P.I.C.E[3] information early in the sales conversation deals with what used to be called customer objections – which usually occur late in the selling process when using traditional sales approaches. Here the buying criteria are discovered much earlier – well before any recommendation is made.

You learn what will shape the customer's decision before the customer ever has a chance to be negative in the buying process. While building rapport and trust, the customer is invited to discuss his or her decision criteria before any product or service is pitched. In this way, the information is not brought up as points of resistance to the purchase, but as information the salesperson can consider before making his or her recommendation.

The following sample questions could be asked to uncover each of the five elements. Learn them all, but only ask one, or at most two questions for each category. Ask the question to direct the customer's attention to the specific element, then get conversational about that element and extend what you learn. Draw the customer out so he or she volunteers more information about each element.

You'll be able to do this using the active listening skills presented later in this chapter.

If you can, work through the S.P.I.C.E^3 sequence in an organized manner. Generally, you would first learn more about the customer's situation, expanding on what you already know about the customer from his or her appearance and initial comments.

SITUATION QUESTIONS

These questions allow you to move into a conversation where you gather data and facts about the customer's status quo. You need to determine if this is a likely environment for the problems your solutions will solve, and to help the customer to better know his or her situation and the resources within it.

- You know your current situation better than I do. Please tell me as much as you can about how you do what you do where you think a new XXXXXX would be helpful?

- I'm curious where you will be using this XXXXXX – personal or business use?

- Tell me about your business? What is it you do?

- How do you do your work now?

- Can you tell me what you'll be using an XXXXXX for?

- What have you been using up till now?

- Who will be using this XXXXXX?

- How did you do that before now?

- Can you please tell me how that works?

- How does your XXXXXX help you do your work today?

- I don't really know enough about your current situation. Could you please tell me more about the environment where you will be using the XXXXXX?

- We've talked a lot about your situation but is there anyone else who will be using this XXXXXX so we make sure we take care of their needs as well?

- Are there any particular resources within the situation now that we should be thinking about as we consider how to be of assistance?

SITUATION INSIGHT POTENTIAL – Asking these questions and having this conversation helps to challenge and reframe the client's perception of his or her own situation. By learning more about the customer's situation, you explore how he or she sees, hears, feels, understands his or her current environment. This process expands the customer's awareness of what is pertinent in his or her status quo. Typically, this helps the customer to discover previously undervalued resources within the current situation that might be useful when a new solution is identified.

Part of learning the customer's situation is discovering what he or she is doing well. It is a good place to start the conversation because the customer knows his or her own situation well and you don't. The customer gains confidence as he or she shares this positive information with you. It's easier to brag about success than it is to admit to problems and failures. You have a chance to build trust as you listen effectively. It will make it easier for the customer when you later ask him or her to share more difficult information.

As you learn more about the customer's current situation (*his or her status quo*), you might get information about the symptoms and problems the customer experiences. All situations have some problems. If the customer isn't giving you clues about such problems, you might have to ask a question or two to direct the customer to tell you what you need to know.

PROBLEM QUESTIONS

You ask these questions to discover the symptoms, difficulties, dissatisfactions, real problems, opportunities and challenges the customer is having in his or her current situation. You want to cause the customer to see his or her problem(s) differently, to ideally realize problems exist that he or she didn't know existed, or to see new opportunities he or she hadn't yet considered.

- Are you experiencing any problems with your current XXXXXX?

- What problems with your current XXXXXX cause you to think about getting a new one?

- How do you feel about your current XXXXXX – what don't you like about it?

- What frustrations do you have with your current XXXXXX that cause you to look for a new one?

- Have you been experiencing the symptoms of (*typical symptoms of the problem your solution resolves*)?

- We've noticed that some customers experience (*typical symptoms of the problem your solution resolves*). Have any of these symptoms been evident in your operations?

- How often do you encounter (*typical symptoms of the problem your solution resolves*)?

- When did you first start to think that your results aren't as good as you wish could be achieved?

- Have you been completely satisfied with how your current XXXXXX has served you over the past few years?

- What concerns do you have about your current set-up that motivate you to want a new XXXXXX?

- What don't you like about the way you currently do things?

- If you were to say your current way of doing things could be improved, what would you improve?

- Typically in every situation there are problems we have to work around and sometimes we don't get the results we're after. Do you have any problems right now you would like to address?

- If there is one negative in your current situation you would like to get rid of, what is that?

- You mentioned you don't like the current performance of your XXXXXX. Are there any other problems you experience?

- Given changes in how you do things, are new opportunities presenting themselves?

- I think I better understand what you are trying to do, but I need to understand what problems you're having doing that. What problems have you experienced?

Work to cause a new insight in the customer as you uncover the real problem. You add value by helping the customer to see his or her problem in a new way. This might be a function of focusing the customer's awareness on previously ignored or under-appreciated symptoms; or directing the customer's attention to the real cause of the symptoms if he or she is not looking in the right direction; or, stimulating the customer's thinking about a new opportunity.

PROBLEM INSIGHT POTENTIAL – By delving into the customer's problems, you may convert what were once assumed to be just "normal" attributes of the client's situation into perceived symptoms of a problem that needs to be resolved and not just accepted. This exploration will likely expose the real problem when that problem has not previously been understood. In addition, you might expand the customer's awareness of neglected opportunities.

If you discover that the potential customer does not have any of the problems that your solutions solve, this is a clue to end your sales interaction. Unfortunately, this may have wasted both your and your customer's time. Discover this as soon as you can. If you learn the customer has a problem your solutions do not address, then make a referral to someone who may have the correct solution. However, the very act of listening to the customer to clarify this much will have differentiated you from your competitors, and the customer might be more likely to come back to you when he or she has a new need that you can fulfill.

As you discover problems, you might also get clues as to the consequences of these problems. There is significant insight potential when a customer considers what the status quo truly costs. This is a critical point in the conversation. You must have established some rapport and trust to be ready to examine implications.

You want the customer to quantify his or her costs as much as possible. The customer has to be comfortable sharing such private information with you. In addition, as the customer confronts the costs of the problems, both tangible and intangible, he or she will encounter whatever emotions he or she has about these costs. The customer must perceive you as sensitive, caring, and non-judgmental, or your customer won't feel safe sharing this information with you. Be comfortable entering these emotional waters with your customers.

If the customer hasn't yet given you clues about the implications, you will have to ask an implication-oriented question to steer the conversation in that direction.

IMPLICATION QUESTIONS

These questions begin the portion of the conversation where determine the implications or consequences of those problems, specifically by discovering the degree of quantifiable cost, frustration, and pain the customer has within his or her status quo.

- What are the costs of using this method?

- What are the consequences for you when your current XXXXXX does that?

- What is the impact on you when you can't do what you want to do with your current XXXXXX?

- Is there a particular cost to you when you can't do what you want?

- Are there any consequences you experience with your current XXXXXX because it can't (*do what the customer wants*) ?

- If things aren't working as well as you would like, what does it cost you to stick with the status quo?

- Are there any particular costs that would result from delaying your purchase?

- Are there any tangible costs in continuing with your current set-up such as extra rent costs, maintenance, fuel costs that you would like to see reduced?

- Do you think you experience lower productivity using the current XXXXXX?

- Do these problems put you at a competitive disadvantage? If so, what is that disadvantage?

- Sometimes there are hidden costs doing things the way we do them now. Are there any you can now identify?

- What do you think it costs you to do it the current way versus upgrading?

- You've identified financial costs for how you do things now, but are there any intangible costs, such as personal satisfaction issues, quality being less than you would like, emotional costs such as disappointment or frustration?

- What does your analysis of this problem tell you about the costs of the problem – tangible, intangible and lost opportunity costs?

- How has this problem affected your success?

- Has this problem held you back in any way from achieving your goals and targets?

- Given your assessment of the real costs of this problem, what do you calculate as the burden of things staying the same?

- Are you experiencing any of the following costs:

  o costs of error or failure,

  o downtime costs,

  o maintenance costs,

  o lost opportunities,

  o negative impact on the people involved, or

o costs of delay?

- I assume you have new opportunities that you aren't yet able to pursue. What benefits and improved results might you be missing by not pursuing that new opportunity?

Learn both the tangible and intangible costs of the way things are now. Ideally, know the financial implications – the dollar costs the customer has to deal with. You want this information because it will be used to determine the value of what the customer will ultimately choose to buy. By taking stock, the customer will see how much not buying will continue to cost. The customer's motivation will rise if he or she concludes these costs are no longer acceptable.

IMPLICATION INSIGHT POTENTIAL – You have the opportunity to deliver new insights as the customer measures the full costs of his or her problems. From this exploration, he or she will likely realize that the consequences of not taking action are too great to live with or accept any longer. The customer, through new insight, might discover costs that hadn't previously been considered or fully understood.

At some point, you will know you've heard your customer's most significant implications. You'll have had an opportunity to empathize with the customer's feelings about these costs. Having realized that the costs are greater than first thought, the conversation might appear to hesitate because the customer bumps up against what is stopping him or her from solving the problems. Or the customer might actually state something like, "But, there isn't much we can do about this." The conversation now needs to focus on what is preventing a solution. Get at this with a constraint-focused question.

CONSTRAINT QUESTIONS

You ask these questions to find out what the customer thinks is blocking him or her from solving the problems. This includes learning what excuses he or she uses for why no change has happened before now. These questions also find out which are real constraints and which are imagined.

- What stopped you from making this change before today?

- So let me ask, what kept you from making a change before now?

- Has there been any particular reason why you haven't yet made a change?

- I gather you've been shopping around, looking for a new XXXXXX. What concerns have you had that kept you from buying?

- I know it's a big decision to make a change like this. How do you feel about that?

- Are there any roadblocks preventing you from making improvements?

- You've been putting up with this situation for quite some time. If you don't mind me asking, what prevents you from making this change?

- As your current XXXXXX got older, what kept you from getting a new one?

- Perhaps you haven't wanted to make a change before now. Can you tell me why?

- Various things keep us from upgrading. What are your reasons for sticking it out this long?

- Change is often something we avoid. If you've avoided making the change before now, please tell me why?

- Given all we've talked about, what stopped you from making a change before now?

- What alternatives have you already tried or considered, and what prevented them from producing your desired outcomes?

- Given that you've been working to resolve the problems, what seems to be the most critical hurdle blocking your progress?

- If your problem persists despite your best efforts, you must be bumping up against some tough roadblocks. What are they?

- Could you please tell me about the constraints that hold you back from getting this problem solved?

- You know the obstacles to successful resolution of this problem better than anyone so I need you to share that expertise with me. What would an effective solution have to overcome?

- Given that you've examined various alternative solutions, can you tell me why you've rejected each of them as unworkable in your situation?

- Sometimes our ability to implement change is constrained by the lack of willingness to change on the part of significant others. What resistance have you encountered?

- There are likely some pretty important criteria that any solution must meet. Please tell me what they are and why you think they are so critical?

Constraints can be quite varied – financial, regulation based, attitudes, lack of skills, contractual obligations, scheduling requirements, beliefs and values, timing, or anything that the customer feels is in his or her way. Constraints may relate to a low level of willingness to undergo change on the part of the customer. Alternatively, the customer might think others are unwilling to take on the risks of change.

Part of the exploration of constraints would include a determination as to the reality of these constraints. Are they real or imagined? To do this, your customer really does have to believe you have his or her best interests at the top of your agenda. If the customer trusts you, invite the customer to do this exploration with a further question like one of the following:

- Of the roadblocks you've identified, which ones most significantly get in your way?

- If we could do something about (*one of the constraints*), would it make it possible to proceed in a new way?

- Sometimes we think a constraint really prevents our taking action, but when we examine it, we realize it's something we can work around. Does this apply to any that you've just listed?

- If you had to prioritize the constraints in terms of importance, what constraints would be the most important and which constraints are less limiting?

- There are times when we limit our own ability to make changes. Thinking about the constraints you've identified, are any of them just excuses you're in the habit of using to keep from making a change, and not real roadblocks?

- As you consider them, which of these constraints is a real roadblock and which might just be an imagined limitation?

- If you had the power to wave a wand and make some of these roadblocks disappear, which would be the easiest to remove?

CONSTRAINTS INSIGHT POTENTIAL – This conversation helps to identify what is truly blocking change and what are only self-imposed or imagined limitations. As this is clarified, the client is enabled to make a choice for change based on the reality of his or her situation. The customer gets to challenge his or her assumptions about what really does prevent change. In turn, the customer's information informs the salesperson as to the full set of requirements the solution must satisfy.

Once you discover what has prevented action before now, shift to an exploration of what might be possible if the constraints were removed and the problems solved. Discover what would really excite the customer enough to make a decision to implement a solution to his or her problems. Discover what the customer would expect to gain if the best possible solution could be developed. You could start that process with one of these sample E^3 questions.

EXPECTATIONS, EXCITEMENT, EAGERNESS (E^3) QUESTIONS

These are the questions you ask to begin talking about what the person expects or hopes to experience as benefits when he or she solves the problem(s) by making a new acquisition. You use these questions to learn what will excite the customer enough to change? The E^3 questions discover what benefits your customer is looking to buy, and how eager he or she is to experience those benefits.

- What are your minimum expectations for the results you would have to achieve if you get a new XXXXXX?

- So what is the most important thing you're hoping to gain with this new XXXXXX?

- What do you hope to gain by buying a new XXXXXX?

- What do you think the benefits would be if you could really solve this problem?

- What would you gain if we could identify a complete solution that solved these problems?

- What do you think is the most important thing that would cause you to feel confident that something is the right solution?

- If you were going to paint me a picture of how you would like to see everything working, how would that look?

- For you, what is the one most important result you would get if a new XXXXXX did everything you wanted?

- What do you think is the most important consideration when making your decision?

- If we could provide a complete solution that meets your needs, what would that mean for you in terms of real gains?

- If you could get everything you wanted within your budget, what would be the most important gain for you?

- If we were able to come up with a solution that exceeded all of the expectations you've had up until now, what extra benefits would you really like to achieve?

- If we could reduce the costs you now experience, and increase the payoffs because you could do what you do better, faster, cheaper, what real benefits would you see?

- If I were to recommend a solution that gave you better and faster performance, what do you think the benefits would be?

- What do you think would be the most exciting benefit of getting a XXXXXX that would meet your needs?

- As you think about getting the new XXXXXX, what's most exciting for you?

- If you were able to get the ideal solution today, what would be the first thing you would like to brag about to your buddies?

- When do you hope to have the new XXXXXX in place?

- How eager do you think you are to achieve these benefits?

- Given the new possible outcomes we have discussed, how ready are you to find the ideal solution?

- How long do you think you can wait before a new solution is put in place?

EXPECTATIONS/EXCITEMENTS/EAGERNESS (E³) INSIGHT POTENTIAL – First, you help the customer clarify his or her minimum requirements that any solution must meet. By having this conversation, you also have the potential of elevating the customer's expectations. You invite him or her to think about the better results he or she might be able to achieve. Doing this brings about a new energy and desire for those higher benefits and shifts motivation to an eagerness to discover how the improvement can be achieved. You have the potential of liberating the customer's ability to consider new possibilities. By doing this, the customer will likely shift from hesitation and resistance to a desire for action. In turn, the customer will shift from wanting an acceptable solution to wanting the best solution.

By getting the customer to talk about his or her S.P.I.C.E³, you open the door for your customer to achieve many new insights. When the customer learns something new and important as a result of his or her conversation with you, you substantially differentiate yourself from any other salesperson that just tries to sell his or her stuff.

Test Your Understanding Of S.P.I.C.E[3]

Given the above examples of questions appropriate for each element, do you understand the differences between these elements? Do you have some clarity as to when you would ask such questions? Do you understand what information should surface when you address each of the five elements?

To test your self, read the following scenario, "Psychologist in Private Practice", and fill in your own S.P.I.C.E[3] sheet (*See Appendix 3*). Although this scenario involves an owner of a small business shopping for personal computing products, you don't have to be a computer products salesperson to do this exercise.

We deliberately use this example involving older technology so you may have some familiarity with the concepts involved, although this is not necessary. The information is about the client and not about products or services.

All the information you need for this test example is available in the scenario. On a piece of paper, list the answers to each of these five questions.

1. What do you know about the Situation?

2. What do you know about the Problem(s)?

3. What do you know about the Implications of the Problems?

4. What do you know about the Constraints?

5. What do you know about the Expected Gain
   (*Expectations/Excitements/Eagerness*)?

Psychologist In Private Practice

The customer is a Psychologist who has a private counseling practice. He counsels individuals, couples, and families. He sees his clients for fifty (50) minute sessions, and charges them $150 per session. He sees between 40 and 45 clients each week, with some of his normal counseling sessions scheduled on Wednesday evenings and his more urgent sessions, if he has any, scheduled on Saturdays. He doesn't work with clients on Wednesday mornings.

During the 10-minute interval before his next session, he dictates his notes about the previous counseling session into a dictation machine. He admits this is old technology but it allows him to move about his office as he talks into his dictation machine. He thinks best on his feet.

Currently, he dictates a week's worth of notes on voice tape and sends them to a typing service to have them transcribed as session reports. They return the type written work and his tapes to him in five to six days. This costs him $600 per month, and $5 per report for every report over 40 in a week.

In the transfer between his office and the typing service, some of his reports and tapes have been temporarily misplaced – not often, but enough for him to have concerns. He is required by law to keep such files and they must be kept confidential and secure. He harbors some worry about a potential lawsuit if a confidential report or tape fell into the wrong hands.

In addition, he uses the hard copies of these reports as his research notes from which he analyzes patterns in his cases and writes articles for publication. Currently, he does his writing work on an old computer. He originally bought the computer about five years earlier when he first set up his practice.

Because he is a weak typist and because he never really learned to use his word processing software, he types his error-ridden drafts on his computer in a simple text editor then sends out printouts of his draft work to the typing service when he needs a proper version typed. This costs him $3.00 per page. Some publications to which he submits his articles have advised him that he is going to have to find a way to submit his papers digitally via the Internet. He does not currently have access to the web on his computer.

When he originally bought his computer, he was told that it was possible to dictate straight into a computer and have it transcribe his speech to text. He bought some software to do this but it didn't work very well. He gave up all attempts to use it and switched back to his dictation machine.

He still wants to be able to dictate his notes, have the computer create the text file, save to disk, and print the hard copy. He then wants to be able to extract notes from his files to use when writing his papers and a book he is contemplating writing. However, he worries that the technology won't work any better now than it did before.

In addition, to support his writing and his casework, he wants Internet access so he can find out about the latest treatment programs for various disorders. He hears from colleagues and his children that he shouldn't be such a Luddite and he should be on the web. They tell him that it's an incredible source of information that would truly help him in his practice.

He takes in an average of 8 cheques per workday from his clients. He uses a bookkeeper to maintain his financial records. For her services, he pays $500 per month. He's heard he could do this with a simple computerized accounting system and save that expense. He wants to finance the computer to spread the payments out. He wants a reliable solution that meets all of these needs. He thinks this could save him money given his current expenses for these services.

He is a reluctant computer user and has indicated he doesn't want to be spending all of his time fiddling with the technology. Every hour spent learning to use the equipment is an hour of lost revenue, plus some dissatisfied clients if they can't get in to see him during that time. As well, he doesn't want to be spending a lot of his evenings learning to use a computer and the software. He must be able to use the equipment quickly. He expects it to be reliable and he expects good service from the dealer who sells him the equipment.

He will be the only person using this equipment. There are no other uses planned. He put off buying a new computer because he has been afraid of it, and the time it will take away from his practice to learn to use it. But, he would do so now if it feels right.

* * *

Read and analyze the above information. Organize your own thinking into the five S.P.I.C.E^3 elements on your S.P.I.C.E^3 sheet. Then write down your answer to this one major question, "Does the purchase price of the combined products and services that solve his problems matter in this situation? Yes or No?" Why do you think price is or is not an issue? How much do you think this customer might pay to get the right solution? Please do this before you read on. Challenge yourself in this exercise to be sure you understand the concepts correctly before you try to implement them in real life situations with real life clients.

* * *

We share below our own organization of the information into the five elements for you to compare with your own work. We do this to give you someone else's point of view – not to say this is how you should have sorted the information.

PSYCHOLOGIST'S S.P.I.C.E³ SUMMARY

Situation

- He is a professional psychologist, counseling his clients, and keeping confidential files about his sessions with them.

- He has an older computer, which he has hardly used and he continues to be a computer novice.

- He sends work out to a service to be typed, including his dictated notes on his counseling sessions and any draft papers he has written in his text editor.

- He needs to keep hard copy records of each counseling session and he uses these notes to write publishable papers.

- He hires a bookkeeper to do his accounting.

- He generates between 40 and 45 reports per week.

- He receives between 40 and 45 cheques per week.

- He doesn't work with clients on Wednesday mornings.

- He types then sends error-ridden drafts of his articles to the typing service that then prepares error free papers that he submits for publication.

Problems

- He has to wait about a week to get his work back from the typing service.

- The typing service has misplaced or temporarily lost some of his confidential dictations on client sessions.

- He is a slow typist and makes spelling errors.

- He doesn't have access to information on the Internet but most of his colleagues do.

- Publishers tell him he must submit his articles electronically but he can't.

- He has a book idea he hasn't been able to pursue.

Implications

- He must wait longer than necessary for access to his dictated notes.

- As a professional, he is at severe risk of an expensive lawsuit if the lost confidential information were to fall into the wrong hands, and this possibility scares him.

- He's not publishing as much as he would like and may be losing some ground as a professional to colleagues who appear to have incorporated computing technologies into their practice.

- He feels some embarrassment when his colleagues hear how he does things.

- He spends at least $1,100 per month on services.

- The quality of the work being done for him is less than it should be as the work of a professional, thereby diminishing his reputation.

Constraints

- He's concerned about his ability to learn to use the equipment quickly and if he can't, he will lose revenue because it will chew up his counseling time.

- His prior experience leads him to doubt that the technology will perform as promised.

- He has some dread about introducing this new way of working and his ability to handle this.

- He doesn't have a lot of extra time to learn how to use new technology.

Expectations, Excitements and Eagerness

- He wants to cut his costs if he can.

- He wants control over his own work – having access to the information when he wants it.

- He wants peace of mind – needs to be able to make sure the information is confidential and secure.

- He wants easy entry of information, working the way he's used to working.

- He wants to enhance his professional reputation.

- He wants to increase his success at getting published both in article and book form.

- He wants to learn to use the new technology as quickly as possible with the least interruption to his practice.

- He's looking forward to being able to gather information from the web and being able to submit quality papers on-line.

- He wants to quit using old technology and is excited about switching to the new methods of work his colleagues use.

- He wants a solution that will truly work this time.

- He wants this to feel right so he can buy now.

* * *

You might have had some small differences in your own work and that's okay. However, you do need to understand that the deepest part of his Reality Trough is about the severe risk he takes when he sends the confidential work out to be typed, the hurt he experiences professionally when not publishing, fear about lost time spent learning, disappointment over his inability to use the technology he bought last time, and the dollar costs he incurs in his current way of working. The constraints in this situation are primarily his doubt about the technology working, and his need to protect his time.

We believe this is a situation where the customer needs a solution, has current tangible and intangible costs, and an affordable solution exists. We don't think price is going to be an issue. The salesperson must provide a solution costing less than current costs. In addition, the solution will provide additional benefits over what this psychologist has now.

For example, this customer might be willing to pay as much as $1,100 per month (*potentially more to avoid the risks of a lawsuit*), if he could get the following:

- control over his own work, along with reduction of the $1,100 in current monthly expenses,

- a guarantee the confidential information is safely guarded,

- the ability to work in a manner he is accustomed to,

- the ability to gain access to the information when he needs it, instead of waiting for the service to send the information back,

- access to a broader database of information by getting on the Internet,

- more cost effective bookkeeping,

- the ability to submit papers electronically for publication,

- the ability to submit better quality articles based on case notes and better quality background research in a more timely fashion,

- the ability to work on his book, and

- training and assistance for full and effective implementation of a solution in the quickest possible timeframe.

All of this value, when compared to the costs of the status quo, could be worth much more to him than the current expenditure of $1,100 per month where he doesn't get these benefits. A solution involving a complete computer system, a digital dictation/voice-to-text translation device, software, supplies, training, leasing to spread payments out, preventative maintenance services and more would cost substantially less than $1,100 per month.

It would provide much more than he has been getting when paying a higher price and provide more than he expects. It will give him exciting benefits he can't have in his current situation. He is eager to achieve these benefits now. Price doesn't matter in this scenario and he is likely to buy a solution that gives him what he wants.

* * *

As a second test, go back to the exercise where you wrote out the S.P.I.C.E.^{3} information for your own client. Examine each point on your list. Do you mostly know product-related information, or do you know about his or her personal and business needs? Does your list include something about all of the five elements, or only about some of the elements?

Have you learned the information that falls within the customer's Reality Trough? Or, have you played it safe and stayed away from the frustrations, irritations, and pain of his or her status quo? Do you think your client is clear about the implications of staying the same and the constraints that block the buying of a solution?

If you know the information for all five elements, do you think your customer does? Have your prior conversations with the customer led him or her to new insights about any of your customer's situation, problems, implications, constraints or possible new results? Has your customer experienced the bottom of the Reality Trough and bumped up against what stops him or her from resolving the problems and experiencing better results? Is your customer excited about getting a solution and eagerly waiting to hear what you will recommend?

If you answer "Yes" to these questions, why haven't you made a sale? If you answer "No", what stops you from taking your customer through the full cycle of change to create a readiness to buy?

ASK QUESTIONS THEN LISTEN ACTIVELY

We presented many examples of questions for each of the five S.P.I.C.E.^{3} elements. We also emphasized the importance of only asking one or at most two questions for each element of the S.P.I.C.E.^{3} conversation. That's because too many questions feels like an interrogation.

Instead, you should be primarily listening to the customer as he or she shares this information with you during this step in the sales process. Use questions like these to start the exploration of each element then use the active listening skills to draw out deeper information.

Your goal is to reach for full understanding. You achieve **full understanding** through the process of listening to the customer, reflecting back what you understand from what the customer has said to you, and checking to see if you have understood.

You achieve full understanding when this active listening process causes the customer to gain new insight about his or her problems, implications, constraints and desired achievements. As you clarify the customer's needs, he or she learns from you and this adds value to working with you versus working with any of your competitors that do not do this.

ACHIEVING FULL UNDERSTANDING

Full understanding involves three accomplishments. Your goal is to achieve all three of these important aspects of full understanding. It is not enough to achieve just one or two.

FULL UNDERSTANDING =

You understand the other person.

+

The other person knows you understand.

+

The other person understands him or herself more completely.

Both of you must understand more deeply than before the S.P.I.C.E^3 conversation and both of you must know that you understand.

First, understand the customer. Understand the deeper meaning of his or her words and behaviors. To understand all of the customer's needs, encourage him or her to give you more information.

Secondly, for full understanding to occur, it's very important the customer knows you understand. Using the "GET SMARTER" sales approach, you demonstrate you understand by listening actively. You aren't just taking information in. You present back to the customer what you think you're getting and check to make sure you've understood. As a result, the customer knows you understand, because you actively demonstrate that you do.

Lastly, to achieve full understanding, the customer must increase understanding of his or her own needs. Your active listening behavior not only helps you to understand the customer. It also helps the customer to expand his or her own thinking and achieve a better awareness of his or her own needs. The customer sees and hears him or herself more completely through what you reflect back. The customer gets to re-hear him or herself through your words, form new insights and deepen his or her own self-understanding.

ACTIVE LISTENING SKILLS

There are particular active listening skills to use to conduct an effective needs assessment and to learn the customer's full S.P.I.C.E^3 without doing an interrogation.

INVITATIONS

An invitation is a specific request for the other person to tell you something about him or herself. Your goal is to keep the customer sharing information so you learn about his or her needs. As examples of Invitations, you could say,

"Gosh that sounds interesting. Please tell me more about what it means to be a (*what the customer is*). What do you do exactly?"

or

> "I don't know how you do what you do – can you please tell me more".

or

> "That's Interesting, I sure would like to know more."

or

> "Please explain what you mean when you say (_and then quote using the words the customer used_).

or

> "Please tell me more about _____ ."

EXPLAINED INVITATIONS

Alternatively, you could use the more elaborate skill of Explained Invitations.

Explained Invitations

> **A statement of the importance of the information you need in order to better understand.**

$+$

> **An invitation to tell you more and give you more information**

In some cases, people might ignore your invitation if they don't understand why they should tell you more. The customer might not yet appreciate your interest in helping him or her to better understand the full set of needs. Give the customer a reason.

First you explain why you want to know more, and then invite the other person to tell you. Be curious about his or her story and explain your curiosity. Get the customer talking and telling you what he or she thinks is relevant.

For example,

> "That sounds important and might influence which product is the right one for you. Could you please tell me more about that?"

or

> "It's critical that I understand the real problem you're trying to solve by buying a new solution today. You've said you have a problem with your XXXXXX. Please tell me more about how you experience this issue?"

Your explained invitation makes it easier for the customer to understand your need and to give you more information.

PARAPHRASING

Paraphrasing is the act of rephrasing what you think the customer means and then asking if you have understood correctly. Give the other person a chance to correct you so he or she can expand on what is being said.

Paraphrasing

> **A statement that shows what you think the other person meant by what he or she said (your interpretation of the meaning of the other person's words).**

$+$

> **A check-out question to determine if you have understood correctly.**

Paraphrasing is a particular skill with a powerful role in the "GET SMARTER" approach. Paraphrasing is an active listening skill. You don't just listen passively to the other person's words. Also, you don't just repeat back what the customer said. Repeating is being like a parrot. Parroting is annoying. Think of how annoying the kids' game is when a child keeps repeating back exactly what has just been said. Instead, you share your interpretation and ask if you have interpreted accurately.

You interpret the meaning first and then you reflect back your interpretation and ask if it is correct. For example,

"I think you're saying that....   Am I understanding you?"

or

"It seems like you mean....   Am I right?"

or

"From what you've said,
I'm guessing you mean....   Correct?"

or

"Sounds like you want...   Is this correct?"

Paraphrasing is reflecting back the full interpretation of what you get so the other person can correct you if you don't understand properly. Typically, we interpret what a person is saying based on how he or she says it, what we already know about him or her, our own history, and the context in which the other person says what he or she says. We have personal filters that adjust the message as we take it in. Our values, attitudes, prior experience, perception of the situation, needs, assumptions, mood and emotions all affect our ability to understand what is being said to us.

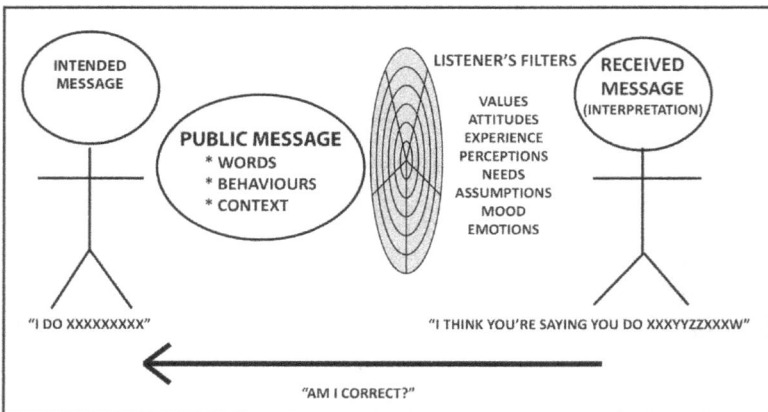

Our interpretation is usually much larger than the words the other person uses. As a result, our interpretation could match what the other person intended to convey in the way of meaning, be close but not quite what the other person meant, be completely inaccurate, or be more than the other person intended but still accurate.

There is almost always a gap between what the other person says and what we think he or she means. So we have to check to see if we have interpreted correctly. For example,

> "Do you mean you will be the primary user, doing work-related activities, but you also expect your children to be using it for school work and Internet access?

The customer can then do one of four things:

- Acknowledge the accuracy of your understanding – "Yes, that's what I mean."

- Correct the inaccuracy of your understanding – "No, what I meant is …"

- Expand on the accuracy of your understanding – "Yes I meant that and also …"

- Acknowledge your accuracy and expand on his or her own thinking – "Yes and that reminds me, I…"

Any of these responses lead you to full understanding because the information is clarified and expanded for both of you.

INFERENCE CHECKING

Inference checking is a skill that uses our natural tendency to form impressions about the other person based on the information he or she gives or shows, from what we know about him or her, or the context and situation we're in. We make guesses, somewhat informed by what the other person tells us, how he or she is dressed, what the other person does, what he or she doesn't do or say.

The skill of Inference Checking allows us to find out if the guesses we make about this other person are accurate. This requires that you pay attention to the inferences and assumptions you are making about the other person.

Inference Checking

> **A statement telling the other person what you infer or guess about him or her based on what you have seen or heard from the other person or have heard about him or her, or otherwise know about his or her context.**

+

> **A check-out question to determine if your inference or guess is correct.**

To check your inferences, tell the customer what you are inferring or guessing about him or her then check to determine if your inferences are correct. For example,

"I'm guessing you ....   Am I correct?"

or

"It's my inference that....   Is this right?"

or

"Perhaps you...   Correct?"

or

"I'm thinking you want...   Am I right?

You disclose the guesses you make in order to check if your guesses are accurate, to keep yourself on track, to learn more about the customer. If you didn't check, you could be forming the wrong impressions, thereby leading you to make the wrong recommendation later.

Sharing your inferences has the added benefit of allowing the customer to give you more information about him or herself. The customer does this as he or she either confirms the accuracy of your guess, or corrects you. In turn, if you surface something important that expands the customer's understanding of his or her S.P.I.C.E[3], the customer achieves greater self-understanding.

Inference Checking works best when you make positive guesses about the other person, and not judgmental or critical guesses. Use your intuitive ability to form positive assumptions about your customer and then check to see if your assumptions are correct. When Inference Checking with your customers, you could say something like:

> "My other customers have concerns about maintenance costs. I'm guessing that's important to you as well?

or

> "Jill, you're dressed quite stylishly now so I'm guessing that you're looking for a new outfit that matches the latest trend for (*desired style*) . Am I correct?"

or

> "I'm guessing you do most of your writing for your book in your spare time. Am I correct?"

The customer can make any of the same four responses as he or she would in response to a paraphrase – acknowledge that you understand, correct you, acknowledge some understanding and expand, or acknowledge and add the new information triggered by hearing your inference.

FEELINGS CHECKING

Feelings Checking is similar to both paraphrasing and inference checking but is focused on the customer's underlying emotions. You want to focus on those underlying feelings because they are clues to the customer's full set of needs.

Feelings Checking is the act of showing that you have empathy for the customer by noticing how he or she seems to feel. You make your guess about the underlying emotions based on observations of the other person's behavior. You listen to voice tone and tempo, watch for facial, body and hand gestures, notice what is said and not said. Your mind is always trying to get a sense of how the other person is feeling based on these observations. Use that natural inclination to add to your understanding of the other person. The Feelings Checking skill is used to determine if you read your customer's feelings accurately.

Feelings Checking

> **A statement telling the other person what you infer or guess about the other person's feelings based on what you have seen or heard from the other person or know about his or her situation.**

$+$

> **A check-out question to determine if your inference or guess about the feelings is correct.**

You state your guess as to how the customer is feeling, and ask if you have guessed correctly. For example,

"I'm guessing you feel...   Am I reading you correctly?"

or

"It seems like you feel...   Am I right?"

or

"You're likely feeling...   Is this correct?"

or

"You're feeling ...   about that?"
(*clearly expressed as a question*)

Your guess is about the other person's emotional state so your guess should be an emotion word – happy, sad, disappointed, frustrated, anxious, hurt, excited, angry, tense, stressed, eager, pleased, etc.

When feelings checking with your customers you could say something like:

"As I listen to you, I sense a confusion about what all of the technical jargon means, and this can be pretty intimidating when making a purchase as significant as this, am I right?"

or

"You seem quite frustrated by not being able to meet your deadlines, is this correct?"

or

"You look somewhat shocked by this calculation of your current costs. I'm guessing the size of that cost startles you?"

Once again, the customer can acknowledge that you're accurately reading his or her emotions, correct you, acknowledge some understanding and expand, or acknowledge and add new information stimulated by the customer's expanding awareness of his or her own feelings.

IDENTIFICATION

Identification is also an active listening skill. It is used to show the other person you understand his or her situation because you've been in a similar circumstance yourself, or you can at least imagine what it must feel like to be in the same predicament.

Identification

> **Your description of your own similar experience and the feelings that you had, or your guess about how you would feel if you were in the same situation as the other person is experiencing.**

+

> **A check-out question to determine if the other person feels the same way.**

Identification shows empathy. This will help the other person open up to you. We have greater trust in people who understand what it means to "walk a mile in our shoes".

Using identification, you think of a time when you were in a similar predicament or you imagine yourself in the other person's situation. Then check your own awareness of how you would feel. Imagine you work and live in similar circumstances, you have the same goals, you have the same problems, and you can't solve your difficulties until you get a new solution. Then ask yourself, "How would I feel if this were me?"

This is a powerful tool you would use no more than once or twice in your conversation to show empathy and caring. For example, you could say something like,

"I remember when I bought my first XXXXXX. I felt lost and confused about the many words I'd never heard before. I guess you feel the same way right now. Correct?"

or

"I remember when I had to buy the XXXXXX for my boss. He expected me to know what I was doing, but I was relatively new to XXXXXXs myself. I found I was frustrated by the many different choices I had to make. I'm guessing you feel the same pressure as you shop for a XXXXXX for your organization, am I right?"

or

"If I imagine myself in your situation, having just realized how much I'm currently paying for less than satisfactory results, I'd feel disappointed about not having had this fixed earlier. Are you feeling that way?"

or

"Janet, when I was looking for a new XXXXXX, I was quite concerned about how much training I would need in order to be able to use it effectively, and worried that I couldn't learn what I had to know. I'm guessing you feel some of that concern right now, correct?"

116

Customers will appreciate your effort to put yourself in their shoes and feel what they feel. If you guess correctly, you expand the trust and rapport within your relationship. If you guess incorrectly, they still appreciate your effort to understand what they're experiencing and will correct your misunderstanding. As the customer corrects you, he or she expands his or her awareness of real feelings, and this increases his or her motivation to do something about these feelings.

EFFECTIVE QUESTIONING

Be skilled at asking different types of questions. The types of questions you ask have an impact on the quality of answers you get. Open questions solicit larger answers. Closed questions get single word answers. Ask more open questions than closed.

A Closed Question such as "Do you own a XXXXXX now?" will likely elicit a single word answer of Yes or No. You could easily get that information and much more by asking an Open Question such as, "What do you use your existing XXXXXX for?"

There's another way to classify question types – direct versus exploratory. Direct questions seek a specific piece of information. For example, "Do you expect to use the laptop on an airplane?" This focuses the customer's attention on that specific thought and a specific answer is being invited.

On the other hand, exploratory questions seek elaboration and an expanded story. For example, "What will you be using the laptop for?" This question is more open in nature and invites a sharing of information by the customer that could cover a broader range. This allows the customer to take the story where he or she thinks it should go. The broad answer could include reference to taking the laptop on airplanes or not, depending on the relevance of that information to the customer.

In general, ask exploratory questions at the beginning, and save your direct questions until you near the end of your discussion of needs. You want an open conversation at the beginning where the customer takes the lead, and a more directed conversation as you near the end. After you know most of the customer's S.P.I.C.E[3], ask one or two direct questions to get those last bits of information you need to know.

This allows your customer to tell you his or her story without the distraction of your specific questions. It increases the likelihood you will learn all you need to know instead of getting focused on only part of the story.

Questions take control of the conversation and can distract the customer from telling you the story in the way he or she wants to tell it. If you ask too many questions, you run the risk that you will not get the whole story. You may get answers to your questions, but if you failed to ask a question about a key aspect of the customer's story, you don't achieve full understanding. Questions are necessary but you only want to ask a few.

Each type of question can be useful. You just need to pay attention and learn the proper timing for when to ask the different question types. There are several types of exploratory questions, and as they get the customer telling you more about his or her full story, learn to use these different types.

Standard Questions start with who, what, where, when, how, and why. A standard question is an open question seeking an elaborate answer. When you ask, "How do you do this now, given that you don't have an XXXXXX yet?", you're asking a standard question.

Status Quo Questions try to get an elaboration of the customer's current situation. For example, you could ask, "How is your day-to-day work affected by your current XXXXXX?" This is a good type of question to help you to learn if the customer is not happy with the status quo.

"Best Of All Possible Worlds" Questions ask the customer to imagine the best possibility and describe what that would look like or entail. For example, you could ask, "If a new XXXXXX could give you a competitive advantage, what would the advantage be?" This is a good type of question to use to learn about his or her expectations and excitements.

Assumptive Questions start with a positive assumption about the customer then finish with a question that relates to that assumption. This works best when you assume the customer has done what you think should have been done in the situation, and ask the outcome. For example, you could ask, "When you measured the

118

costs of that problem, what did you discover?" or "When you asked your partner to solve that issue, what happened?" or "When you did (*what the customer could have done*) , what took place?"

Multiple Choice Questions help your customer to answer a question by giving several answers to choose from. Give the other person several possibilities and then ask which might apply for him or her. When people have choices, they feel more freedom. As an example of a multiple-choice question, you could say,

"People choose to use an XXXXXX for different reasons. Some people use it for recreational purposes, while others use it for their work. A few use it for both. Which applies in your case?"

or

"When choosing their delivery supplier, some people are more concerned about delivery costs than the time of delivery, the method of delivery, or the tracking of the delivery. Which is most important to you?"

or

"Have you noticed any dryness of skin, itching, an increased tendency for your skin to break and bleed, greater need for moisturizing cream, changes in your color?"

Alternatively, you could help your customer to answer by asking an explained question.

Explained Questions start with a clear declaration of your reason for asking a particular question. This gives the other person a reference point to better understand the reason for giving you the information.

To use this skill effectively, you must first understand your real reason for asking a particular question. This requires an expanded awareness of your own motives and your own requirements for certain bits of information. Consequently, you should have a specific purpose behind each question that you ask. It helps if you have the full intention to learn the customer's S.P.I.C.E[3] as this structure gives you the reasons to gather specific information.

Explained Question

> ## A clear statement of the full reason that you wish to ask a question.

$$+$$

> ## An open question to draw out all of the customer's thoughts in response to your need to know that information.

As an example of an **Explained Question**, you could say,

> "In order to make a proper recommendation, I need to know what you'll be using the XXXXXX for and what you hope to gain by using it. What benefits are you looking for?"

or

> "In order to make sure our solutions are relevant to your situation, I would like to know more about any problems you experience right now. Have you noticed any particular difficulties when you are (*doing what the customer does*) ?"

In effective selling, having the ability to make good use of questioning skills is an art. Know:

- when to ask a question,
- what to ask about,
- how to choose the type of question to ask in order to make answering the question easier for the customer, and
- when to use the active listening skills instead.

Experiment with different questions and different question types. Notice how your customers react. Pay attention to their non-verbal responses. If there is any hesitation, or apparent reluctance, there may be a problem with your question. Do you see the other person relax as you ask the question, or get tense? Does the customer move toward you ever so slightly, or move back? Does he or she show excitement about answering the question, or suspicion?

Learn to use your questions effectively and you'll differentiate yourself from your competition. You add value just by being someone who draws out information and listens, making the conversation more comfortable to the customer.

MATCHING

If you really want to build rapport with another person, if you really want to show you understand, if you really want to get into the other person's shoes to achieve full understanding, then subtly and gently use the skill of matching. This is a skill best used only after you've mastered the preceding skills.

We share it here for the sales professional who really wants to master the relationship building and needs assessment process. The skill can be used deliberately to achieve and deepen rapport. Rapport helps the customer to feel comfortable opening up with you. Matching works when your matching behavior is below the other person's conscious awareness.

Matching involves subtly adopting some of the gestures, posture, voice tone and tempo, eye movement patterns, and words and phrases used by the other person. The key word is "subtle". You match enough but not too much.

Matching is an act of becoming the other person, stepping inside his or her shoes to see and feel the world the way he or she does. When done properly and with a positive intent, matched behavior feels familiar. Familiarity leads to trust and rapport. This enhances one's feeling of safety.

Used incorrectly, the customer can be put off, sensing he or she is being mimicked or even mocked. Matching isn't mimicry when done effectively, but it typically is when done poorly. If people sense you are copying them, they can become suspicious of what you are doing. This is particularly likely if you are not genuinely trying to experience the world the way they do. Hence you want to use this skill carefully and preferably naturally. Get into a state of rapport with your customer by using the active listening skills, and subtly continue the rapport building with matching behavior.

Before you actually try to use the skill, check out the validity of this skill as a natural form of human behavior. Start paying attention to your conversations. Do this in informal situations where friends chat with each other or with family members engaged in conversation. Particularly notice how the two of you look and sound when you think you experience trust and rapport with each other.

When in rapport, you will notice similar gestures, pace, voice tonality. Posture will likely involve some form of lean toward each other. Conversely, when not in rapport, pace of speech might be disparate, gestures dissimilar, body posture closed and distanced from the other person. Our body language says something about how open, safe, and close we feel to the people we talk with.

As another way to see matching in action, watch two people who seem to be comfortably engaged in conversation. First watch one person's behavior and then watch for similar behaviors as the other responds. If you can videotape the behavior then turn off the sound and run the video at a faster speed, this similarity of behavior between two people in a state of rapport becomes very apparent.

Matching must be done with a desire to empathize, understand and respect the other person. If your intention is to manipulate in some way, it likely will not work. Use this normal human behavior to deepen your relationships with your customers. Use matching to step into the other person's world and better understand his or her needs.

USING THE ACTIVE LISTENING SKILLS

A key element of the "GET SMARTER" sales process is the notion that you don't move on to selling your products and services until you fully understand your customer's needs. Half of the time that you have available with this customer should be spent on the first three steps. In these first three steps, you take the time to "GET" the information you need in order to make an effective recommendation. Being any less informed before you attempt to sell a solution is not an effective way to take care of the customer.

The goal is to work through the S.P.I.C.E[3] sequence so the salesperson will likely start with a Situation Question to learn more about what the customer is trying to do. Once the customer has offered information, the salesperson's interpretation of that information is reflected back and checked to see if understanding has occurred.

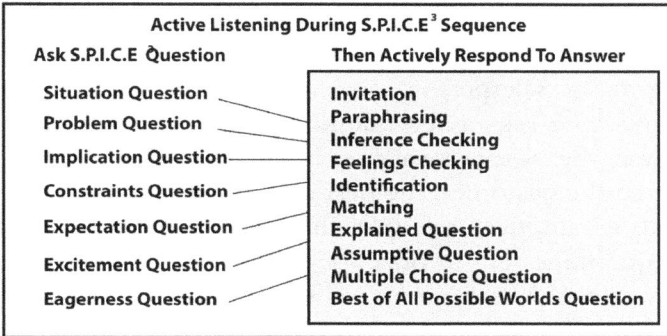

Active Listening During S.P.I.C.E[3] Sequence	
Ask S.P.I.C.E Question	Then Actively Respond To Answer
Situation Question	Invitation
Problem Question	Paraphrasing
	Inference Checking
Implication Question	Feelings Checking
Constraints Question	Identification
	Matching
Expectation Question	Explained Question
	Assumptive Question
Excitement Question	Multiple Choice Question
Eagerness Question	Best of All Possible Worlds Question

As the customer gives information, skilled salespeople use paraphrasing, inference checking, and summarizing to actively listen to the information. Effective salespeople keep their customers talking by actively following what the customer says. The salesperson reflects back what he or she is receiving from the customer so the customer can correct if the salesperson misunderstands, or the customer can further elaborate if the salesperson does understand.

During this process, the best salespeople pay attention to the customer's non-verbal behavior as well as to what the customer says, because these can be important clues about the customer's feelings about the benefits of solving his or her problems. In turn, feelings are the windows to any subconscious and underlying expectations the customer might have, even though the customer may not be fully aware of all of his or her expectations.

These highly proficient salespeople use the feelings checking skill to make sure they're reading the customer's emotions correctly, and to show respect for those feelings. The best also know it can be very helpful to use the skill of identification with the customer to show empathy, and to help the customer feel safe in talking about him or herself.

This process continues through each of the five elements. Focus on each particular element by starting with a question appropriate to that element then clarify with the active listening skills until you know what you need to know about that element. Then ask a question for the next element in the S.P.I.C.E[3] sequence. Get these answers in a conversation where the customer does most of the talking and you listen actively.

Once the customer has elaborated as much as possible in response to the salesperson's use of the active listening skills, the salesperson then asks a few questions to get the remaining bits of information the salesperson needs. To make the questions more palatable to the customer, the best salespeople will favor the use of explained, assumptive, multiple choice, and "best of all possible worlds" questions. Try to only ask questions to get the needed bits of information the customer failed to tell you spontaneously as you actively listened.

During this conversation, the best salespeople deflect both themselves and their customers away from talk about specific products. Products do not matter at this stage. The salesperson is trying to learn what the customer wishes to accomplish so the salesperson can recommend the best solution.

BEHAVIORS THAT INTERFERE

There are certain behaviors that will get in the way of listening for understanding, and you have to guard yourself from using them.

- **Pitching Your Product** – offering information about your products, services, and solutions in response to something the customer has just said.

- **Listening For Just The Facts** – focusing so much on the facts that the position, ideas, or emotions that the facts are intended to convey are missed.

- **Not Taking Notes** – relying on memory, which gets harder to do when the story gets more complex, and consequently important parts of the story are forgotten.

- **Distractions** – putting up with or causing distractions like the clicking of a pen, talking with someone else while the speaker is talking, or doing something else while listening

- **Emotional Distractions** – having specific feelings in response to something the speaker says that trigger your own thoughts about prior situations, thereby taking your attention away from what is being communicated.

- **Preconceptions** – not listening to what the customer says because of some preconceived idea (*i.e. hearing something that makes you think he or she is just like other customers*).

- **Embarrassment** – missing something the speaker said and being too embarrassed to ask him or her to repeat it, or being too intimidated to give back your interpretation out of fear that you are wrong.

- **Interruptions** – cutting off or otherwise interrupting the speaker because you think you have something more important to say or ask.

- **Premature Directive Questions** – cutting off the flow of the customer's story by asking a pointed or direct question that changes the subject and directs the customer to attend to what you think is important before the customer has had a chance to tell you what he or she thinks is most important.

- **Criticizing** – privately thinking about or publicly commenting on negative aspects of the speaker or what he or she is telling you instead of learning his or her full meaning.

- **Faking Attention or Rehearsing** – thinking of something other than what the customer is saying, or mentally preparing what to say next, or thinking about the next question.

- **Prejudging** – adopting a negative attitude and tuning the speaker out (*for example, by deciding the customer probably won't buy much*).

Discipline yourself to avoid these behaviors. They just get in the way of open conversations. Notice what happens inside you when others do these things to you as you tell your own stories.

125

NOT ABOUT PRODUCTS

None of these elements involves discussion of products or services. Simply put, it is best if you have a self-imposed rule against talking about product or solutions at this stage. In the "GET SMARTER" approach, you don't ask questions about which products the customer wants, likes or needs, or even which features the customer wants, likes or needs. Steer the conversation away from a product focus if you can, to a focus on what the person wants to accomplish with the products.

Your encounter with the customer might start with the customer asking, "How much is your Product X?" Answer the question then take charge to steer the customer toward a discussion of his or her needs. The question about price, and your answer, would ideally be the last mention of product in the discussion of needs. Instead of asking the customer which features he or she is looking for, find out what the customer hopes to gain by using the new product.

No matter how technical the products or services you sell, it's your job to have a plain language conversation about the customer's needs. If you talk product during this discussion of needs, you make the customer responsible for being a product expert. If this happens, you're not doing your job. If the customer has to be the product expert, what does he or she need you for? If the customer has to be the expert, he or she will likely just gather information from the Internet then shop for the best price – you offer no additional value. Get your customer to participate as the expert who knows about his or her own personal information and needs, while you concentrate on understanding those needs so you can later determine which solution is best.

PERSONAL USE OF THE ACTIVE LISTENING SKILLS

You've just been shown effective interpersonal skills for listening, and achieving full understanding:

- invitations, and explained invitations,
- paraphrasing,

- inference checking,

- feelings checks,

- identification,

- exploratory questions including assumptive, multiple choice, "best of all possible worlds", and explained questions, and

- matching – subconscious paraphrasing showing the customer you really want to understand what it means to be him or her.

We hope you choose to use these skills, as active listening will enrich your sales interactions with customers. Use these skills to get customers talking and help your customers to find the reasons and motivation to buy.

However, these skills will also enrich your personal life if you use them more often in your own relationships. Your spouse, your children, your friends will appreciate you when you give the gift of listening to their needs with the goal of full understanding. Using these skills will mean your significant others will open up with you to disclose generally private information. When you use these skills, the other person feels he or she can trust you.

Use the skills wherever you have an opportunity to listen to others. This will build your proficiency with the skills and make such use much more natural when you engage in your sales activities. If you get so comfortable with the skills that you don't have to think about them, you become unconsciously competent. This frees you up to pay more attention to your customer than to your own responses.

It's a safe assumption you already know how to use these skills. However, most people use them all too seldom. We urge you to deliberately use these skills in Step Three, where you take time to learn your customer's needs and get his or her S.P.I.C.E[3]. We also urge you to increase the frequency of use of these skills with those you love and care about.

Using active listening skills is significantly better for your own well being, the well being of your customers, and the well being of your family and friends. Active listening is better than using the behaviors known to get in the way of achieving rapport and understanding.

YOUR OWN COMFORT WITH FEELINGS

When you use these skills with customers, some of what they disclose to you will be the problems they have within their status quo. In turn, if you help to explore the consequences of these problems, feelings will be triggered by the customer's expanded awareness of the costs. You must be able to handle these feelings and to treat some level of negative emotions as a normal outcome of expanded awareness of the problems and their implications.

When we train salespeople to use these skills, some trainees say, "We're not therapists. We don't need to handle customer feelings. We don't even need to know what the feelings are." This is a typical response from people who early in life learned to shut the door on feelings and to act as if their own feelings didn't exist.

However, we think it's better for the customer to confront those feelings. This allows the emotions to surface as the customer realizes the need to take action. This helps the customer get to the point of saying, "This sucks. Let's do something about this. What have you got as a solution?"

This isn't therapy. We aren't asking you to fix "broken" people. But buying is about making a change. To be motivated to make the change, the customer benefits when the full cost of not changing is known.

Bringing the implications of the status quo into full awareness will surface negative emotions along with the realization that the costs are higher than the person was admitting to him or herself. Assist the feelings to surface and the motivation to change will rise. These skills make it easier for the other person to listen to your recommendation when it is time for you to make it.

MULTIPLE PERSON CUSTOMERS

In some retail situations, customers might be representatives of small businesses or special interest groups, or the customer might be a couple or an entire family. For example, a couple might visit an auto dealership looking for a new vehicle. A special interest group might visit a sports equipment store to look for equipment for a team. A member of a small business might visit a cell phone store looking for a viable cell phone alternative for all members of the business.

If you frequently sell to small businesses, groups or families, you will have to learn about the S.P.I.C.E^3 of all people who will participate in decision-making and those who will be most significantly impacted by the changes arising from implementation of a new solution. The first half of the selling process will be longer as you speak to each V.I.P. involved in the purchase process.

As you move from person to person, identify the problems from each person's perspective then find out how each person experiences the implications and constraints. Learn what each person would ideally like to see as results when a new solution is applied. Help each party to achieve insights about the real problems; the true costs; the real constraints and those just imagined; plus the results and benefits that could potentially matter.

Make sure each person understands you are listening to each other person in the organization, group, or family so you can arrive at a solution that has total support. When you think you know enough, share what you've learned about the needs of the total group. This will give you an opportunity to once more review the S.P.I.C.E^3 and make sure you have full understanding.

If you are meeting with the whole group or family at once, each person will hear what every other member thinks. Make eye contact with each person you speak to. Use the active listening skills to check for and demonstrate understanding. It will be your responsibility to encourage all parties to listen for understanding and you will have to work harder to keep the whole group moving through the exploration of their S.P.I.C.E^3 in an organized process.

Even though you work in a retail environment, if you are selling a potentially complex solution to a small business, you may want to have different meetings with different individuals and possibly a group from the business. Again, you will have to work hard to keep everyone together as you move through the S.P.I.C.E^3. After you have talked to many, getting individual perspectives and small group input, share what you've learned and review a collective S.P.I.C.E^3. Your summary will show that there is some consensus about the needs.

WHEN TO MOVE TO THE NEXT STEP

Recognize when it's time to move to the next step. You are ready to move forward when you have indications from your customer that you fully understand him or her, and that your customer has a better understanding of his or her own S.P.I.C.E^3. You are particularly ready if the customer has achieved new insights.

Move forward when the customer trusts your intention to satisfy his or her needs. You are both ready when the customer sees you as an expert who wants to provide only the right solution and not just sell something you have in stock. By behaving like an insight-oriented consultant who first wants to understand your customer's needs, you will be seen as working for your customer, and not working on the customer.

Option 1 Half Time Before Summary	Option 2 Summary Before Half Time	Option 3 Before and After Half Time
Greet	Greet	Greet
Engage	Engage	Engage
Take Time To Learn The Customer's S.P.I.C.E^3	Take Time To Learn The Customer's S.P.I.C.E^3	Take Time To Learn The Customer's S.P.I.C.E^3
Half Time	Show Full Understanding - Summarize The S.P.I.C.E^3	Show Full Understanding - Summarize The S.P.I.C.E^3
Show Full Understanding - Summarize The S.P.I.C.E^3	*Half Time*	*Half Time*
Make Your Recommendation	Make Your Recommendation	Summarize The S.P.I.C.E^3 Again
		Make Your Recommendation

You have a decision to make at this point. You must decide whether to follow getting your customer's S.P.I.C.E.^{3} with either Option 1 – moving to Half Time where you use a break in the interaction to prepare for your summary and your recommendation, or Option 2 – summarizing what you've learned before Half Time, or Option 3 doing the summary of your customer's S.P.I.C.E.^{3} both before and after Half Time.

This decision is as much about the art of selling as it is about the sales process. You have to use your judgment in each situation to determine which option to utilize.

The decision depends on how clearly both of you understand the customer's S.P.I.C.E.^{3}, how deeply the customer has felt his or her Reality Trough, and how eager the customer is to receive your recommendation. It also depends on how long Half Time is going to be. If a long Half Time, do the summary both before and after.

In general, you can likely move to Half Time if you've been using the listening skills with a fair degree of checking to see if you have full understanding, and if you worked in a sequential fashion through the customer's S.P.I.C.E.^{3}. If so, you've been summarizing what you've learned as you continued the conversation. You know it's time to move to Half Time when you're confident you both know the customer's S.P.I.C.E.^{3}. Go to Half Time if he or she is eager to hear your recommendation.

On the other hand, if you aren't sure the customer knows you fully understand his or her S.P.I.C.E.^{3} or if your customer hasn't fully experienced the Reality Trough, then proceed to Step Four where you concisely summarize what you know about his or her problem(s), costs, constraints, and what would be most exciting. Talk the customer through his or her S.P.I.C.E.^{3} so the customer clearly feels the lows of the Reality Trough and the highs of his or her expectations, excitement and eagerness before you go away for Half Time. Leave the customer eagerly waiting to hear your recommendation.

A third option is to do Step Four before you break for Half Time, and then once again when you return. By skillfully doing the summary twice, you can increase the customer's eagerness to hear what you have to recommend. However, there is a risk that you will be too repetitive, which could diminish the customer's anticipation. It's best if you do this when Half Time is a longer interval.

In the retail context, you would probably start Half Time right after you've learned the customer's S.P.I.C.E[3] because you've been actively listening and summarizing as you did so. Your Half Time is likely to only be a few minutes and the customer isn't likely to lose his or her eagerness in that interval.

THE TRANSITION TO HALF TIME

Use Half Time to prepare yourself for the second half of the sales process. Ask for a moment or if necessary, a longer time away from the client to do your preparation. When working on a retail floor, you might indicate you wish to gather everything together that you would like to recommend. Alternatively, you could tell the customer you wish to prepare a computer generated quotation, or tell the customer you want to check your ideas with one of your colleagues to ensure you have the best solution.

> "I think I have an understanding of your needs and expectations. If you agree, I'd like just a few minutes (*hours, days, weeks*) to prepare my recommendation. If you're okay with the wait, perhaps you could (*complete this credit application while you wait, or read this information to help you determine what to consider when making your decision*). Is that okay with you?"

If you'll be only a few minutes, give the customer something to do. This could be completing a credit or lease application, reading some material that relates to the solution you will suggest, or having a coffee in a waiting area.

> "Jack, I really appreciate the conversation we've just had. You've been very kind letting me know what you're trying to accomplish and what it's currently costing you to not get the results you want. I think we have a great way to take care of you, and I'd like to gather the elements of that solution together. It will only take me a few minutes to do so. Earlier, we talked about the benefits of spreading out the payment, so while I'm getting

everything ready, you could fill out this credit application. If you elect to proceed with that option, filling it out now will speed up the process. Sound okay to you?"

or

"Sue, I need a few minutes to get my recommendation organized. I'd like to get you a cup of tea or coffee and a seat in our customer waiting room. Can I do that?

or

"Sam, I think we both understand the benefit of getting a solution right away. We have everything you need, but I want to gather it together to show you how we can take care of this, and get you the increased benefits right away. While I do this, I suggest you fill out this lease application so we have that as an option to spread out your payments and get a tax advantage for your business at the same time. It will only take a few minutes for each of us, and then we can review what I have to suggest. Sound okay?"

If you've made the decision to break for Half Time, you want your client waiting with anticipation for what you'll bring back as your solution. You want your customer to be curious about how you will reduce costs, meet all expectations and clearly increase his or her benefits. Let your customer know how much time you will need to be away. Keep Half Time as short as you reasonably can. This will sustain the customer's anticipation for the short interval the customer has to wait.

If there is a long delay between your gathering of his or her S.P.I.C.E³ information and your return, the customer might be tempted to take his or her new understanding to a different supplier. If you are pretty sure you have the right solution available, give a clear time frame for when you will present your solution.

However, if you don't yet know what solution you should recommend, or if you aren't sure you have the solution right now, advise the customer that Half Time will take longer as you search for a suitable solution. Emphasize that the customer's situation is complex and deserves the best possible solution. Tell him or her you will use the time to find that solution.

> "Bill, we've discussed a lot today, and it seems particularly important that we provide a unique solution to your needs. I have some ideas as to what we could propose to best solve your problem(s), but I want to organize my thoughts. It will also help me to speak with our specialists to get their advice as to the best way to solve this problem, so I'd like to set a time about three days from now when you could return and I could present and discuss our proposal. Would that be acceptable?"

or

> "Jill, I really appreciate your openness today. I'm excited about getting you the best solution for your needs. We don't have the complete solution in stock so I need to do some research and find out where and when I can get what you need. That will take me a day to get the information, so I'd like to meet with you again tomorrow, if that works for you?"

Once you have the customer's approval to break for Half Time, thank your customer and get to work on your recommendation right away. You want to be seen to be working with some urgency to provide the best possible solution as soon as possible. You reinforce his or her eagerness by demonstrating your own eagerness to get what your customer needs.

THE TRANSITION TO SHOW FULL UNDERSTANDING

On the other hand, if your conversation hasn't been as organized as it could have been and your customer needs to have a clear description of his or her S.P.I.C.E.[3] along with a chance to more deliberately review the emotions of his or her Reality Trough, you need a way to transition to a summary of what you learned. Make this transition to Step Four by telling your customer you think you understand what he or she needs, and then ask for permission to summarize what you've learned. Do this to confirm understanding.

> "Before I make my recommendation, I want to be completely sure I fully understand. I'd like to summarize what you've told me. Is that okay? "

If okay, move to Step Four and summarize his or her S.P.I.C.E[3] clearly taking your customer through the Reality Trough. Leave your customer in that state of anticipation for what you are going to recommend.

Half Time

(Getting Ready To Make Your Recommendation)

Half Time can be as short as a few seconds while you gather your thoughts, or as long as months if the solution isn't yet available. The client will wait as long as it takes – if you've done the first half effectively.

During Half Time, you review your own understanding of the customer's needs, determine the right solution for those needs, and prepare to present your solution. If you have initiated Half Time before doing Step Four, you will also need to rehearse doing the S.P.I.C.E[3] summary to show full understanding.

G	Greet	Greet and approach showing interest in the customer and beginning a conversation.
E	Engage	Engage in conversation allowing relationship building to occur.
T	Take Time to Learn the Customer's Needs (Get The Customer's S.P.I.C.E[3])	Get the S.P.I.C.E[3] in an open discussion of the customer's needs, reaching for new insights and taking time to actively listen to the customer as the customer does most of the talking while you clarify for understanding (*reach for deeper insight*).
	Half Time	*Identify the best solution, prepare to recommend a complete solution, and if necessary, rehearse your summary of the customer's S.P.I.C.E[3].*

GOALS OF HALF TIME

You have several goals to achieve in this break between the first half of the sales process and the second:

- acquire the expertise (*either on your own or by turning to in-house or supplier-based experts*) that allows you to determine the best solution for the customer's needs,

- determine if you have a solution that fully satisfies the customer's needs,

- locate all of the components of that complete solution,

- prepare to make your recommendation, and

- if you have initiated Half Time before doing the summary of the customer's S.P.I.C.E[3], then prepare to return with an organized summary that will take the customer through his or her Reality Trough.

THE SIGNIFICANCE OF HALF TIME

Half Time is a significant aspect of this sales approach. Half Time emphasizes that half of the time normally spent with a client would be spent getting critical information to effectively determine what to sell. Half of your selling time should be invested in learning about the customer and his or her needs. The second half would be spent completing the sale – delivering your solution.

If in your retail environment, it typically takes twenty minutes to sell your solution, then ten minutes would be spent learning the customer's S.P.I.C.E^3. If you sell smaller solutions, you might spend only five minutes learning the S.P.I.C.E^3 in a ten-minute total sales process. Do not move beyond Step Three into Half Time if you don't know the customer's S.P.I.C.E^3.

Half Time is significant in another way. It conveys to the customer you now want to think about and determine what is the best solution for his or her needs. This emphasizes once again you're there to help the customer to succeed. You aren't just "flogging" your products and services. You're very focused on finding the best solution. Use Half Time to step away from the client and organize yourself for the second half of the sales process.

This stepping away could be as simple as telling the retail customer you're going to gather the products you intend to recommend, or as comprehensive as arranging a second visit with your retail client so you have time to prepare a presentation to be made in the next encounter. In other words, Half Time could be a few moments or last several days, depending on the situation. Even a retail sale could involve a break of several days so the salesperson can arrange for a proper presentation of what he or she will recommend.

If Half Time is initiated before the salesperson has summarized the customer's S.P.I.C.E^3 (*as in Step Four*), then Half Time can be used to rehearse or write up such a summary. Refer to the notes you took during the discussion of your customer's needs. Organize these notes into a S.P.I.C.E^3 summary either mentally or in written form so you have the clear flow of information through your customer's Reality Trough.

Do not make a recommendation until you've completed the first half – the "GET" half. Get information that allows you to know and solve the customer's problems, before you present or pitch any product or services. You will truly differentiate yourself from your competition by sticking to this part of the model. Doing this makes you more valuable than your competitor.

THE DURATION OF HALF TIME

The time you take will depend on the complexity of the customer's needs, what you sell, your knowledge of your solution options, the problems each option can solve, who you're selling to, and the availability of the complete solution.

Your knowledge of the most appropriate solution will influence how long Half Time will take. You might have to use this time to conduct research to find the best solution. You might have to call suppliers to see if they have the products and services that would satisfy the customer's needs.

However, in most cases where customer problems are not so complex, your employer is likely to have all of the goods available and on display. You would only need a few moments to get everything ready. Instead of walking your customer around to show the various components of your complete solution, gather everything together and present the complete solution all at once.

In a computer store, within minutes, the salesperson could place the boxes for an appropriate computer system, monitor, printer, software, cables, supply items, and extended warranty on a dolly and wheel the goods up to the customer. A cell phone salesperson could smoothly gather the phone, a protective case, extra cables, a car charger adapter, cleaning supplies, extended warranty package, and a training guide appropriate to the phone. A cosmetics salesperson could quickly collect together the skin-care creams, lotions, powders, perfumes, lipsticks, eyeliner, nail polish, blush, and other items that fit the particular needs of the customer.

Alternatively, Half Time could involve a much more comprehensive preparation of the complete solution. As has been demonstrated by more than one clothier, a salesperson in a clothing store might schedule a next appointment to show off the wardrobe he or she intends to recommend. In preparation for the appointment, the most appropriate clothes given the customer's needs could be arranged into outfits. These outfits could be photographed showing different ways to mix and match the clothing items. A booklet to take with the clothes could be created providing prompts showing how to dress for success with the new clothing.

Later during the presentation of the recommendation in a specially scheduled appointment, the customer could see the clothing laid out the way the salesperson would recommend. This process involves the showing of a complete solution and not just one outfit. When you're able to sell multiple outfits, the size of the sale justifies the time this approach would take. In addition, the booklet serves as a record of what the customer purchased so the salesperson can subsequently follow-up and recommend complimentary items.

Half Time to prepare in this way could possibly take one or two hours of time. For other examples, consider the following:

- Rather than take the customer for a test drive in a generic version of a possible solution, a car salesperson could indicate he or she has the best solution for the customer in mind, but the specific car with the necessary features needs to be prepared for a test drive.

- A furniture salesperson could indicate he or she wants to set up a display to simulate what the customer's particular room will look like with the new furniture in place.

- A farm equipment salesperson could indicate she will bring over the proper equipment for a demonstration on the farmer's own property, or at least ask for time to set up the equipment she will be recommending.

- A cell phone salesperson might develop a report comparing costs of the old plan used by the client, with the costs of a new plan the salesperson is about to suggest, and do this comparison report on the screen of the new phone.

In such situations, Half Time would involve preparation of such presentations that will be made later in the "GET SMARTER" approach.

Some trainees have asked why one would go to this expense before completing the sale. The answer is two fold – first, because the sale is likely a larger sale of a complete solution, making this worth the effort; and second, because doing the first three steps effectively leaves you knowing you already have the sale. If the customer is eager to receive your recommendation, and it's the right one, he or she will buy now.

The customer wants to do this because it will save him or her time, reduce their current costs, and yield more benefits and better payoffs. You show the customer what you believe he or she will want to buy. By getting everything ready in this manner, the customer can see and buy the best solution right away.

Taking such initiative requires a degree of confidence that the expense is justified. This confidence comes from knowing the customer really wants to receive your recommendation. This eagerness is the clue he or she will buy the right solution. You also have the necessary confidence because you know your solution is the right one. By preparing in such a way, the purchase process is expedited because the solution is right there.

However, it is not necessary to do such elaborate preparations during Half Time for all sales. A working demonstration may not be required. It may be enough that a stack of all items to be included in the solution has been gathered together, or it may be enough to prepare a verbal or written presentation of what the salesperson is going to recommend.

If a proper solution is not yet readily available in your retail setting, the customer will wait longer to get the right solution if the problem is known to be very complex. If the salesperson has done a great job of learning the customer's S.P.I.C.E[3] and has demonstrated great understanding, thereby building rapport and trust, the customer will wait until the salesperson let's him or her know the perfect solution is available.

The nature of your complete solution will influence how long Half Time has to be. Think about the solutions you could sell, and then consider how long Half Time would likely take in your own situation. How much time would you need to prepare to make your recommendation – minutes, hours, days or longer? You need to decide if you're just going to tell the customer what you recommend, present a written proposal or quote, gather up all the components that make up the solution to show to the customer, or make an in-action demonstration of your solution. Choose the approach that adds the most efficiency to your sales process.

In turn, the customer's needs may determine the length of Half Time. Your customer may require an interval that allows him or her to get a meeting organized to receive your presentation and proposal.

THE SALESPERSON DURING HALF TIME

You will have several tasks to complete during this time away from your client.

DETERMINE IF YOU CAN SOLVE THE PROBLEM

Obviously, Half Time allows you to step away to determine if you actually have a solution that best meets your customer's full set of needs. Throughout the first steps in this sales model, a promise has been implied. The salesperson will only recommend the best solution.

Half Time is an opportunity to fully assess your ability to provide a complete solution that truly satisfies all constraints and fully realizes the results and benefits the client expects to achieve. If you're not able to do this, you will have to return to the customer and make this declaration.

IDENTIFY THE SOLUTION

In most retail environments, the required solutions will be comprised of the products within your retail showroom. You will use your knowledge of your inventory to determine which mix of products and services best solves this customer's unique problems. By knowing what you have in your inventory, you can select those products that meet the full set of the customer's needs. However, in some retail situations, the customer's problems may require a more complex customized solution.

When selling large-scale custom solutions, Half Time will involve significant problem-solving activity and require more time. For problems requiring a complex solution, Half Time can, and probably should be used to meet with any of your company's technical experts, potential suppliers, your sales manager and your sales team to have a creative discussion that leads to an innovative solution. Unlike research and development which innovates new products, such meetings are about finding the best mix of existing products and services to provide a unique solution for the customer's particular situation and problems.

Identifying a solution unique to a particular customer must come from strong product knowledge, knowledge of what worked for other customers, a deep consideration of the unique situation and problem(s) of this particular customer, and a brainstorming mentality allowing full consideration of ideas that might not first appear practical, acceptable, effective or affordable. The goal is to identify an optimum solution and the best solution might not at first seem possible. In such situations, creative problem solving is often required to solve the problem in ways that your competition can't. You aren't just selling a few products or services supplied by your company. You're selling custom solutions to each unique customer.

When dealing with highly complex problems, ask yourself these questions:

- What can we combine within our mix of existing product(s) to make a workable solution?

- How could our products be implemented with under-utilized resources already owned by the client to produce the desired results?

- What could we remove from the problem situation to make our solution appropriate?

- Who has complimentary products and services we can bundle with our own to provide an effective solution?

- Is there a supplier we don't usually buy from that might have the solution this customer requires?

- Is there a manufacturer that might be interested in producing a solution that will meet this customer's needs?

- How could we easily re-engineer our solutions so they have the abilities required by the customer?

- How can we share the risk of a new solution with the customer – delayed payment structures, loaned personnel, rental as opposed to sale, immediate product replacement if failure?

- What changes could we make to our ordering processes, inventory management, packaging, quantity requirements, delivery, financing, warranty, maintenance services, installation schedule, training services, mix of products, end of life services to make our solutions more acceptable to the customer?

As a salesperson, you don't create new products but you can work to create new solutions with a creative mix of existing products and services. The key is creative thinking. Consider many options. Think beyond normal practice. Look for something that is obviously good once you identify it, but one that hadn't even been considered as within the traditional realm of possibility. Even though you work in retail sales typically selling smaller items to individuals, you can still get creative in how you put your products and services together to arrive at complete solutions.

LOCATE THE SOLUTION

Do what you have to do in order to locate the source of supply for the best solution for your customer. Determine what is the best solution, ascertain how this solution will solve the customer's problem, and search for its availability. Within your store, find the collection of products and services that make up the solution. If your company manufactures the solutions you sell, then locate where that item is stored. If your company does not manufacture or does not manufacture all that your solution would require, find an alternate manufacturer and determine how to get what that company would produce. If your company resells goods provided through distributors, then find the sources of the products and services that would make up your solution.

A housing realtor could tell the customer, based on his or her needs, the perfect home is not currently available and that the salesperson will search for the right home and contact the customer once it has been found. A car salesperson might have to canvas other regional dealers looking for just the right vehicle for his or her client. An art dealer might have to seek out an existing owner of a particular piece of art and inquire if that owner wants to sell. A retailer that sells products from many manufacturers may have to canvas suppliers to see if they have a solution that will work in the customer's specific situation.

DEVELOP SOLUTIONS

Perhaps, the current product offerings that the salesperson and his or her company sell might not be adequate as the solution. A new supplier might need to be found. Alternatively, another retailer might sell goods that could form part of a solution. This would require forming a partnership with other providers to create the complete solution that meets the customer's needs. As a complete solution is likely to be at least somewhat unique for each client, Half Time may be needed to put these alliances in place.

QUOTES AND PROPOSALS

"To quote or not to quote" is the question. This is a tough decision to make. In making this decision, you have to have a pretty good understanding of the quality of the relationship you've achieved in your interaction with this customer. You place yourself at a competitive risk both by giving, and by not giving a quotation.

By refusing to give a quote when asked for one, you disrupt the trust you've built in the relationship. On the other hand, when you freely give a quotation without being asked for one, you provide ammunition for any competitor who is shown the quotation and asked to match or beat your product or pricing.

In some industries, it is very normal to provide customers with quotations. For example, if a customer discusses home renovations with various contractors then it is likely that each will give a quote describing the services they will perform and the price they will charge. If you are a competing contractor, you likely put yourself at a competitive disadvantage if you differ from this norm.

Using the "GET SMARTER" approach, you may not have to give a quote. But you do need to be alert to your customer's expectation. The work you do in the first half of the sales process may have the customer committed to buying your solution so no formal quotation may be necessary.

Some of the best salespeople will **not** provide customers with a quotation unless specifically asked. They don't want to give the customer a tool to use to shop around on price. In addition, they don't want the customer talking with significant others only about the solution, without also discussing the S.P.I.C.E[3] that led to the recommendation. When the customer asks for a quote, the salesperson then works to clarify why the customer feels he or she needs a quotation.

There are specific occasions where you might agree to present a quote instead of presenting the goods and services that make up the solution. You would do this when:

- the customer stipulates that such a written proposal is required to satisfy his or her buying process,

- the customer is making a complicated purchase to solve a serious problem,

- the customer has to get buying approval from others involved in the decision process, and

- you're doing a consultation for a business to solve a comprehensive business problem.

By submitting a proper quotation, you help the customer in his or her decision-making and you impress the client with the quality of your work.

If your customer has shown a lot of positive responses to how you've helped but needs to talk with someone else before making the decision, trust in the quality of the relationship you've built and give a quote. Prepare a formal quotation during Half Time so you can return and hand the customer a one or two page quote that summarizes the customer's S.P.I.C.E^3 and lists the components of your solution.

Presumably, this quote process within your organization is computerized. Unfortunately, it's our experience most quotation software used by retail organizations doesn't yet incorporate the information you would want included when using the "GET SMARTER" sales approach. Take initiative within your company to get the software changed so it does.

If you aren't able to do this, try to get the software to output the quotation as a text file. Import this file into a word processor and modify it. Your quote would ideally include:

- the customer's S.P.I.C.E^3 emphasizing the insights your customer achieved, particularly regarding the problem, implications, constraints, and the most exciting benefits,

- a description of the solution which could include all of the elements of the solution in a list, but without line item pricing,

- a clear description of the benefits to be realized by this solution,

- the total price and the recommended payment strategy such as financing, leasing or staged pricing based on the installation period,

- a summary of the net gains the customer will realize,

- a description of what would happen after the customer decides to buy,

- an indication of your eagerness to earn your customer's business, and

- an indication you will call to follow-up at a specific date and time.

We suggest you also place the word "Confidential" on a cover followed by:

"The information, ideas and format contained in this proposal are the confidential property of (*name of your company*) and should not be disclosed to any competitor of (*name of your company*) or other individual not directly involved in the purchasing decision."

This will not protect you against an unscrupulous client but it will cause the good ones to protect your intellectual property.

PREPARE YOUR S.P.I.C.E³ SUMMARY

If you intend to return from Half Time to do "Step Four – Show Full Understanding", you need to organize what you know about your customer's S.P.I.C.E³, and prepare to make a summary presentation of that S.P.I.C.E³ once you return to the customer. Rehearse what you will say so you can take the customer into the lows of the Reality Trough and the highs of the E³ expected gain. Make sure you prepare to do this succinctly and with clarity and passion.

THE CLIENT DURING HALF TIME

Half Time could involve work on the part of the client. If you only need a few moments to organize yourself to make your recommendation, give the customer something to do during this brief break.

Assign some related activity that prepares the customer for the next step. For example, the client could be given a video demo to watch or asked to watch a fully automated PowerPoint presentation. Or, it may be useful to have the customer read materials to increase his or her expertise as a buyer. You could ask your retail client to fill out a credit application while he or she waits.

On the other hand, you may need more time to prepare your recommendation and schedule a subsequent meeting. If so, the client could be asked to return to home or office to talk with others who will be influenced by the buying decision. Ask your customer to find out if significant others have additional information to clarify the S.P.I.C.E³. Your customer might be directed to get detailed costs of the problems he or she experiences to heighten his or her motivation to get a solution. This allows the customer to determine what a new solution would be worth.

In some instances, there might be value in asking the customer to contact other customers who have purchased from you. Such positive testimonials will increase the customer's eagerness to hear your recommendation.

In turn, the customer may require a Half Time interval that allows him or her to get others to come to a meeting with you to receive your proposal. Half Time allows the customer to get organized enough to receive your recommendation.

By having the customer engaged in the sales process, he or she becomes an ally in finding the correct solution. In undertaking these activities, the customer is working with the salesperson and not focused on preparing an argument against what the salesperson will recommend.

WHEN TO MOVE OUT OF HALF TIME

You are ready to move out of Half Time when you're ready to make a recommendation and the customer is ready to receive it. In most situations you will have the solution available for your customer. Depending on the choice you made at the end of Step Three, you will either transition out of Half Time to revive your customer's eagerness by going to Step Four – Show Full Understanding; or, out of Half Time to Step Five – Make The Recommendation.

However, other possibilities might exist. In some situations, you may have discovered during Half Time that you do not yet have a solution for this customer's situation. You know that one is coming but is not yet available. If this is the case, you will need to transition from Half Time to a postponement period during which the customer waits until you can find the proper solution. You will need to provide some indication as to how long it will take to have the best solution available to the client.

Alternatively, your assessment of your ability to provide a complete solution that truly satisfies all constraints and fully realizes the results and benefits the client expects to achieve might indicate that you don't have that solution. If you are not able to provide one, you will have to return to the customer and make this declaration.

TRANSITION WHEN YOU DON'T HAVE A SOLUTION

If you do not have the best solution available at this time, you will have to do one of the following:

- refer the customer to a supplier that does have the solution,

- indicate that you need more time to find the solution because the solution isn't readily available, but you have some ideas where to find it, or

- indicate that the solution does not yet exist and that you will contact the customer as soon as it is available.

If your company does not sell the right solution for your customer's needs, you may have to return and say something like:

"Fred, I've done my research and I've discovered that my company does not have the best solution to your needs. However, "*Competitor X*" does, in stock and ready for you to pick up. I've spoken with them and they're holding it for you until you make your decision. I trust that their solution will give you the benefits we've discussed. I regret that we didn't have this solution ourselves because I was looking forward to helping you get better results than you're getting now. I really appreciate the opportunity to earn your business and look forward to working with you again in the future.

Making a statement and referral like this will build your customer's trust and appreciation for what you've done to clarify the customer's needs. You may not get this sale but you will get this customer to return to you when there is a future need, and this customer will likely make referrals of family and friends.

However, where your competitors don't have the proper solution either, because that solution isn't yet available in the market place, you may return and say something like:

"Jill, I was so excited about finding the best solution for your needs but my technical experts have advised me that what is available on the market at this time doesn't yet do what you need. They strongly suggest that you wait for the next round of product releases. What comes out then may do what you need. We suggest you wait and get the solution that does meet your needs. I'll watch for such a solution and contact you as soon as I know it's available, whether through us or through a competitor. I want you to succeed. Is that okay with you?"

Hopefully, you will be returning to deliver good news and won't have to deliver such a request for more time. But if you do, and if you have faithfully followed the "GET SMARTER" steps:

- showing that you fully understand the customer's needs,

- having brought about new insights so the customer more fully understands his or her needs, and

- if you built substantial rapport,

most customers will trust you and wait for you to find what they need.

Most of the time, you will likely have a solution for your customer and will not have to ask the customer to postpone his or her acquisition. If you have what your customer needs, transition to the next step in the sales process.

TRANSITION TO MAKE THE RECOMMENDATION

If you completed Step Four before Half Time, then you'll likely return from Half Time to present your recommendation. First, transition to this next step by asking the customer if he or she is ready to hear your recommendation. You might learn the customer is ready and eager.

S: "Bill, thank you for your patience. Have any other thoughts come to you while I was away that we should discuss before I present my recommendation?"

C: "No. I'm ready if you are."

or

S: "Sally, I've gathered everything together that will help with your skin problems. If you're ready, let's take a look."

C: "I'm really eager to see what you have."

or

S: "Thank you for waiting. Have you completed the credit application?"

C: "Yes" handing the forms to the salesperson

S: "Great, I'll get that entered right after I present my recommendation. While away, I found myself feeling even more excitement. We can help you to realize significant cost reductions and increased benefits. Are you ready to hear what I have to offer, or do you have any questions about what we discussed?"

C: "No, I'm ready. What have you got?"

or

S: "Jane, are you ready to hear what I have to recommend or did some new information come to light that I should know about before I propose our solution? I appreciate your willingness to give me time to get ready."

C: "While I was waiting, I called and had a chance to speak with my colleague. He agrees with all that we discussed. He really appreciates the insights you brought to light in our discussion. We're ready to see what you can do."

or

S: "Thank you for coming back in for this second meeting. I met with our specialists and we've come up with a solution that reduces your costs and increases your profitability. I'm excited about how this can make a difference to your bottom-line, and relatively quickly. Shall we proceed?"

C: "Yes. I'm eager to hear what you suggest."

At this point, present what you prepared during Half Time by moving to "Step Five – Make Your Recommendation".

On the other hand, you might discover something new came to mind for the customer since he or she last spoke with you. If so, you will have to determine if your intended recommendation has already addressed the needs presented by the new information. If it does, you can proceed.

S: "Thank you for waiting. Have you had any additional thoughts about your needs since we spoke?"

C: "Yes, I called my boss who reminded me that we need some way to spread the payments out over time so we can manage this under our budget."

S: "That is useful information. I did build a financing consideration into my recommendation that would both spread the payments out over a three-year period and provide a tax benefit. Should I present my recommendation or do you want to wait until we can involve your boss in our discussion? "

If you discover new requirements that your intended recommendation does not satisfy, you may need to back up to learn the new information.

S: "Thank you for waiting. Have you had any additional thoughts about your needs since we spoke?"

C: "Yes, I'm wondering if your company can take my older equipment in on a trade-in? "

S: "That is important information. I confess I failed to address that need when I built my recommendation. As I understand it, you want us to assess the value of your existing equipment, give you a trade-in allowance and take it off your hands. Correct? "

C: "That's correct. I know it has lost a lot of its original value but I'm hoping both that it is worth something that could reduce my costs today, and that you will get it off my hands. I have no further use for it and don't know where to dispose of it."

S: "I apologize for not having clarified this earlier.

C: "Yes and there is no need to apologize. I failed to bring that up in our earlier discussions. I'm glad you gave me a chance to bring it up today."

S: "Bill, this information means I have more work to do on my recommendation before I present it. Could we set up a meeting for next Monday and I will address this new concern?"

C: "That would work for me."

If anything like this happens, prepare the new recommendation, taking care to cover off all the new needs that you just uncovered, then return as scheduled to make your presentation. Understandably, any increase to your costs would be addressed in a changed price.

TRANSITION TO SHOW FULL UNDERSTANDING

If you've undertaken Half Time before Step Four, you will need to return to the customer and transition to this next step to show full understanding and take the customer through his or her S.P.I.C.E.^{3}. You could say something like,

"Thank you for waiting. I think I've found a great solution for your needs. Just to refresh both of our memories, we talked about (*then summarize the S.P.I.C.E.^{3}*)."

or

"Thank you for agreeing to meet with me again to discuss my recommendation. I know it wasn't convenient to have to come back to our store. I'm really excited about what I've discovered as a great solution, and will get to that shortly. But to make sure nothing has changed since we last spoke, I want to run through what I understand about your needs. (*Then summarize the customer's S.P.I.C.E*[3]*).*"

Once you have the customer's permission to summarize, move to the fourth step and hit the high points of his or her S.P.I.C.E[3]. This review will be done to revive a high motivation to get the problem solved and to increase eagerness to hear your recommendation.

STEP FOUR – SHOW FULL UNDERSTANDING

(SUMMARIZE WHAT YOU'VE LEARNED ABOUT THE CUSTOMER'S S.P.I.C.E³)

In this step, take the customer through his or her Reality Trough by summarizing what you've learned about:

- his or her situation,

- his or her problems,

- the implications of those problems,

- what has stopped the customer from finding a solution before now, and

- what he or she will gain by solving his or her problems.

This should highlight the customer's new insights and involve a movement through the emotions of the Reality Trough arriving at excitement, anticipation, and eagerness.

This step truly differentiates your sales approach from anything your competitors might do. Before trying to sell anything, you summarize what you've learned about the customer's needs and expectations and ask if you have fully understood.

GOALS OF STEP FOUR – SHOW UNDERSTANDING

At this step, you have multiple goals. You aren't yet trying to get the sale but you're moving in that direction by making sure both of you know the customer's existing needs and what an optimum solution should deliver. The goals of Step Four – Show Full Understanding are to:

- prove to yourself you've achieved full understanding of your customer's S.P.I.C.E[3],

- prove to your customer you've achieved full understanding,

- help your customer realize he or she learned more about his or her needs through conversation with you,

- determine if you know enough to make a proper recommendation,

- show your customer you know enough to make a good recommendation,

- prove to yourself you've achieved a relationship where the customer will value and trust your recommendation,

- create an anticipation or looking forward to what you will recommend, and

- take your customer, in an organized fashion, through the lows of his or her Reality Trough, finishing on the emotional high associated with hope and a deeper expectation that he or she can gain the desired extra benefits.

Many poor salespeople assume they understand and skip this step. The salesperson may not have a complete understanding and if the customer thinks the salesperson doesn't understand, the customer can't and won't trust the salesperson's recommendation. Failing to show full understanding is where objections are created.

The customer sees the flaws in any recommendation that comes from a failure to understand his or her needs.

Some salespeople assume the customer understands and jump ahead. But if the customer is confused, he or she is not yet ready to make a decision. If the customer doesn't understand his or her own needs, there won't be motivation to change. The customer won't listen to your recommendation with intent to buy. You'll likely be wasting time – yours and the customer's.

In the customer's state of confusion, he or she will just object to the recommendation in self-defense. Instead of being in a state of anticipation and eagerness to hear what you have to offer, he or she is going to be stepping back, wary about what you're going to do next. The customer will build a resistance in anticipation of what you will suggest.

THE PROCESS TO SHOW UNDERSTANDING

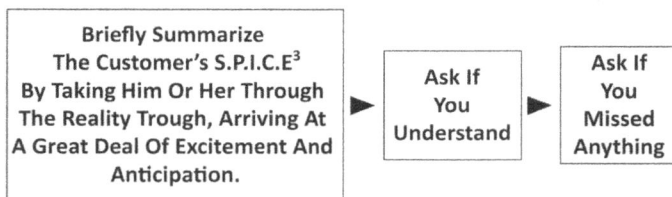

Summarize what you learned during the earlier conversation where you discussed your customer's needs. Organize your summary in terms of the information that is the customer's S.P.I.C.E^3 and work to surface the underlying emotions so you take him or her through the Reality Trough in the few moments of your summary. This summary should induce the range of feelings from the low point of the Reality Trough to the excitement and anticipation of his or her desired E^3 outcomes.

The Process To Show Understanding

Briefly Summarize The Customer's S.P.I.C.E^3 By Taking Him Or Her Through The Reality Trough, Arriving At A Great Deal Of Excitement And Anticipation.	►	Ask If You Understand	►	Ask If You Missed Anything

This summary should be brief and yet touch on the highlights of what you and your customer have learned. If you've taken notes as you listened in the first steps, use the notes for guidance. Don't just read your notes. Quickly summarize with feeling. If learning this information took you ten minutes, give it back in crisp form within about a minute.

Once you have summarized the S.P.I.C.E^3, ask if you have understood correctly and if you have missed anything. You want your customer to clearly indicate that you fully understand his or her needs, and that it is time to get to the recommendation. This is your chance to check for readiness to buy.

For best results, your summary should be brief and organized as follows:

1. Make a brief reference to what you learned about your customer's current situation. The key is to reference the highlights only, focusing on two main aspects – where in your customer's situation the problems occur, and any underutilized resources you discovered that may facilitate a solution. As the situation is well known to your customer, you'll just bore him or her if you summarize too much situational information.

2. Remind your customer about key symptoms that indicate the real problems that reside within his or her current way of doing things.

3. Then summarize what those problems cost – both tangible and intangible costs. Be really clear about each problem and the costs of that problem. Make sure to emphasize anything that you uncovered that was a new insight for your customer. This is where the prime motivation to solve the problem resides.

4. Describe the perceived constraints that have justified not taking action before now. If you can, point out what are real constraints and any constraints that appear to be imagined and not real. You likely wouldn't use the language of real versus imagined but you would say something addressing the realization that a previous concern is no longer a roadblock. Acknowledge that you will make sure your solution alleviates the real constraints.

5. Cover any underlying expectations your customer would have about whatever he or she will buy. This could include thoughts about the most important criteria that the solution should satisfy, what the new solution must minimally accomplish, how he or she will pay for the new purchase, about warranty coverage, about service from you and your organization, about getting the best deal, and more.

6. Most critically, enthusiastically summarize the exciting benefits or results your customer now expects to get by using the new tools. If you helped your customer to achieve any new insights about what he or she would like to achieve, stress these benefits as they are likely the most exciting to the customer. Focus attention on what he or she expects to gain by any solution you will recommend. Address the value of getting the problem solved now. Set up a frame of hope and excitement, where your customer is eagerly waiting to learn what you're going to recommend.

7. And lastly, ask if the customer believes you have understood his or her needs, ask if the customer thinks anything important has been missed, then ask if your customer is ready to hear what you intend to recommend.

As you proceed through the summary of needs, periodically ask if you've understood everything so far. This keeps your customer involved, and sets up a "yes" framework when you demonstrate you understand well. Each time he or she says, "Yes", there is a greater sense that you are working together.

Look for any clues indicating you've misunderstood or missed something. Determine if there is anything else to cover before you make your recommendation. If so, back up to finish the needs assessment. Ask more questions or use active listening skills to learn what you need to know.

Let's look at an example of Step Four – Show Full Understanding in a retail environment where the salesperson is selling cell phones.

S: "I want to be sure I fully understand. Let me summarize what I think you've told me."

C: Nodding. "Okay."

S: "You need a new cell phone because your old one fell into the lake this weekend. You liked that phone. You delayed getting a new phone before now because your old phone was working fine. Correct."

C: Head down. "That's pretty much it. Now I have to, and I'm going to have to enter in all my contact information by hand again."

S: "I also understand four of you in your household have been paying on average about $70 more per month because someone goes over their data limits. Much more frequently than you had realized. Correct?"

C: "Yes. I'm the one who gets billed, and it bugs me."

S: "As well, getting a new phone doesn't excite you because you're feeling intimidated by all the bells and whistles of the new phones, correct?"

C: Smiling. "I mostly just used my phone as a phone."

S: "However, you've started doing some texting, e-mailing and with your brand new grandchild, you wish you had the camera capability that your son has in his smartphone. Is this right?"

C: "Definitely."

S: "Now you also mentioned you envied your buddy because he's able to get up-to-the minute updates on stock prices, and he doesn't have to pay extra data charges when he does. He brags about the extra money he makes doing trades when he can easily see changes in stock prices. Being able to check your favorite stock prices on your phone would be a real advantage, correct?

C: "As long as I don't have extra charges. They can be pretty high if you use too much data."

S: "Bill, if I understand correctly you want to access the stock market, to take high quality pictures of your granddaughter, to prevent service charges for over use by your family, to quickly learn to use the features of your new phone, and to protect all of your data so it can easily be copied to a new phone. Is this correct? Oh, and based on this experience, you also don't want to pay any service plan penalties or the price for a new phone if this phone gets lost in the future?"

C: Looking at the salesperson, "Right. So what do you recommend?"

S: "Have we missed anything important?"

C: "No. Give me your recommendation."

This summary takes the customer through the most critical aspects of his S.P.I.C.E[3] thereby resurfacing the low feelings the customer associates with the costs of his lost phone and his family's previous phone use, and then the feelings of excitement about what might be realized if the salesperson can deliver the right solution. The customer reaches a state of eagerness to hear the salesperson's recommendation. With this process, this is not a resistant customer.

REQUISITE SKILLS

To be effective at this stage, we advise you to build the following skills:

- Hone your ability to organize the information both on paper and in your head.

- Consciously stop yourself from skipping this step until it's a habit you do every time.

- Develop your ability to summarize in S.P.I.C.E^3 chunks and ask the person if you summarized each chunk correctly.

- Get skillful at covering the highlights and the customer's new insights to emphasize what really matters to the customer.

- Enhance your ability to move quickly through the cycle of change as you review the S.P.I.C.E^3 so you place your final emphasis on an enthusiastic summary of the benefits and gains your customer hopes to achieve.

While doing this brief summary, you also need to use your ability to paraphrase any new information that comes up. Be patient and cover all of the important parts. Lastly, learn to recognize non-verbal cues of resistance or hesitation. If you get any, back up to Step Three to further discuss your customer's needs.

If you don't address any evidence of resistance at this stage, you will get objections when you present your recommendation later in Step Five or ask for a decision in Step Six. You want such issues addressed now before you make your recommendation. In this way, you maintain rapport and further develop the alliance with your customer, as you both work to make sure you know what a complete solution must accomplish.

NOT A SUMMARY ABOUT DESIRED PRODUCTS OR SERVICES

If you're summarizing the products and product features the customer is looking for, you've failed to perform a proper needs assessment. As an example of what a summary in this step is not, let's look at a couple of summaries presented by salespeople who only discussed desired product features during the needs assessment stage.

"So as I understand it, you're looking for a Crochet 26 megapixel digital SLR camera with metal body weighing less than 1.5 lbs, a shutter mechanism rated for at least

500,000 shots, and using Ultra SD memory cards. And you want it at the best price. Correct"

or

"If I understand correctly, you're telling me you want an Asusian Cruiz Hybrid with leather seats, leather covered steering wheel, the speed wing, hood scoop, brushed aluminum wheels, black racing stripe, diamond coat over cherry red paint, and the 7 year extended warranty?"

If either of these examples looks like what you imagined this step to be, you could be selling the wrong things to your customers, and you won't even know why. With all that focus on product specifications and features, you aren't being an insight-oriented consultative salesperson.

The customer likely had to tell you what products and features he or she wanted. This means the customer had to be the expert. The customer had to move through the cycle of change on his or her own.

In the first example, the summary is focused on just the camera, not on a complete solution. The sale will be less than it could or should be. The camera needs lenses, storage media, a carrying kit, maybe a shoulder sling, or possibly protective coverings for use in poor weather conditions. The customer may need training in the use of the camera, software to properly edit the images he or she has taken, or extended warranty coverage to protect the investment. But none of that will be offered because the focus wasn't on the needs but on the camera.

The second example looks like it is pointing to a more complete solution but may not be, and what is summarized may not be the right products for the customer's real needs. For example, the customer may think he or she wants the sporty car, but needs a car more practical for a young family.

If all you learned, and if the only thing you summarize is the product and features the customer is seeking, you won't have added any value so the buying decision will get down to price. You'll have failed to learn about your customer's real needs and will have reduced yourself to the role of retail clerk. No value there. The customer may as well turn to a provider who offers a lower price.

It's All About Value

People really don't want to buy products or specific services. They want to buy the benefits or value the products or services will provide. In Step Four, you're summarizing the value the customer wants to buy, not the products he or she wants. Realized Value is the benefits the customer will get versus the price to be paid for those benefits.

Realized Value = Benefits Minus Price

To get real value, the customer wants the benefits to be greater than the total price. In fact, the customer will think he or she is getting a great deal if the customer believes the value far exceeds the price.

Too many salespeople make the issue price or allow their customers to make price the issue because the salesperson fails to create value. When asked to consider their decision criteria, customers seldom rate price as higher than fifth (5th) in importance when determining what to buy.

Weaker salespeople typically worry that price is the number one consideration when customers think value is most important. Too often, price-conscious salespeople try to keep the price down, undersell and fail to satisfy customer needs.

As a salesperson, learn to make value the number one consideration in your own mind. Sell the benefits because people buy benefits. Start by summarizing what those desired benefits are, right here in Step Four, well before you make your recommendation. Do that before you make your recommendation so the customer knows what criteria to use in evaluating your solution.

When To Move To The Next Step

It is your responsibility to move the sales interaction forward to provide your customer with the appropriate solution. You will know it's the right time to move to the next step when:

- the customer indicates you have full understanding,
- the customer is showing positive non-verbal clues and an eagerness to hear your recommendation,
- the customer is showing a readiness to buy, and
- you have the product knowledge necessary to make the right recommendation.

Depending on the order in the sales process in which you have done this Step Four, you will either move to Half Time or to the step where you present your recommendation.

TRANSITION TO HALF TIME

If you don't know what to recommend but you understand the customer's needs, or if you need time to get the solution ready, tell the customer you'll find and prepare the solution and get back when you're ready to make your recommendation. Initiate a Half Time break to get the knowledge and the solution worked out.

Leave the customer in a great state of anticipation for what you're going to recommend, and keep him or her busy. As previously discussed, give your customer an assignment to complete during Half Time so he or she isn't just waiting for you, or even worse, leaving to go shop around because of a growing impatience to get a solution. You can say things like:

"George, I'm excited about getting you the best possible solution. I need a few minutes to get it organized. While I'm gone, please complete this leasing application to allow us to proceed as soon as possible. As we learned in the discussion of your needs, there would be real value in spreading out the payment. There's no reason to delay when you can realize greater value right away. I'll only be a few minutes."

or

"I want to get everything together that I'm going to recommend to you. While I do, you could expedite the process by completing our credit application. You indicated financing might be of benefit to you, and this will allow the application to be processed quickly."

or

"Jeff, I'm really excited right now because I know we can put together a complete system that will substantially reduce your costs while giving you increased productivity and greater success at what you're doing. To give you a preview of what I'm going to recommend, I'd like you to take a look at this demo video on this iPad while I get everything organized. Sound okay to you?"

Delivered effectively, your transition statement hitchhikes on the higher degree of eagerness you created as you summarized the customer's S.P.I.C.E^3. This leaves the customer with a positive expectation that what you return with will be the solution he or she needs to buy.

TRANSITION TO MAKE YOUR RECOMMENDATION

On the other hand, if you took your Half Time break after learning the customer's S.P.I.C.E^3, then returned to the customer and completed an effective summary of his or her needs by taking the customer through the Reality Trough to the emotional highs of his or her S.P.I.C.E^3, then it's time to move to Step Five and Make Your Recommendation. The customer is eager to hear it.

If you've created a positive readiness to hear your recommendation, tell your customer you're ready to present it. This transition is simply asking your customer if he or she is ready to hear, see, touch your proposed solution. For example,

"Jacob, I'm confident I can solve your problems, get you benefits you don't get now, and reduce your costs. Are you ready to hear what I propose?"

or

"I'm sure glad you've given me this chance to earn your business, because what you need is directly addressed by the solution we've come up with. Let's look at it out right now, okay?"

or

"Wow. This is a great match – we have what could make a significant difference in your exact situation. Shall I show it to you now?"

or

"Gwen, I'm very excited about our recommendation, because we have what you need. It's like our two companies were designed to work together. What we've planned will more than solve this problem. It will give you competitive advantages and produce very positive results on your bottom line. Ready?"

There's no reason to delay presenting your solution. Move to the next step and share your recommendation. The customer is ready. You're ready. Both of you are busy people and want to get on with this sale/purchase. Having asked, you now have permission to present your products and services to your customer in the form of a complete solution.

THE SECOND HALF OF THE SALES PROCESS

Now, you're going to provide a complete solution to satisfy your customer's expectations, excitements, and eagerness, while further enhancing your relationship with your client. You're also going to get this sale.

Step Five – Make Your Recommendation

Present your complete solution and fulfill all of your customer's needs (his or her S.P.I.C.E^3) – nothing less.

It's time for you to achieve the sale. It's time for your customer to get his or her benefits. Give your customer the recommendation he or she is eagerly anticipating.

Goals Of Step Five – Make Your Recommendation

In this step, we also have multiple goals. We aren't just focused on getting a sale. When you "Make Your Recommendation", your goals are to:

- recommend what you think is the best solution for your customer *(to help the customer achieve greater success)*,
- suggest a complete solution,
- make one full recommendation, not many, as it confuses the customer *(only offer the one right solution)*,
- match your recommendation to the benefits your customer wants to buy,
- convey your enthusiasm for your recommended solution, and
- get it so right the only decision can be, "Yes".

Present everything the customer needs in order to realize the full range of benefits and savings you've promised. You implied this promise by learning his or her S.P.I.C.E[3]. You can't recommend anything less.

In the "GET SMARTER" sales approach, the recommendation is preferably made without talking about the products and services you are selling. This is a significant difference between the best salespeople and average salespeople. The best recommend a complete solution by emphasizing the results the customer can expect. Less effective salespeople talk about products and features.

Recommendation Process

You want to be as careful when you make your recommendation as you were in the preceding steps. To effectively make your recommendation:

1. Tell the customer this solution will yield the benefits of (_restate what your customer previously told you he or she expects and wants in terms of results_).

2. With enthusiasm, specify the complete solution that would best fit your customer's needs. Do not get caught up in product detail. Stay focused on the complete set of products and services as the correct solution.

3. Give your customer the total price and compare this price to the costs of his or her status quo to show how your customer can afford this change now and how he or she can't afford to delay.

4. Tell your customer again how this solution gives him or her the exciting benefits and relieves the costs or the pain of the status quo.

5. Lastly, invite and answer questions in a manner that educates your customer so he or she can make an informed decision.

DO NOT TALK PRODUCT – TALK COMPLETE SOLUTION

Even though you recommend a complete solution that contains several or even many products and services, we recommend that you not talk about individual products and features at this stage. Talk about everything together as a solution. If the customer asks a question about a specific product, then answer that question.

If you do mention a product or feature, attach a benefit to every product or feature you mention. Only focus on those features and benefits relevant to the customer's needs. The features important to you, or to any other customers, do not need to be mentioned if they aren't important to this particular customer.

You only need to talk about those aspects of the product the customer asks you to talk about. Stay focused on the complete solution and the benefits that matter to this particular customer.

Prevent the discussion from becoming product focused by keeping it solution and benefit focused.

Speak in a language your client understands. Most people don't relate to the professional jargon of your industry. When the customer knows you fully understand his or her needs, the customer may not even care about the technical specifications of the products. If the customer does care, this will surface in the questions he or she asks and you will answer those questions, but only if asked.

Customers care about benefits like getting a specific task done, achieving a particular result, increased productivity, improved profitability, product quality and reliability, ease of use, overall functionality, the total costs of ownership, pride of ownership, enhanced reputation, etc. Use plain language to talk about what the customer cares about and understands.

INVOLVE YOUR CUSTOMER

Throughout your presentation, check with your customer about his or her understanding of your recommendation. As you mention a benefit, ask if your customer agrees the benefit you've mentioned is important. For example, a salesperson presenting a solution containing a color gel printer to his or her customer, could say,

"This will reduce the cost of producing your final color print outs, and that's important to you, correct?"

Convey your enthusiasm for the fit between your customer's needs and the solution you present. Check periodically to see if the customer shares your enthusiasm. You could get your customer to tell you why he or she is enthused. This gesture keeps your customer involved.

Be aware of the communication between the two of you while you make your presentation. Watch your customer's body language to make sure he or she isn't confused, hesitant or losing interest. Evaluate yourself throughout this step and make any necessary adjustments. If you lose the customer's attention, understanding, enthusiasm, or trust, stop your presentation. Ask what your customer thinks so far and shift into using the active listening skills.

PRESENT THE COMPLETE SOLUTION

Make a recommendation of the complete solution. Present the total suggested package of goods and services. No surprises. Don't recommend the primary item, get your customer's decision to buy, and then spring another recommendation to buy a bunch of add-ons. People don't like such negative surprises.

Emphasize that this group of products and services represents a complete solution to the problems identified in your earlier conversation. This solution will reduce costs, increase benefits and add profitable value to what your customer is doing in his or her pursuit of business profit or a more successful personal life.

Reinforce the message that the customer is getting more than a product by buying from you. Talk about the advantages the customer will get when he or she buys from you and your company. Don't be shy. Sell yourself and sell your company's competitive advantage as part of the complete solution.

TALK TOTAL PRICE AND TOTAL VALUE

Tell your customer the total price and specify any payment amounts. Outline the payment schedule. Avoid talking about specific prices for each item unless asked. Compare the total price to the costs of the status quo, the desired benefits, and the anticipated financial gains he or she can expect to achieve.

> S: "Bill, the solution I have for your family can save you an average $65 per month or $1,560 for the term of this new two year plan. This savings will cover the cost for the new phones. Plus, you won't have any negative surprises because your data limits were too small. Your subscriptions allow sharing of total data capacity amongst all family members. You wanted to reduce your monthly costs, correct?"

> C: "Yes. That's very important."

> S: "And I can do this with the latest smartphone technology, running apps tailored to each of your preferences. The phones are protected for the full two years so you get replacement phones if any phone is

broken, lost or stolen, and because of Cloud technology, your data from your old phones will be quickly transferred over to the new phones while you wait. That benefit would have been very useful when you dropped your phone in the lake, correct."

C: "Yes, this would have been a very different conversation if it was just about a free replacement."

S: "In addition, on your personal phone, we will install an app that gives you great visual access to the stock market and your own stock portfolio. You can easily accomplish what your friend has been bragging about.

C: "Great. According to him, that will allow me to make more than enough money to cover the cost of these phones."

S: "That's right. The price is $340 per month for all subscriptions and an initial outlay of $1,476 for the new phones, protective cases, protection plans, and selected apps. Remember, that initial outlay is recovered by what you save in monthly fees. Do you have any questions?"

You want to clearly show your customer how buying your solution is substantially better than not buying. In turn, you want to be able to show your customer how what he or she saves or gains makes the purchase affordable. Your sale will be much more likely if money freed up by reduced costs or money gained by implementing the new solution will pay for the purchase. Any new intangible benefits will further make the value greater than the price.

ANSWER THE CUSTOMER'S QUESTIONS

Answer any questions or concerns (*and only those questions or concerns*) about your recommendation. Before you answer, paraphrase the question to be sure you understand what your customer wants to know.

Many weak salespeople hear a question and answer that question plus three others the salesperson thinks relate to what the customer asked. Such salespeople talk too much. The customer may not have initially been concerned about the other questions. Hearing the information, the customer might just tune out, or start to think about the extra information and get deflected away from an enthusiasm to buy. Either way, this reduces your effectiveness.

Too many salespeople tell their customers things about products and services the customer does not care about. Because the salesperson thinks the information is important, he or she talks too much in offering it. Such talk can create customer concerns.

Because the information does not seem relevant to the customer, a doubt creeps in that maybe the salesperson doesn't really understand the customer's needs. Or the new information can spark uneasiness because the information wasn't initially wanted and the customer may begin to worry that the information is more important than the customer thought. This can cause the customer to retreat in order to consider the significance of the information.

A COMPLETE SOLUTION

Know what you can offer as your complete solution. A complete solution should contain all products and services necessary to resolve the customer's S.P.I.C.E[3]. Put together a solution containing all or some of the following:

- specific goods including all accessories,
- related services such as delivery, installation, maintenance, integration with other goods already in place, training, disposal of old unwanted goods, investment protection plans, subsequent end of life disposal of the goods you are selling,
- supplies, and
- financial arrangements.

For complex solutions, it is wise to include the services of one of your company's experts so implementation is done properly and everything works as you've promised. Look for ways to add value to your products and services by building in some form of installation or implementation services, on-going supplies, training, or preventive maintenance. This goes a long way toward sustaining customer goodwill as the solution works properly from the beginning.

Our organization used to sell a "SmartStart" with the computer systems we sold. A technician with people skills would deliver and install the equipment in the customer's home or place of business, and do a quick "show and tell" on how to use the equipment. We also sold more extensive training services to shorten the learning cycle associated with the new technologies.

If you formed a solution by creating an alliance with another organization, be clear with your employer and your customer that you've done so. Your organization is totally responsible for the solution, and will have to do what it takes to make sure the customer gains all of the promised benefits and savings.

"George, today I'm recommending a solution comprised both of products we make ourselves, and products from a supplier that has allied with us to make it possible to solve your problem today with an optimum solution. Because we're selling you the solution, we stand behind all of the components and will provide you with any ongoing support you may need. You will always be able to deal with me."

If you're unable to deliver a complete solution that truly meets the customer's needs at this time, then make this clear to the customer in an open declaration.

REQUISITE SKILLS

You require specific skills for making effective recommendations. Make sure you build your proficiency with these skills. It is part of being a professional to make sure that your expertise is as high as possible.

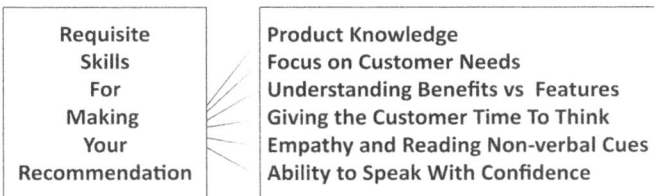

Requisite Skills For Making Your Recommendation	Product Knowledge
	Focus on Customer Needs
	Understanding Benefits vs Features
	Giving the Customer Time To Think
	Empathy and Reading Non-verbal Cues
	Ability to Speak With Confidence

The number one skill is having enough product knowledge to make the proper recommendation. If you don't have enough technical expertise to determine the right solution for this customer's needs, use Half Time to get the product knowledge you need.

You don't personally have to have detailed product knowledge, but your company does. After you learn the customer's S.P.I.C.E^3, you could meet with a team of specialists within your organization. Tell the experts what you've learned about your customer's needs and get them to come up with the complete solution. You may also need to involve these experts in the actual presentation of your recommendation. If this is how it's done in your company, then you have to excel at both getting the customer's S.P.I.C.E^3 and at relaying the information, without data loss, to others who have to know enough to determine the best solution.

You also need the ability to think about the products and services only in terms of your client's needs. The bells and whistles don't matter. What matters is what the products and services will do for your client. Pick those products that satisfy the customer's S.P.I.C.E^3. Too many salespeople focus on products with features they think are important, neat or exciting. If particular features don't matter to your customer, you would just bore the customer, or worse, show you haven't paid attention to his or her needs.

Know the difference between a feature and a benefit. Many sales models encourage you to present a feature, advantage and benefit when selling products. A feature is one of the characteristics or qualities of the product. An advantage is a feature unique from any other products. A benefit is the actual positive outcome the customer will realize as a result of buying and using the product. If you ever mention a feature or an advantage of a product, always tell the customer which benefit the feature or advantage provides.

In the "GET SMARTER" approach, focus on the benefits, and particularly the benefits of the total solution not individual products. Include the benefits of buying from you and from your company. These benefits should be the benefits the customer told you he or she expects out of a solution to his or her problem. Do this in the customer's language with an emphasis matching his or her own so your customer knows it is exactly what he or she wants.

Describe or show your recommendation, state the benefits, and then be quiet as your customer thinks about what you have proposed. Give your customer time to think, and then ask if he or she has any questions. Too many salespeople talk too much – and talk themselves out of a sale. Keep your presentation short and concise.

Maintain your empathy at this stage. Develop your ability to read a client's non-verbal cues and look for behaviors that suggest disagreement, uneasiness, or confusion. Fundamentally, develop your willingness to suspend your selling efforts if you detect any client resistance or objection. The most resistant person to the "sell" should be you – the salesperson. (*See Appendix 5: The SMART Mantras*).

Don't let your customer buy until you both know it's the right thing for him or her to buy. If you see any clues suggesting your customer might be uncomfortable, distracted or irritated, stop immediately and do a feelings check. Find out if the customer is having a reaction to you, your recommendation, or to the time you're taking.

Develop your ability to speak with excitement and confidence about your recommendation. Present enthusiastically so your customer can feel eager to own the solution. Your zeal and certainty can be highest when you've done an effective needs-assessment, and when your product knowledge allows you to know you've recommended the right solution. It's easier to be energized if you've discovered real problems, with real costs, and you're able to offer the right solution to take care of the problem for your client.

EXAMPLES OF SOLUTION PRESENTATION

Let's consider a few examples of how effective salespeople make the recommendation using the "GET SMARTER" approach.

> S: "Mr. Jones, this excites me. I believe this complete tablet system will fully meet your needs. You're concerned your children are falling behind at school because they don't have a tablet to use in the classroom. With this system and the software applications that I've included, your children will have

great performance, high-speed access to the Internet, and all of the tools they'll need to accelerate their learning in math, reading, and science. That's critical, right?"

C: "Yes"

S: "Financed, for all three of them, you'll be paying $140 per month for 24 months, and this covers the cost of the tablets, the wi-fi installation and data services.

C: "That's doable."

S: "As an added bonus, you won't be seen as the bad guy because you make them do their homework. Now, they'll have lots of fun learning on the tablet, and playing with the educational games as a reward for getting their school work done."

C: "Great."

S: "I also recommend an application that allows each child and you, from your smartphone, to see where each tablet is located. This gives you security knowing you're able to find the tablets if they're misplaced and it allows you to know your kids are safe."

C: "Awesome."

S: "I've included an in-home tutorial to get all of you comfortable with your new tablets, as well as the productivity, educational, and recreational applications. You'll be productive right away, which is important to you. Correct?"

C: "Yes. I don't want the kids just using the tablets for games, so they need to know how to use everything."

S: "Our installers will visit tomorrow morning at 10:00 to set up your high-speed Wi-Fi for effective Internet access from their rooms. Sound good?

C: "Let's do it."

The recommendation is presented in terms of the benefits and with very little reference to features. The language is not about technical specifications and avoids use of technical jargon. The salesperson emphasizes the benefits of the whole solution rather than the technical details of the different parts.

The same occurs in this second retail example. While standing beside the full stack of all the products the computer salesperson is recommending to this customer, he or she says,

S: "Jim, this stack is everything you need in the way of equipment and this gentleman here will deliver it to your place, set it up, and show you how to use it. You'll be able to change the way you do things as soon as the next few days, only costing $250 per month with this lease arrangement."

C: "Sounds too easy."

S: "Hard to believe, I know, but the new equipment gives you three new ways to increase your revenues doing work you couldn't do before. You only win with this solution, and as soon as this week. Any questions?"

Earlier in an exercise where you tested your understanding of S.P.I.C.E[3], you learned the S.P.I.C.E[3] of a particular psychologist in private practice. A salesperson might make his or her recommendation to this client in this way:

S: "Phil, with this solution you'll reduce your risk of lost materials, gain the ability to keep your confidential client information in your office, and be more productive in your writing while saving at least $725 per month. That's pure increase in profit plus you'll increase your ability to publish. Important, correct?"

C: "Very much so, as long as you aren't just blowing smoke like the last guy that sold me my computer."

S: "Phil, this solution works because it includes a key element. You want to... need to... quickly learn to use this technology and I've included the installation and training services to make that happen. With your participation, it will be installed the first Wednesday morning after you say, "Yes". The installer will set it all up and spend one-on-one time with you to make sure it works as you expect. Then, for five weeks, a trainer will come to your office each Wednesday morning to sit with you and teach you what you need to know to get the desired results. You'll learn how to dictate your session notes and turn your voice recording into digital data for use in your word processor. You'll set up the accounting software for your own use and learn how to make your entries. You'll learn how to use the Internet for your research and how to submit your writing to publications that require on-line submissions. This training is critical, right?"

C: "Yes and Wednesdays would work out beautifully."

S: "Given your high motivation to make this work, I'm certain that within one month you'll be able to cease your use of the typing and bookkeeping services. With this solution, you'll save money, gain much more control over your own work, have the peace of mind knowing your confidential information is safe, reduce your dependence on expensive services, work the way you like to work, enhance your professional reputation, and learn to use the latest in technology. Spend $375 a month now by leasing this new solution for three years and you'll no longer pay $1,100 per month for services that frustrate you."

C: "I can start Wednesday this week if you can make it happen that fast."

Because your recommended solution is the right one, there is no need to cover the specific technical products that would allow the psychologist to achieve these benefits, but there is a need to stress the installation and training services. This assures the customer your solution will work. The customer alluded to his prior purchase where he was unable to get the results he wanted because he hadn't learned how to use the technology. The nature of the service and the concurrent benefits would be stressed to make it clear that the solution will get him the results he wants.

ABOUT BENEFITS – NOT ABOUT PRODUCTS

The recommendation you make in the "GET SMARTER" approach would definitely **NOT** sound like this,

> "For you, I suggest this system with a quad core i7 processor which makes it much faster, 8 gigabytes of memory which also enhances speed, a 4 terabyte solid state drive for lots of storage, mirrored to a second drive through RAID for constant back-up, a Gemstone Res80 graphics accelerated video card also for speed, and the ZForce FX360 audio card for surround sound. This is a fast computer."

This is not emphasizing the benefits but presenting the features, all aimed at the one benefit of speed. The customer wants to achieve results using this computer. Talk about what those results will be. And be sure to talk about the benefits that matter to this client. Because you learned the S.P.I.C.E.^{3} for this customer, you know what his or her priorities are so stress those benefits.

PLAIN LANGUAGE

Avoid using jargon as you present your solution. This is easier if you talk about expected results and benefits as opposed to product features. Speak clearly about the benefits in plain language. As much as possible, use similar language to what the customer used when telling you his or her S.P.I.C.E.^{3} information. Such language is readily understood, and given the familiarity, can be more readily trusted by the customer.

CONVEY YOUR BELIEF IN THE SOLUTION

Practice so you present your recommendations with confidence and enthusiasm. Experiment with different phrases showing commitment to your recommendation. You can't expect your client to commit to your recommendation if you don't fully believe this is the best solution to the customer's problem. If you are recommending the right solution, believe it fervently and show that belief.

Of course, you must be recommending the right solution. This process of focussing on benefits and not the products requires that the solution will result in the desired benefits. If the solution is not fully capable of yielding the benefits the customer now expects, you shouldn't be recommending it, and definitely should not be presenting it in this way. You must **not** stay away from the products just to mask any inadequacies of your solution.

If there are any limitations to your solution that mean you can not provide all of the benefits the customer has come to expect, you must be completely clear with your customer about those limitations. Insight Sales and the "GET SMARTER" approach require full integrity on your part.

PRESENT THEN STOP TALKING

Master making your recommendations concisely and with style. Say enough to explain why the solution you're recommending meets your customer's needs, then shut up and let your customer digest the information. After sufficient pause, ask if there are any questions, answer those questions and only those questions, and then transition to the next step. The more comfortable you are when doing this, the more credibility you have with your customers. The more credible you are, the more trust will lead to sales.

WHEN GIVING A QUOTE

If you do choose to give a printed quotation to a customer that you know is leaving, indicate you want to earn his or her business. Emphasize the importance of making sure alternate suppliers fully understand his or her needs, and remind the customer of the insights you helped the customer to achieve through your conversation.

"George, when shopping around, remember that you discovered you need a solution that does __X____Y____ and __Z__ . We determined that this is critical for you to get the benefits you want."

Invite your customer to come and talk with you after he or she has gathered more information by checking out your competition. Arrange to call the customer in a couple of days to discuss his or her decision.

BREAK OLD HABITS

To build your "GET SMARTER" mastery at making recommendations, you may need to break out of the trap of old habits. If you've been spending a lot of time talking about products or services and their features, with maybe some emphasis on specific product or service benefits, you need to force yourself away from talking about products.

Using our approach, your focus is on the whole solution as opposed to its parts and components. If this is very different from your current style, we encourage you to practice making a recommendation without mentioning, even once, the specific products within your complete solution.

In the "GET SMARTER" sales approach, Step Four – Show Full Understanding, Half Time, and Step Five – Make Your Recommendation, all relate to each other. Your customer's eagerness to hear what you have to offer grows when you check for understanding by summarizing his or her needs. Half Time gives you the ability to prepare a complete solution. The recommendation relates directly to the customer's needs and the benefits he or she is looking to buy.

If you do this effectively, there's little reason for your customer to say, "No". You'll have shown that your solution gives the customer the benefits he or she wants. Because the value of those benefits exceeds the price of your solution, your customer can afford to buy. In fact, if done correctly, your customer will see that he or she can't really afford to delay the purchase. If your customer delays, he or she would have to live with current costs and without the benefits the new solution will yield.

It's critical that you recognize when to move to the next step. Too many people keep trying to "sell" their recommendation by talking about things that don't need to be said. Stop recommending when you know you've made the recommendation and the customer is ready to take action.

WHEN TO MOVE TO THE NEXT STEP

Once you have presented your solution, direct your customer to a decision. It will be time to move to the Action step when:

- You've uncovered all of the relevant information about your client's needs.

- The right solution for those needs has been identified.

- You've presented your complete recommendation with enthusiasm and a clear demonstration of how benefits exceed price.

- Buying cues are evident, such as the customer nodding his or her head in agreement throughout the presentation of your recommendation.

and

- All of the client's responses to your presentation ratify that you've matched the benefits of the solution to his or her needs.

If you've done the right stuff to this point, naturally move to the next step. If your customer's behavior is positive, assume that he or she is ready to decide to buy.

If you aren't here yet, and see hesitation on the part of the customer, back up and clarify any reservations the customer might hold. Customer hesitation or resistance should move you back to Step Three to clarify his or her needs.

TRANSITION TO THE ACTION STEP

Move to Step Six by declaring you believe your recommendation meets your customer's needs and provides real value resulting in extra benefits compared to his or her current situation.

> "I'm pleased this solution meets your needs, reduces your costs, and gives you added value by (*producing desired benefit*). Do you agree? Do you share my excitement?"

If you feel the need to do so, you could remind the customer the price is well below the extra value the solution will provide, or that the expected profits exceed the price. But do so positively so you don't direct your customer to think about the price and the need to compare your price with that of a competitor.

> "And the beauty of this solution is that it saves you more money than you've been spending. What you'll be spending to put this solution in place costs a great deal less than what you spend now. In other words, this really adds to your bottom line. That's what you want, right?"

or

> "Well folks. I have nothing more to add. This solution does what you want, will yield great results, and provides benefits that will more than cover your investment. Does this excite you like it excites me?"

or

> "Bill. I'm truly pleased this solution gives you all you want, and for less than you pay now. Are you feeling the same eagerness I feel?"

If you sense any hesitation, or disinterest, or stiffening as the customer readies to object, then you need to back up to the process of listening to what your customer has to say. Get the customer talking about his or her reaction and look for more clues about his or her needs that you might not have uncovered.

If your client appears to share your excitement, then move to the next step and lead the customer to his or her decision. You want to exit this step with both of you feeling excited about getting the solution put into place as soon as possible. If you have done all of the previous steps effectively, this is where you will most likely be. It will be time to stimulate the decision to buy.

STEP SIX – ASK HOW TO PROCEED

(INVITE THE CUSTOMER TO MAKE A PURCHASE DECISION)

You don't need a tool chest full of manipulative closes. You just ask the customer what he or she would like to do next.

Once you've presented your recommendation to your customer, the next step is the action step. You initiate a call-to-action because it's time for the customer to decide.

GOALS OF STEP SIX – ASK HOW TO PROCEED

Once again, you go into a step in the "GET SMARTER" sales approach with more than one goal. In this step, your goals are to:

- move the customer to take the next appropriate action,

- make it clear what is going to happen next so you both know what to expect,

- initiate the purchase in a way which is comfortable for the customer, and fits with the information the client has given you about him or herself,

- deal constructively with any customer questions, concerns or objections, and

- win the customer's business in such a way he or she will make referrals to others because the customer knows you can be trusted to look after friends, family members, and colleagues just like you've taken care of him or her.

Your goal is to continue to sell and be seen to sell with integrity. Be ethical in your approach. Proceed with the sale in such a way the customer is glad he or she chose to buy from you and from your organization. This isn't going to be the end of a sale. It's the start of a long-term relationship and you both should expect this.

TIME FOR THE CUSTOMER TO DECIDE

"Step Six – Asking How To Proceed" is the stage at which you invite the customer to simply make a decision. If you diligently followed the "GET SMARTER" sales model, provided a solution completely meeting the customer's needs, and if you've earned the customer's trust, the customer will buy. However, if your customer isn't ready to decide, provide the customer with any assistance he or she needs to make a decision.

189

At this stage, if you didn't completely discover your customer's S.P.I.C.E^3, he or she may have questions, concerns or objections as you ask for a decision. Dealing with these questions, concerns and objections at this stage takes up valuable time. In fact, dealing with objections at this stage typically takes more time than first learning the customer's needs during Step Three.

At Step Six, this is about resistance. At Step Three, this is about getting information. Consequently, learn how to do an effective needs-assessment and deal with this information in Step Three. Totally learn the customer's S.P.I.C.E^3 before you make your recommendation.

If you do get some resistance, you'll need to remain true to what you've done in the first half of the sales process to establish trust and rapport with your customer. Don't suddenly undergo a personality change and switch to persuasion selling. Be consistent, back up to learn what you failed to learn earlier, and then change your recommendation accordingly.

Unfortunately, once you reach Step Six, you're at the stage where many salespeople struggle. Asking for the customer's business seems to frighten many rookie salespeople. Too many salespeople fail to ask the customer for his or her business.

We think this fear comes naturally when the salesperson knows he or she has been pursuing his or her own goals and not those of the customer. This dance of opposition comes to a head at this step. Because of the tension of opposition, the salesperson typically expects resistance and avoids asking.

As a salesperson, you're expected to sell. You will be measured on your sales performance. To sell, you have to be able and willing to initiate a call-to-action. You're unlikely to be a successful salesperson if you avoid this step.

The way we see it, if you know your customer service and your complete solution is better for the customer than not buying at all, you have the responsibility to take care of your customer by getting him or her to buy now. If you know your customer service and your complete solution is better than what the competition offers, it is your responsibility to get the customer to buy from you instead of from a competitor. You have an ethical responsibility to get your customer to choose an optimum solution that delivers the results he or she wants.

If a change would relieve the problems, reduce the costs, and give the customer added benefits, it's irresponsible for you to quit now. It's poor service to let your customer stick with the status quo just because you didn't invite him or her to make a decision. Remember, you're recommending a solution with real value that exceeds the price the customer will have to pay. You aren't pushing your customer into something he or she doesn't need. You're helping your customer to make a decision for his or her own good.

We think you've earned the right to do so because you've provided the value-added service of an insight-oriented consultant. You've identified your customer's real needs and recommended a solution that saves the customer from the costs of his or her status quo, and yields extra benefits.

We admit it's reasonable to be concerned about the customer's resistance to buying because asking for the business could trigger any of the following concerns:

- Do I really need this product?

- Will buying this product really make a positive difference?

- Does this product measure up to what the competition has available?

- Should I postpone buying?

- Will this supplier stand behind the product?

- What will my friends/peers think if I buy this item?

- Is this person trying to get me to buy the right solution?

However, if you've matched your presentation to the needs of the client and have presented the complete solution while clearly indicating the benefits the customer will realize, all of these concerns will have been dealt with. The customer will clearly know he or she needs the solution, and needs it now.

The customer will see your solution as directly related to his or her needs and this will stand in stark contrast to a competitor's products, which were promoted without knowing the customer's

S.P.I.C.E.[3]. Your customer will realize there is an urgency to buy because something can be done now to significantly reduce costs or increase payoffs.

Your customer will have established a relationship of trust with you and will know you're presenting the solution that fits his or her needs. You aren't pushing the customer to decide to buy. You're asking your customer to decide what he or she wants to do next. There's nothing scary about that.

If you properly use the "GET SMARTER" sales approach, you'll find your confidence to initiate the call-to-action will go up. You'll know you've earned the right to ask. You'll know your chances of getting a "Yes, I'll take it" are much better when you've effectively fulfilled the role of insight-oriented consultant for your client.

If you've been effectively using the "GET SMARTER" sales approach, we think you can call the customer to action and get a "Yes Let's Do It" response ninety percent (90%) of the time (*or more*). Results are highest particularly when dealing with repeat or referral customers. "Yes" is a response given without objection.

Remember, you get these results because, by this stage, the customer is ready. The customer felt the need to go shopping because he or she felt a need to solve a problem with the types of products and services you sell. By talking to you, the customer crystallized his or her needs and wants. You've recommended the proper solution for those needs. In the customer's buying cycle, he or she is ready to take action. You served the customer with integrity. Now, you encourage the customer to make a decision for his or her own good.

WHEN TO ASK

The process is actually very easy but this step really does require putting in good honest work in all of the preceding steps before you get to this point. If, and only if, you and the customer fully understand your client's needs, if you've summarized to demonstrate full understanding, if you've made a recommendation matched to those needs and desired benefits, if you've explained the benefits with enthusiasm, and if you've attended to the client's responses to your information and detected a positive response, initiate a call-to-action.

CUSTOMER BUYING SIGNALS

There are many ways a customer can let you know he or she is ready to buy. The customer can say so or give direct clues by what he or she says. For example, the customer could ask a question about the product you've recommended, about when you could deliver, about price or financing. He or she could make a positive comment about what you've recommended, or could stipulate his or her requirements, such as **"I need five of these by Wednesday, can you do it?"**

Alternatively, the customer could simply let you know through non-verbal clues. For example, the client's facial expression might change – eyes widening, smiling more, looking at you with a facial expression showing a genuine interest. Or the customer might begin nodding his or her head in agreement, or lean forward, intent on hearing your message. If the customer is a couple or family, one person might look to others for their nod of acceptance.

It's also a good sign when the client begins to study either the product or any written materials you've provided. This behavior is gaining some thinking time. Be silent. Allow the customer a moment of privacy. Then when he or she looks up, ask what he or she wants to happen next.

Recognize the customer's buying signals, display a high degree of self-confidence in the "rightness" of your recommendation and ask a very straightforward question. Stop "selling" when you get the signals. Too many people talk themselves out of the sale by continuing to talk past the signals, thereby losing the customer's attention and readiness.

When you see a buying signal, try a call-to-action. It's your responsibility to either:

- move forward to the next stage in the customer's decision-making process, and get the sale, or

- back up to gather more information if your customer isn't satisfied your recommendation meets his or her needs, or

- get feedback from your customer as to why you didn't earn his or her business.

In truth, you really don't have any other choices. It's not acceptable to stop after making your recommendation and not have a clue whether or not the customer is going to buy from you, and if not, why not.

HOW TO ASK FOR A DECISION

Just ask the customer what he or she thinks should happen next. Put control of the situation completely in the customer's hands. You've performed your function to this point. You've managed to get the customer to the place where he or she can make an informed decision to purchase a complete solution. Now it's up to your customer to decide.

OPTION 1 – ASK DIRECTLY

If you're fairly confident you built sufficient rapport, and you see positive responses to your recommendation on the part of the client, ask directly. For example,

"George, this solution excites me. Shall we go ahead?"

or

"Have I earned your business today?"

or

"What do you think? Does this solution look right to you?"

OPTION 2 – DECLARE AND ASK

Again, if you've done all of the preceding steps well and can tell that the customer is truly ready and receptive to your recommendation, assert the appropriateness of your solution, indicate you want to win the customer's business and then ask for the sale.

"Samantha. I'm glad that this solution was available because it gives you all of the benefits we discussed. I want to win your business. Have I done so?

Option 3 – Assume The Business

If you believe the customer is absolutely ready to buy, based on all of his or her responses to your recommendation, both verbal and non-verbal, just assume the customer is ready to buy what you've recommended. Initiate the transaction. If everything you need for this complete solution is available in the store, gather everything together, then say,

> "I've gathered up everything you'll need, let's go to the till."

or

> "Should I set up the appointment for delivery tomorrow?"

If some elements of the solution need to be ordered in, set the process in motion by saying to the customer,

> "I need to order in a few of the components of this solution and that will take a few days, so I'll initiate this order and get our purchaser working on it immediately."

Some of the best salespeople are very good at assuming the sale. Such salespeople use the "GET SMARTER" approach and know the customer is ready to do business just with them. It's easier to assume the sale when you know you've been working for the customer's success, using the best sales process. Assuming the customer is ready comes naturally when you've been paying attention to the customer throughout the process and noticed the customer's trust in you.

Option 4 – When Uncertain Of Customer Readiness

If you think the customer is ready, but you aren't quite sure, ask for the business by saying something like,

> "Shall we do it?"

or

> "Have I met your needs?"

or

"Looks like this will do it, right?"

Your call-to-action can be as simple as asking what the customer wants to do next.

"How do you wish to proceed?"

or

"How shall we proceed from here?"

or

"Shall we go ahead?"

or

"This solution is right for you. What do you want to do now?"

MORE CALL-TO-ACTION EXAMPLES

The call-to-action is a simple and straightforward question. Pick the words that fit your style but your words should basically ask, "How would you like to proceed from here?" This can be said as,

"Well Dan, I think we've covered what we needed to and sorted out what's best for you. What do you think... is there anything else we need to do or should we just go to the till?"

or

"What would you like to do now, think about this some more, talk with your advisor, or go ahead with the purchase?"

or

"Is there anything else I can do to help you make your decision, or are you ready to proceed to the next step?"

or

"I'm excited about how this fits your situation, meets your needs, and gives you the benefits you're looking for, but now I need to follow your lead. What do you think should happen next?"

or

"We've discussed your needs and I've recommended what I think best meets them. You seem excited about the possibilities, but to be sure... how do you want to proceed at this point?"

or

"I think this solution could really make a difference for you, but you've got to feel comfortable with what I've suggested. How are you feeling about this? How do you wish to proceed now?"

or

"So you have significant costs within your current way of doing things that can be substantially reduced. You now have before you a solution that will make that difference. Are you ready to proceed?"

The key is asking for the customer's decision with integrity, believing your solution is a complete solution that matches the customer's needs. You know you're doing your best to look after the customer. If you've done the right stuff and believe you have your customer's best interests at heart, we think the customer will believe this as well.

In my opinion, the safest alternative is just to ask the customer what he or she wants to do next. Assuming the sale, or asking for the sale both work well if you're reading the customer accurately. This is easier to do if you have a great deal of sales experience. But you might have misread your customer, especially if you're new to selling, or new to the "GET SMARTER" approach to selling. To ask, "How should we proceed from here?" is a mistake-free question and your safest strategy.

No manipulation is intended. No deceit is perpetrated. No competition with the customer is undertaken. You provide a value added service, and then ask the customer how he or she wants to proceed next. This behavior is quite comfortable to the client.

SUCCESSFUL CALL-TO-ACTION OUTCOMES

Your call-to-action question should take the two of you to one of four possibilities acceptable to you as the salesperson. The customer could:

- decide to buy,

- ask a question or express a concern or objection,

- negotiate a specific time frame within which you will call to follow-up (*to help the customer with his or her decision making, or to discuss the actual decision*), or

- give you feedback about how you failed to earn his or her business.

Your call-to-action should not end up with a "wishy-washy" outcome where the customer promises to get back to you because he or she is going away to think about it, and quite possibly shop around. Get the sale, get an appointment to follow-up, learn about any questions, concerns or objections and deal with them, or get feedback about how the customer feels you failed to meet his or her needs.

If the customer's response is a decision to buy, then complete the transaction and shift to the next step.

IF THE CUSTOMER HASN'T YET DECIDED TO BUY

If you detect any reservation on the part of the customer, stop and check.

> "I sense a hesitation on your part and I'm wondering if I've failed to take into consideration one of your needs. As your consultant, I want to help you get the complete solution to the problems we discussed, and get it implemented so you experience the benefits sooner than later. So if I haven't done my job, please let me know what concerns you."

or

> "I agree this is an important decision and you wish to take time to think it through. Is there anything I haven't given you as information that would help you to make your decision?"

or

> "It's important to me that I provide a solution that meets all of your needs. From your reaction, I think I may have missed some key concerns. I really need to know what they are so I can properly match your needs to the right solution."

or

> "You're making a significant investment here, and it's important you get the right solution. I think you have reservations about what I've recommended. If so, please tell me what concerns you?"

THE CUSTOMER THAT WANTS TO DELAY

The customer might want time to think about what you've discussed and your recommendation. Respect this need. Review what you have talked about, re-state your recommendation and the reasons why, assert that you really want to earn your customer's business and that you want to help him or her successfully solve the problem. Then ask for a time when you can call to follow-up.

> "I agree that you should take the time to think about what we talked about today. We reviewed the problem you are having with (*the problem*) and how this is costing (*the implications*). You haven't resolved this problem before because (*the constraints*) but you're excited about getting a solution that would give you (*the E^3 Benefits*). I've recommended (*your complete solution*) so that you can achieve (*the E3 Benefits*). I really want to help you get these benefits sooner than later. I want to earn your business. Take time to think about this and I will call you to follow-up our discussion. Given that each day you

delay has those costs we've discussed, would it be appropriate to call you tomorrow?"

or

"Mrs. Cressman, we've discussed the problems you're trying to solve, the costs of those problems, and the benefits you're hoping to achieve. It's important that you get a solution that allows you to (*summarize the E^3 Benefits*). I really want you to realize the gains a proper solution can give you, and will follow-up with you. I think we both recognize the sooner you begin to experience the benefits, the better it will be. The solution I've proposed will get you going right away. When can I call you to follow-up?"

or

"Sue. I know this is a big decision for you and I respect your caution. Take a few days to think about what we've discussed – the costs you experience now, the benefits my proposed solution will give you, and how the results you achieve will more than pay for this solution. Remember that you want to be able to (*summarize what the solution will do and the E^3 Benefits*). I will call you on Wednesday at 9:30 a.m. to see how your decision- making is progressing."

THE CUSTOMER THAT WANTS TO DISCUSS WITH SIGNIFICANT OTHERS

Alternatively, if your customer just needs to discuss his or her decision-making with someone else, then give room to do so. Ask if there is any way to help the customer share what you've discussed so he or she can make an effective presentation to the other parties. You could offer to meet with his or her people and do this for the customer, or to be available to answer questions and deal with concerns. However, you need an agreed upon time to make a follow up contact with the customer.

"This is a significant investment and I understand the need to discuss this with your spouse. If there's any information you need from me to help you do so, let me know. Given the significance of the benefits you would realize by making this change, when can I contact you to follow-up? Is Tuesday okay?"

Remind the customer you want to earn his or her business. Simply summarize the benefits you understand the customer is looking for and set a specific date and time when you will call.

"Remember that the solution I proposed will give you (*summarize the E³ Benefits*). I want to help you get going with that solution so you can reduce your current costs and add the extra payoffs. I will call on Friday to discuss what your team thinks about all of this."

THE CUSTOMER THAT WANTS TO SHOP AROUND

If the customer tells you he or she intends to shop around or check with your competition, acknowledge this is an important decision and you respect that the customer wants to be sure to make the right one. It's appropriate to support your customer in his or her decision to check with a competitor. Never say anything disparaging about the competition.

You could offer to help the customer review any new information he or she might be given. Ask the customer if you could have done anything to be more helpful in your preceding discussion. Given that the customer hasn't made the decision to buy yet, set a time and date when you will call to follow-up.

"Sally, I understand you have an important decision to make, and you don't want to make a mistake that you have to live with for a long time. I appreciate the desire to check competitors so you make the best investment possible. They'll likely give you new information, and some of it may be confusing or contradictory. I'd like to meet with you to review what you learn, and to match this up against the benefits you're trying to achieve. It is important that you can (*summarize the solution and the*

E³ Benefits). Do you have a time frame in mind when I can contact you to follow-up? And if there's anything you can tell me about how I could have been or still can be more helpful to you, I welcome your feedback."

or

"Jim. It's a large investment and you want to know you're making the correct decision. I can appreciate the wish to shop around. Make sure the people you talk with take the time to discuss your needs. They should get to know your particular expectations and desired outcomes. Check out pricing but the real issue is getting all of the results we discussed today by putting a complete solution in place. The solution you buy should give you (*the E³ Benefits*). I'll call you tomorrow at 10:00 a.m. to see how your visit to our competitors turned out for you. If you get new information that appears to conflict with what I told you, I'll help you sort out the differences."

You can still say particular things to bring your customer back to you. Your parting comments could include the reasons your other customers choose again and again to buy from you.

"Mark, I understand the need to see if a competitor can offer a better solution. I urge you to consider the nature of our conversation today as you do so. Our customers know that we have their best interest at heart and this is reflected in how we work to deliver new insights through our conversations, to bring new solutions to problems they haven't been able to solve, to work together to increase our customer's success. Please make sure the competition delivers those same benefits before you make your purchase decision."

or

"Adele, I'm glad you're looking for the best solution for your needs. You will truly benefit by putting the right solution in place. I respect your decision to shop around but before you go, I just want to give you a few reasons why our customers prefer to do business with us. They feel comfortable with our pricing because we have a price matching program in place, buy nationally and get good deals ourselves that we pass along to our customers. They know we have a strong commitment to our ongoing relationship and provide exceptional after sales support. And lastly, our customers know the solutions we sell deliver the desired results."

or

"Rama, I look forward to helping you after you've checked with our competition. I want to earn your business so that you get the benefits our other customers have experienced. It's our goal to take better care of you than anyone else, to enhance your own success, and to earn your trust for the long term. Shop around, then contact me before you decide to buy and I'll help you like I've helped you today."

In these last comments, you may have to use your enthusiasm and confidence in the solution you've recommended to bring the customer back. However, don't do anything more than offer this information. Don't try to persuade the customer to buy now. Just give the reasons why he or she would benefit by returning to you.

Before the customer departs, you could ask for his or her impressions of how you've helped (*or not helped*) him or her. For example,

"And if there is anything you can tell me about how I could have been or still can be more helpful to you, I welcome your feedback."

THE CUSTOMER WHO RESISTS A FOLLOW-UP CALL

If there is any resistance to scheduling a follow-up call, ask for feedback. You've given a significant amount of time to this customer with a pure intention of being an effective insight-oriented consultant. If you failed to achieve a sale, the least you want to accomplish is a learning experience.

Ask the customer for his or her impressions of you and what you've done in this conversation. For example,

> "Frank, it was my intention today to get to know your full set of needs so I could make a proper recommendation, one that would give you the benefits you deserve. It would appear I didn't do my job as effectively as I could have, and I've somehow disappointed you. I want to learn to be a more effective consultant and would like your feedback as to how I failed you today."

or

> "Mr. Dotto, I'd hoped to fully understand your needs so I could recommend a complete solution to reduce your current costs, give added benefits, and increase your profitability. I wanted to build a relationship of trust and rapport where you know I have your best interests at heart... but from your reaction, I don't think I did this today. Could you please help me to develop my skills as a consultant and tell me how I missed this opportunity with you?"

or

> "Bill. I thank you for giving me the opportunity to earn your business, but it appears I haven't gained your trust and respect, or what I've recommended to you was not appropriate. Please help me to grow my own skills and tell me how I failed to meet your needs."

If you hear the words, "I need to think about this for awhile. I'll be back." and sense the person isn't entirely comfortable with you, say something like,

> "Mr. Augustini, I agree thinking about your decision is important. This is a significant investment, and you want to spend your money wisely and get the right solution. However, I also sense you think I may have made the wrong

recommendation. Perhaps I failed to do something for you and you aren't comfortable. I want to be a good consultant to my clients, so if I've failed in some way, please help me to learn and tell me where I missed the boat here?"

Don't be afraid to solicit feedback if the customer isn't going to buy from you. It would be a fair trade for the time you've spent with the customer. If you don't get the sale, learn something from the interaction.

However, for this request to be acceptable to the client, it must have been clear to both of you that you were really working to understand his or her needs. If you weren't actively listening to the customer, he or she will think this request for feedback is unfair. It will feel like a push for something you didn't earn.

DEALING WITH QUESTIONS, CONCERNS AND OBJECTIONS

Find out if there is any confusion, concern, or objection to your proposed solution. If none, ask your customer how he or she wants to proceed. If there are questions, concerns or objections, deal with them.

Customer questions, concerns or even objections should not be a reason to lose control of the sales interaction and shift out of the "GET SMARTER" approach. Keep your head about you, stay consistent with what you've been doing up to this point, and help your customer to make his or her correct decision.

Sometimes, it's hard to tell whether a comment is a question, concern, or an objection and whether the customer just needs additional information or needs you to make changes to your recommended solution. However, questions, concerns and objections are all indications the customer does want to buy from you. Otherwise he or she could just walk.

DEALING WITH QUESTIONS

A question is a request for more information so the customer can decide whether or not to buy. A question should be treated as a buying intention on the customer's part and should be treated with respect and validated. The customer could ask a question such as:

"Is this the best recommendation you can make?"

"Is this the best price you'll give me?"

"Will this XXXXXX last a long time?"

"Does this XXXXXX have enough _____ for what I will be using it for?"

"What if this doesn't work with my existing _____ ?"

"Your competitor sells _____ brand and it has a good reputation. Why are you trying to sell me XXXXXX?"

If the customer intends any one of these as a question, it's not an objection as it's not a resistance to buying. It's a request for information and the best way to deal with it is to understand the question and then provide the needed information.

By asking a specific question about your recommendation, the customer may be trying to make up his or her mind to go ahead and buy. The customer may need one last piece of information. Perhaps your customer wants to hear a response that can be used when he or she justifies his or her purchase decision to others. The customer may be asking just to create a delay while he or she thinks through the decision. The customer may be slowly taking ownership by asking questions about particular things he or she thinks are important. The customer may need to check something against what he or she heard from a competitor, or the customer may just be seeking peace of mind about going ahead.

It would be a mistake to treat customer questions as impediments to getting the sale. Respect and value these inquiries. Get the customer the information he or she requires.

Dealing With Questions

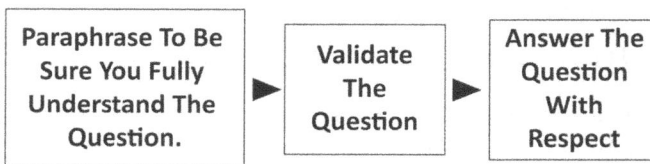

Paraphrase To Be Sure You Fully Understand The Question.	▶	Validate The Question	▶	Answer The Question With Respect

206

First paraphrase the question. Make sure you understand the question, validate its importance and then answer what is really being asked. Answer questions informatively and with care. Avoid offering more information than what the customer has asked for as this can just add confusion.

> S: "It sounds like you're asking me if I think there is something better about this brand than the one sold by our competitor, or if I think the other brand is inferior in some way, is that correct?"

> C: "Yes, is there something better about this brand that I should know?"

> S: "That's a good question. Actually, both are good brands. I recommended the solution I did because this particular model has all of the features you need to achieve the benefits you value the most. You want to be able to (*desired result*) and this XXXXX will do that very well."

Remember, there is a lifetime relationship at stake, so answer with integrity. Do not fall into persuading the customer you've made the best recommendation. Answer truthfully. If the correct answer means the recommendation is not the best one, then change the recommendation.

Questions may be expressed with strong emotion and seem like rejections. It is harder for you to respond effectively if you just focus on the emotional intensity of the customer's question. You need a process that allows you to understand and answer with the proper information. Hear the question, interpret the customer's intent, paraphrase to make sure you understand the question, acknowledge the importance of the question, and answer it.

For example, the customer might ask a question that seems like an aggressive challenge of something you recommended.

| C: (*raising his voice and pointing at the camera*) "So why did you recommend this camera when the one in the advertisement is $100 less?" | |

S: "Sounds like you aren't comfortable with my suggestion, thinking you'd be paying more than you should have to pay?"	Paraphrase
C: "Yeah. It seems like bait and switch."	
S: "I can appreciate your question. I recommended this more expensive camera because you said you wanted to take wildlife pictures. It's often tough to get close enough to take a good picture without disturbing the wildlife, so I've recommended a camera with better zoom capability than the one in the ad. This way you'll get a good shot without scaring the animals away."	Validate Answer
C: "That's important. Okay let's do it."	

or as another example:

C: (with a hard stare at the salesperson and pointing at one of the items in the stack of items recommended by the salesperson) "What do I need this UPS for?"	
S: "Sounds like you don't know why I included this uninterruptible power supply with the computer system I'm recommending, and you're worried about the extra cost. Is this correct?"	Paraphrase
C: "Yeah. It seems like an unnecessary expense."	
S: "I can appreciate your question especially if it seems like something you don't need. I included it because you said you live forty miles outside the city in a rural setting. Frequently in such settings, the power isn't steady — brownouts where the lights dim, power surges, or actual power outages. Such	Validate Answer

fluctuations in power can damage electronic devices, or cause a mess up in the file allocation table of the computer, particularly if power drops when a file is being saved. If this happens, you could lose access to all of your important data on the computer. In the case of power surges, our service center has seen computers with damaged motherboards because the spike in electricity reached the computer. All of this is prevented by a UPS, which levels power before it reaches the computer. "	
C: "So that's what's been happening to my neighbor. Yes, I agree, the UPS is important."	

The explanation of the reasons for these two recommendations in our examples satisfied the customers and each customer made the decision to buy.

Alternatively the question might seem to be critical of the scope of your recommended solution.

C: (*with an angry look on his face*) "What the hell? I came in to buy a suit and now you're telling me I need this whole outfit?"	
S: "I hear your frustration. Sounds like you think I'm trying to sell you much more than you need. Correct?"	Feelings Check
C: "I just don't understand why you think I need a complete outfit?"	
S: "Fair enough. I wouldn't want to just do an up-sell to take more of your money. It's not a good way to treat customers. You told me your wardrobe is generally older, and you typically wear brown suits. You also indicated you feel excited about making a	Validate Answer

209

change and you now have an interest in blues and grays. I heard you say you wanted to catch up with fashion, so I'm recommending a dark blue suit, three dress shirts, three ties, and some socks and shoes. They all work together to give you the dynamic look you're seeking. I've staged them in these Polaroid pictures to show you how they go together, and I think they look terrific. How do they look to you?"

C: "I agree. They'd be a whole new look for me. Okay, you're right. I'll do it."

A reasonable answer, given with integrity, satisfied the customer's question and a decision was made to buy.

DEALING WITH CONCERNS

Alternatively, the customer might express concerns. A concern is an expression of worry about one or more aspects of your recommendation. This gives you new information about something that influences the customer's decision-making. A concern tells you the customer wants to buy but needs something specific to be addressed before he or she can do so. The customer might declare a concern such as:

"I need this by Friday at the latest and you said it isn't in stock. Are you sure you could get it here by then."

or

"I'm concerned I wouldn't use all of this stuff right away. Perhaps it doesn't make sense to buy everything now."

or

"Whenever I buy new technology, I have this long learning curve where I feel less productive than I was before."

or

"I wouldn't want to buy this today and discover it went on sale right after I bought it."

or

"These products change so fast now-a-days. I'm worried this will be obsolete as soon as I buy it?"

Again these statements do not express a resistance to buying. They may express a need for reassurance that your solution is right for the customer. These statements may also indicate a need to know you'll live up to the promises you've made either directly or by implication. The customer wants to know if you'll really meet his or her needs. Possibly, the concern is a clue that something additional needs to be added to your recommended solution.

Expressions of concern are likely just buying signals. By offering his or her opinion about your recommendation, the customer may be trying to make up his or her mind to go ahead and buy. The customer may need you to give your opinion. The customer may want you to offer any last pieces of information that will allow him or her to decide it's the right solution.

As with questions, the customer may be saying this just to delay while he or she thinks through the decision. The customer may be slowly taking ownership by commenting on particular things he or she thinks are important. The customer may just be seeking peace of mind about going ahead. Value these concerns because the customer is telling you he or she is ready to buy from you if you make the commitment to the customer that this is the right choice for him or her to make.

Dealing With Concerns

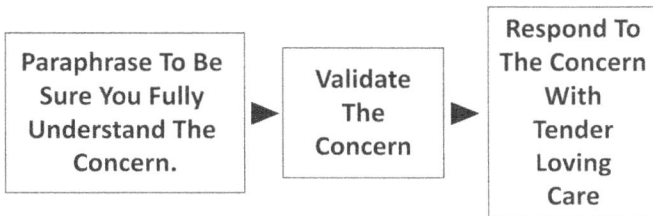

Paraphrase To Be Sure You Fully Understand The Concern.	▶	Validate The Concern	▶	Respond To The Concern With Tender Loving Care

Paraphrase the concern first. Summarize what you think the customer means then ask if you've understood his or her concern. Once you know you understand, validate the concern. Agree with the concern as an important issue or consideration. Make sure you keep an open mind. Then respond to the concern with tender loving care.

Concerns may be expressed with intensity and may seem like a real challenge to you and your proposal. This isn't a time to be defensive because the customer is actually expressing trust in you by bringing out his or her concern. If the customer's concern isn't addressed by your recommendation, find out if the concern is important, and if so, change your recommendation. Understand, validate and respond.

C: *(with exasperated voice)* "Boy I sure would hate to buy this today and then find out it went on sale right away. I wouldn't want to discover that if I waited, I would have gotten a better price."	
S: "So Jeff, I sense you're concerned about whether or not we're giving you a good enough deal today."	Paraphrase
C: "Yeah, I wouldn't want to buy because you're such a great sales guy, and miss out on a better deal."	
S: "I understand. We share the concern as well. We don't want you to pay more than you have to. Actually, we do a lot to make sure you get the best price. We're part of a national chain and as such we get the advantage of large volume buying. That's part of the savings we bring to you. We shop our competition every day to check their prices against ours. In addition, we have a price guarantee. If you find a lower price on any of these items within the next thirty days, come	Validate Answer With Tender Loving Care

back to us, and we'll refund you the difference.	
C: "Sounds good."	
S: "However, remember if you don't put this solution into effect as soon as possible, you do have costs right now. We talked about your current situation – how you aren't able to get some of your work done within your deadlines, how you're spending long hours of personal time just trying to keep up. This will get you working faster and spending your time more effectively. There's a lot of benefit here exceeding the price of your investment in this solution. We protect you on price so you can get this today, and make the necessary changes in how you do your work."	Answer With Tender Loving Care
C: "You're right. Let's proceed."	

Questions and concerns are just a natural part of the conversation you've been having with the customer to this point, so be careful to not over react. Don't be intimidated by questions and concerns. Just deal with them. When you paraphrase for understanding, you discover whether or not the customer has a real question, a concern to be addressed, or an objection.

DEALING WITH OBJECTIONS

An objection, like a concern, is an expression of a problem or a reason the customer isn't yet ready. An objection usually has more intensity than a concern. An objection is likely a signal the salesperson failed to uncover a significant aspect of the customer's needs and expectations during the first half of the sales process.

When selling, particularly if you aren't skillfully using the "GET SMARTER" sales approach, you may hear comments like these, expressed with emotion that suggests rejection of you and your recommendation:

213

"Come on, am I just paying extra for this brand name, or does it really add any value?"

"I saw this same unit at your competitor, and it was $200 less."

"What if this doesn't work with my existing set-up?

"Thanks but no thanks. I don't think this is right for me."

"Whenever we buy new technology, we have a long and expensive learning curve. We just don't want that right now."

"Wow, that's a lot to pay, way more than I expected. I don't think I can afford that much."

"As I look at what you've recommended, you've missed something important. There's nothing here to address our needs for _____ ."

Shaking head. " Eahh, No!"

"This technology changes so fast and will be obsolete before I even buy it."

"I'm not sure the life span of this XXXXXX justifies the investment."

"Well thanks for the information. I'm used to the way I do things now, so I'll just stick with what I've got."

"I've got a pretty good relationship with my current supplier. I'll talk with them about this."

Respond to these comments in a fashion that retains rapport with your client and allows you to sell the right solution for your customer's needs.

Remember, the customer doesn't have to object. He or she could just say thanks and end the conversation. A customer that departs with an unexpressed objection is a lost sale and a walking negative advertisement when he tells others of his dissatisfaction. As nasty as they might seem to you, objections are a good thing. An objection means the customer is:

- still in relationship with you,

- trying to figure out what to buy,

- making sure that he or she gets the best solution, and

- determining whether or not to buy from you.

Remember, objections are your opportunity to help the customer to decide to buy the right solution.

It's better to know the opinions, points of resistance, and priorities of your customer. Preferably you'll learn enough from your customer to address the reasons for resistance. It's better to learn about the objection before the customer buys elsewhere, better to find out key information and adjust your recommendation to properly meet the needs, and it is better to learn how you failed to properly meet your customer's needs in order to learn to do a better job with the next customer.

An objection differs from a question or concern because it is a resistance, a serious challenge to your recommendation, or rejection of you. The customer may believe your solution failed to overcome one of his or her constraints. He or she may think you didn't understand his or her needs and priorities. The customer may think the solution is flawed in some way. He or she may reject the price of the solution because the customer doesn't yet see that value exceeds price. The customer may have a different preferred supplier. Alternatively, the customer may be suspicious of your motives and protecting him or herself from making a buying mistake.

If the customer is truly objecting or resisting what you've proposed, you have an opportunity to learn why. This objection probably means:

> You didn't do a complete needs-assessment, and failed to learn about all of the customer's needs and concerns.

or

> You didn't establish enough rapport during your discovery of the customer's S.P.I.C.E[3].

or

> You didn't recommend the right solution.

or

> You didn't present the solution in terms of the benefits the customer will get from the solution.

or

> You didn't create a clear picture of the value of your solution (*the customer doesn't know how the benefits far exceed the price*).

or

> You asked the customer to buy before he or she felt ready.

or

> Paradoxically, the customer wants to buy but needs something more from you before he or she decides to do so, such as assurance, information, a way to buy, or a small change to your recommendation (*however the customer is not necessarily looking for a better price*).

or

> All of the above.

On the other hand, what appears to be an objection may only be a concern or a question masked as resistance. Also, as with some questions and expressions of concern, an objection is sometimes a vehicle to gain time and space, so the customer can make an unpressured decision or gather more information elsewhere – such as by shopping your competitors. In all cases, we suggest you begin by clarifying what the customer is saying to you.

A customer may be close to deciding to buy even though you didn't do your job as effectively as he or she might have wished. An objection is a buying signal; so see this as a positive indication the customer may still choose to buy from you.

As we explore dealing with resistance or objections, we're assuming you've taken the time to discover the customer's needs and expectations in the first half of the selling process. We believe if you have, you'll get fewer objections in the second half. In general, we believe effective insight-oriented salespeople will encounter very little client resistance or objections.

If you do hear an objection, have enough personal awareness of what you've been doing to quickly ask yourself, "Have I made a mistake, or is this a clue the customer needs a few moments to decide?" If you didn't do full discovery in the first half, then we aren't suggesting you "deal with objections" in the manner most sales books recommend. This isn't a time to get persuasive, to challenge the customer, to intimidate him or her in any way. Back up. Get the S.P.I.C.E[3] properly.

Understandably, it is wiser to prevent objections in the first place. Remember, you prevent objections by:

- building an open relationship where the customer tells you his or her full story,

- listening for full understanding,

- facilitating new insights about the customer's situation, problems, costs, constraints and expectations to the point the customer reaches an excitement about what could be achieved,

- uncovering the customer's needs so you both know there is a reason to buy,

- checking your understanding with a summary checkout, and

- recommending the right solution, a complete solution providing the benefits the customer wants to buy.

Even if there is an objection after doing these steps, having done so will help you to respond to the objection constructively and sustain a quality relationship with your customer.

Don't get anxious and uptight. Just deal with the objection as an indication to back up and get more information. Return to the needs assessment stage and learn what you didn't learn then. Discover what's behind the customer's objection. Be calm. Be the most resistant person to the sale. You only want to sell what's right for the customer. So find out what's right.

In general, we think you will have the most success by using the four step "GET SMARTER" approach for dealing with objections:

Dealing With Objections

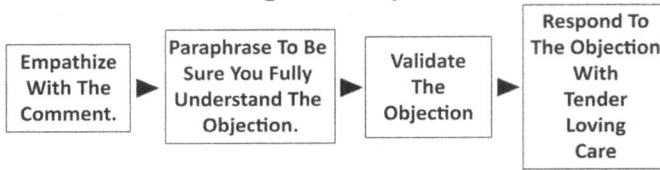

Empathize With The Comment.	▶	Paraphrase To Be Sure You Fully Understand The Objection.	▶	Validate The Objection	▶	Respond To The Objection With Tender Loving Care

1. First **empathize** with the comment. You might say something like, "I sense a major concern regarding what I recommended, and your concern is important to me."

2. Secondly, **paraphrase** to see if there is an underlying meaning to address. Perhaps, the objection is different than it might first appear.

3. Thirdly, **validate** the objection you uncover. Say something like, "I agree with your concern. It's important and should be addressed."

4. Lastly, **answer** the concern or objection. This might mean either changing your recommendation, or just explaining it differently so the customer is more comfortable. It should not mean reducing your price. If your solution has real value (*benefits exceed price*), then price is not the issue.

Empathizing with the comment shows the customer once again that his or her needs are paramount. It is an effective way to respond to the more intense emotions that usually accompany objections. If you imagine yourself in the customer's situation, you can appreciate his or her concern and show respect. Say something that shows how you recognize the importance of your customer's concern.

Clarifying gives the customer a chance to say what was intended and this gives you an opportunity to address the proper concern. It shows respect, maintains a humble attitude, and reaches for information you need in order to make the correct recommendation. Clarify with a paraphrase and then, from a place of understanding, deal with the real concern or objection.

For example, the retail customer might say, with a bit of disgust in his voice and a grimace on his face, "Is this your best price?" As a key person influencing the profitability of your company, you need to enhance your ability to ask the call-to-action without having to discount your already competitive pricing. Reaffirm to yourself that you've added value to the customer and he or she would be better served by buying from you, rather than from your competition.

1. First, **empathize** with the comment.

    "I can appreciate you want to get the best deal possible, that's important isn't it?"

2. Secondly, **paraphrase** for underlying meaning.

    "I'm guessing you're either wanting to check to see if we negotiate on price, or worried this will go on sale next week and you'll have paid too much, is either of these correct?

3. Thirdly, **validate** the concern or objection.

    "No one wants to pay more than they should, and we certainly appreciate your concern."

4. Lastly, **answer** the concern or objection.

    "This solution will reduce your costs and give you benefits exceeding the price you pay. You can't afford to delay getting a solution. However, we do several things here to give you peace of mind about the price you pay. We shop the competition to make sure our prices are as good as you can get. We price match – if a competitor does have a lower price, we'll match their price and provide our exceptional service. In addition, we price protect for thirty days. You'll pay a fair and competitive price for this solution and get the benefits right away. Our reputation depends on it. Does this address your concern?"

Consider the retail customer who says "I'm not comfortable buying from a start-up company."

1. First, **empathize** with the comment.

    "I might be leery about buying from a new company myself."

2. Secondly, **paraphrase** for underlying meaning.

   "I'm guessing you're concerned we're new in an already competitive market place and may not succeed, leaving you in the lurch if you have problems with what you buy, correct?"

3. Thirdly, **validate** the concern.

   "You shouldn't invest your money on a solution your supplier can't properly deliver and support. It would increase your costs instead of reducing them, and neither of us wants that."

4. Lastly, **answer** the concern or objection.

   "Our company is new, but the people in the company have extensive experience providing and supporting what we sell. The response we've received from our customers since we opened has been phenomenal, exceeding our expectations. We fully expect to be highly successful because we do things differently, and that difference has proven significant to our customers. I think I've demonstrated some of that difference in our conversation today. Does this address your concern?"

Here is a transcript where a retail salesperson used the "GET SMARTER" response to an objection, which actually appears to be a complete rejection.

C: "Thanks but no thanks. I … just don't want to do this right now." (*Shaking his head*)	
S: "Okay… I sense your discomfort. You're telling me you don't think I recommended the right products for you?"	Empathize Paraphrase
C: "Yeah, it's all kind of new to me and I don't understand it all. It's kind of like… I'm thinking… maybe not."	

S: "You have concerns about what I've suggested. Anything in particular?"	Paraphrase
C: "You mentioned a tablet and … it surprised me because I'd been thinking I'd get a computer. This tiny little thing. How does it do what I need?"	
S: "I apologize for creating the confusion, and maybe I have recommended the wrong solution. You're hesitation is because my recommendation surprised and confused you, correct?"	Validate Feelings Check
C: "Yes, I was expecting something more powerful?"	
S: "I can see why you would have major reservations. No one wants to buy less than they need. Correct?"	Validate Paraphrase
C: "I sure don't."	
S: "However, you told me you wanted something portable and indicated you were worried about having to spend a lot of time learning to use a computer, just to keep some notes and reminders, organize your schedule, access the internet, and get and send e-mail. Well, all of those things can be done on this tablet with a very short learning curve. The time to learn to use it will be even shorter because I included a one-hour instructional session. With those benefits and the substantially lower cost for the tablet, this seemed like the best choice. You'll be using this much more rapidly than you would be learning to use a computer, which would be overkill for these needs."	Answer
C: "So this will do everything, cost me less and be	

easier to use?" S: "Yes, it will do what you said you want to do, and be much more portable than even a laptop computer. You'll be much more comfortable traveling with it."	Answer

The salesperson showed empathy for the customer, clarified to make sure he understood the concern, validated the concern, and then gave an answer to address the objection and ratify the recommendation.

However, there may be occasions where the concern can't be addressed by re-affirming the recommendation. The process may surface new information, which means the recommendation should be changed. In any objection where the customer suddenly brings up new information, possibly a condition or requirement for whatever the customer intends to buy, accept that you failed to gather this information earlier. If you missed it earlier, get and understand it now.

Your customer objects because he or she thinks your recommendation failed to address something important. This might happen even though its something the customer didn't tell you when you discussed his or her needs. The customer may not have brought it up earlier because he or she forgot about its significance then, and your recommendation has now triggered the memory. Treat this new information as key to finding a successful and acceptable solution. Understand it, validate it and then use it to change your recommendation.

C: "I just don't think this is right for me. It doesn't meet any of our company standards in terms of brand, and the required configuration. They're pretty sticky about that stuff."	
S: "Sounds like I missed a key piece. Your company has specific brand requirements. Is this correct?	Empathize Paraphrase

C: "Yeah. I didn't bring it up earlier because I forgot it was an important consideration. I didn't realize until I saw what you're recommending, and this isn't a brand they would support. Without their support, I'm kind of useless. I don't know enough about this stuff."	
S: "That's pretty significant. It's important we follow your company's preferences. It seems to me I need to know more about this. Can you explain the requirements to me?"	Validate Address the concern by gathering information

The salesperson then learns what he or she needs to know and subsequently changes the recommendation to meet these specific requirements. You want to recommend the right solution – not push what you originally recommended.

If you're presented with an objection you're able to address by reaffirming your recommendation, do so. Your customer will accept this because you paraphrased to make sure you understood his or her concern. If you don't first show empathy, paraphrase and then validate your customer's concern, any other response will be experienced as arguing. By showing your respect for his or her concern, the customer will likely listen receptively to your answer.

On the other hand, if you find new information illustrating a problem with what you've recommended, make changes to arrive at the proper solution. Be flexible and make sure the customer gets the right solution. If the customer recognizes you worked to better understand, and then changed what you propose, he or she will have greater appreciation for your commitment to your customer's well-being.

"Call-To-Action" Versus "Closing"

In some sales models, this step is called "closing". "Closing" is about inducing the customer to buy now so the sale can be closed. Often techniques are used to coerce the customer to buy right now. Through certain psychological processes, attempts are made to manipulate the customer into deciding to buy what the salesperson is selling.

In the "GET SMARTER" sales approach, we don't use the term "closing". We see this as the beginning of a long-term relationship, not the closing of a short-term encounter. We use an ethical sales approach committed to taking care of the customer for the long term. As a result, we suggest you never use the term "closing", and also urge you to never use "manipulative closing" techniques.

Customers resent being "closed". Let your competitors use the manipulative closing techniques and turn people off. You shouldn't. Be different. Use a straightforward question such as,

> **"It seems to me we understand each other and what I've recommended meets your needs. How would you like to proceed?"**

Things Not To Do

Be aware of what **not** to do in response to what appears to be an expression of objection or rejection. Objections can often feel like an attack on you as a person and trigger your defensiveness and a response involving an argumentative statement.

Don't argue! If you do, you will move instantly into the Persuasion Selling approach, lose all rapport, and probably lose the sale. Certainly you will not have a happy customer who wants to return and buy again and again. Don't put yourself in an adversarial and intractable position.

> **C: "That's a lot more than I expected when you said you had a good solution for me. Are you really sure about your recommendation?"**

S: "Well... I pride myself on being a skilled salesperson. I've been doing this for a long time. I've developed expertise in this area. You've got to trust me. I'm doing the right job for you. It's the right thing to buy."

or

C: "The price is pretty steep. That's a lot of money."

S: "It's not much really. It's a pretty inexpensive model now. We just got a good buy on it ourselves, and that's why the price is now much lower than it was."

Don't ignore the objection.

C: "I don't know. This is an awfully high price."

S: "Did I mention to you this is an awesome gaming system – fantastic graphics, high speed performance, fast controls? If you want gaming, this is the one to get. "

Don't minimize the significance of the customer's objection.

C: "That's a pretty impressive recommendation, but you're making some incredible promises this will meet all my needs. Sounds too good to be true."

S: "Don't worry about it. We have tremendous selection, and I've put together the right package. I've covered everything for you."

Don't use the "what if" approach to deflect the objection.

C: "I don't think I can wait the two weeks you're talking about to get the custom unit made. I'm just going to check your competition and see what they've got in stock right now."

S: "Okay. What if I changed my recommendation to something we have in stock? Would that be of value to you?"

or a persuasive reply such as,

S: "What if I took $50 off the price if you order today?"

Don't just give up on the customer and leave.

C: "The price is a lot more than I can afford. I sure wasn't expecting to pay so much when I came in."

S: "Okay. Here's my business card. I see another of my customers has just arrived. You know if things change for you, just give me a call."

Don't plead with the customer.

C: "You've been a pretty good guy to talk with, but your bundle of stuff has a pretty big price tag. Can't you roll something off the price? Just give me a bit of a discount here."

S: "I'd like to, but the guy over there watching us is my manager, and my sales this month have been a little bit behind. I don't want to give you a big sob story but I'm worried about my job. I tell you what – I'll come over to your place and set it up for you at no additional charge if you buy it today?"

Don't capitulate and break company rules to satisfy the customer just to get the sale.

C: "I think I could get a better deal from your competitor because he wants to keep my business. He'll do anything to keep me happy."

S: "What kinds of things does he do for you?"

C: "Well, he gives me free stuff when I make a purchase this big."

S: "Well, I'm not supposed to do that so you mustn't tell anyone. I could throw in a XXXXXX for free if you buy right now. I'll just have to tell the cashier not to charge you for it. "

Don't criticize the competition.

C: "There's a lot of competition out there. Everybody is selling this stuff. Why should I buy from you and not from _____?" (*said with a challenging voice tone*)

S: "Well, we haven't gotten big, fat and lazy like they have, so we work harder to earn your business. I've heard from their customers how the quality of their service has dropped dramatically. They're just flogging product and don't have the expertise we do."

Don't belittle the customer's concern in any way.

C: "Wow. That's a lot more than I can afford."

S: "Oh, you're just thinking of something cheaper. Well you know what we can do. We've got our clearance table over here. We could look at less expensive products for you. Still do the job I suppose. And what if I could chop up the purchase price and give you 36 equal monthly payments?"

or a briefer reply such as,

S: "I guess I didn't understand you wanted to go the cheapest way possible and you weren't that worried about quality."

Don't make exaggerated claims about what your solution can do.

C: "I've never heard of this brand."

S: "Well Brand Y is all we sell. The other brands are not the same thing. This is **the** best – faster, more powerful, more durable, best product life span of anything out there! Using this, you'll be years ahead of your competition. I only use Brand Y myself."

Don't criticize competitive brands.

C: "I'm confused. Your company is listed as one of those selling Brand X but you've recommended something else. Why?"

S: "Well, I've got to tell you this Brand Y is far superior to Brand X. Have you checked the stock prices for the company that makes Brand X – they're going downhill fast because the market place doesn't think so highly of their chances of continuing. Part of the problem with them is they build products with fewer features, and don't give users much flexibility. Brand Y is way more customer friendly."

Don't try to persuade the customer away from his or her concern by appealing to his or her ego.

C: "That's a pretty hefty investment. You've presented the product with the biggest price tag, haven't you?"

S: "Oh well yes. But you know… you're a serious professional, and it appears your reputation matters. This is a very prestigious XXXXXX. The people around you will be impressed. In fact, doesn't the price add to the prestige – not everyone can afford one."

or the reply a salesperson once gave me when I asked about price,

S: "If you have to ask, you can't afford one."

You can use one of the above behaviors that would turn off your customer, end the relationship, and lose the sale; or instead, you could respond to many different types of objections using this formula:

1. empathize,
2. clarify,
3. validate the clarified objection, then
4. answer or address the concern.

We think this approach reduces misunderstanding and tension.

MAKE THE FOLLOW-UP CALL

If your customer didn't buy when you presented your recommendation and asked for his or her business, make sure you call to follow-up. You arranged this follow-up call, so do it. Remember, you're working to be part of an on-going relationship. If the customer left with a quote, or a promise to discuss with others before deciding, or indicating he or she would compare your offer against offers from the competition, call the customer at the arranged time.

If you call and find out the customer has concerns about your recommendation, you have an opportunity to use the active listening skills to draw out the concerns. Fully understand how your recommendation is failing to satisfy your customer. Use this information to consider what changes you need to make to your recommendation in order to meet these clarified needs. If the customer sees your attentiveness as further evidence of your commitment to get him or her the right solution, you will sustain the customer's trust in you. Once you have addressed the concern, ask the customer how he or she wishes to proceed.

If the customer hasn't yet purchased, then discuss what the customer learned from his or her discussions with others, from comparative shopping, from mulling over the decision. Use the active listening skills to understand any new information.

PREVENT BUYER'S REMORSE

The key intention in this call-to-action step is to prevent buyer's remorse. You do this by accepting any question, concern or objection as potential new information critical to arriving at the right recommendation.

Using selling techniques that trap, trick or manipulate the customer into buying creates buyer's remorse. Alternatively, recommending and selling a solution that does not provide desired results will also cause customer disappointment. In some cases, a customer may buy from a convincing sales person even though the customer is in a state of confusion, not fully understanding why he or she is buying a particular solution.

If a buyer regrets having purchased, he or she will either attempt to return the item or tell their friends and colleagues about how you provided the wrong or inadequate solution. Some will do both. Returns add costs to your employer's business. A besmirched reputation hurts future sales to new customers. Minimally, disappointed customers won't come back to buy from you again. This also hurts your employer as competitors win that business. To prevent buyer's remorse:

- greet in a way that builds rapport and openness,

- discuss the customer's needs thoroughly,

- summarize what you learn about those needs to be sure you have full understanding,

- recommend the right solution, and only the right solution to your customer's needs,

- present the benefits your customer will get when he or she buys your solution,

- ask a call-to-action question that leaves the customer in charge of the decision process, and

- resist the sale yourself if you see or hear any clues suggesting the customer doesn't feel right about your recommendation.

The customer's needs must come before your own, and your customer must know this.

RECOGNIZE BUYING DECISIONS

Retail examples of positive signals the customer has decided to buy include behaviors such as:

- smiles as the customer reads your proposal or listens to your presentation,

- members of a couple looking at each other and nodding in affirmation,

- looking at a personal organizer to determine the best time for delivery or to schedule training,

- asking for testimonials from other customers,

- questions about installation,

- verifying your commitment to solve any problems that might arise after your solution has been purchased, or

- straight out comments like, "I'll take it." or, "Can I pay by credit card?" or, "Let's check to see if I qualify for your delayed payment program."

These, or behaviors like them, all say, "Yes, let's proceed."

WHEN TO MOVE TO THE NEXT STEP

When you see a non-verbal buying signal or hear a direct statement indicating the customer has decided to buy your recommended solution, move to the next step. You've made the sale. Now, solidify that sale. You have an indication the customer wants to buy so move forward.

Unfortunately, you'll also know its time to transition to the next step if the customer declares that he or she isn't going to buy at this time. If the customer has elected to not buy today, you'll know it's time to move to the next step once you've negotiated a specific day and time to call in order to review the customer's decision, or to help the customer with his or her decision-making process. Whatever the customer decides, respect and accept his or her decision and move to the next step.

TRANSITION TO REINFORCE THE CUSTOMER'S DECISION

Make this transition relatively seamlessly once you hear the customer's decision. No matter which decision the customer makes, congratulate him or her on making a decision, then launch into comments confirming the customer has made the right choice.

Yes, in the "GET SMARTER" approach, you will agree with whatever the customer decides. You will even do this whether he or she has decided to:

- buy,

- delay,

- shop elsewhere, or

- reject your recommendation.

In the next step, you will tell the customer you appreciate his or her decision especially if the decision is to buy from you, but even if he or she has elected to buy elsewhere or has simply rejected your recommendation. You may have lost the sale, but you still want to retain the relationship. This investment can pay off in future sales if you handle this well.

Acknowledge the decision with enthusiasm and in just a few words. For example,

"Bill, that's great. I'm glad you've made your decision."

or

"Jane, it's good you've made a decision to (_customer's decision_) ."

or

"Sam, good choice for now. I think I would make the same decision."

or

"I understand and appreciate your decision to (_customer's decision_) ."

Make a brief comment acknowledging that a decision has been made, and then launch into Step Seven to reinforce the validity of that decision.

If you've used the "GET SMARTER" approach, we're confident that in most cases, you'll be congratulating the customer for deciding to buy your solution because it will produce the desired benefits and reduce costs. Value will have been well demonstrated and the customer will want to take action. It's easy to transition to the next step when this is the case.

It's harder to make that transition to the next step if the customer hasn't yet decided to buy from you. But, if you've reached this point and a decision has been made to delay, shop your competition, or to not buy from you, you still want to transition to the next step. This will keep the relationship alive and well, thereby retaining the potential to earn the customer's business – either now or in the future.

Even if this particular opportunity is lost because the customer chooses to buy elsewhere, you still have the potential of future sales because the relationship remains healthy. It is your goal to support the customer in his or her efforts to succeed, and in continuing to provide that support by moving to the next step, you sustain your ability to win future business.

STEP SEVEN – REINFORCE THE DECISION

> Let your customer know he or she has made the right choice. Show respect for your customer's decision by affirming it.

Regardless of which outcome you've achieved, fortify the decision with a positive comment saying your customer has done the right thing. This is a very short and simple step.

GOALS OF REINFORCING THE CUSTOMER'S DECISION

In this step, when you're confirming the wisdom of the decision the customer just made, you have specific goals to:

- cement your customer's understanding that what you've recommended really does meet his or her needs, priorities, and buying criteria,

- give your customer the words to say if anyone else challenges or questions his or her decision,

- remind your customer of your commitment to make sure he or she gets the best solution for his or her full set of needs,

- demonstrate your respect for your customer and the decisions he or she makes,

- sustain the glue in the relationship so the client will want to return to buy, either now or in the future, and

- show your customer he or she can feel good about the decision.

The sale doesn't end with the customer's decision to buy or not buy, nor does the relationship. You will have more to do after this step and you want to make sure the rapport that has been established to this point remains intact.

DIFFERENT DECISION TYPES

There can be several different decisions you could be faced with, and you must be comfortable reinforcing each of them. The customer could decide:

- to buy from you,

- to buy elsewhere, or

- not to buy at this time.

Trust in the "GET SMARTER" approach, and feel okay about reinforcing whichever decision the customer makes. In this model, you support the customer's decision with respect and caring.

IF YOUR CUSTOMER HAS DECIDED TO BUY FROM YOU

It's easiest to reinforce the decision when a customer has decided to buy from you. Even though your customer has decided to buy, and particularly because your customer has decided to buy, do this step. Make sure to head off any potential buyer's remorse. Even after the customer has decided to buy from you, he or she can still come to regret that decision as doubts creep in.

Prevent this by confirming the customer has done the right thing. Remind him or her about the benefits he or she wanted, and how this solution will yield these benefits.

> "Bill, I agree with your choice. You wanted a solution that does ____X____, _____Y____, and ____Z____. This will do that for you. I think it's the perfect choice and I'm pretty excited about the results you'll get. Your colleagues will wish they had their own. The benefits will far exceed your investment."

Reinforcing the decision once your customer has decided to buy from you involves the following steps:

1. Reinforce the correctness of your customer's decision.

2. Express envy or say something about how others will think your customer made a great choice.

3. Remind your customer about the benefits and value he or she will realize.

4. Congratulate your customer.

5. Transition to the next step of thanking your customer and arranging follow-up.

Do this with sincerity and the same commitment to the customer's success that has taken you through the previous six steps. For example,

S: "Ron, you've made the right choice. This is going to reduce your costs, give you more and better output for your work, keep you in-line with the technology for the next three years, save you money, and make you even more profits. Your colleagues will think you've made a great choice. I want to hear some grand stories about how you put this stuff to work."

C: "Thanks Shirley. Thanks for your help."

S: "I'm not done helping yet. I want to continue to make sure you're achieving the success we talked about. I'll call you to check on your progress, but this is my business card in case you want to reach me to brag about how things are going."

or

S: "Bill, the more I think about what you've purchased, the more I love it as the best fit for your situation. It's a great choice. As a top end XXXXXX, I wish I had one myself."

C: "Thanks for your help. I think this is the right one for me."

S: "It certainly is. You wanted to be able to reduce your current monthly charges while receiving more services and getting a new phone. This new plan gives unlimited calling, no charges for long distance calls, and free data use up to 2GB per month. The monthly fee is on average $20 per month less than you've been paying. And this new phone has a much better camera, screen, sound, and more storage. And the extended warranty coverage gives two-year replacement for damage or loss. This is a great package.

As you help the customer through the transaction at the till; or if your products are heavy and you help the customer to load the items into his or her car; once again, reinforce the decision.

> "Bill, you've made a great choice and this XXXXXX will really pay off."

Or if you sold a solution to a small business,

> "George. You've made a wise choice to take action now, reduce your costs, and open up new opportunities for your business. Well done."

A "significant other" may challenge the customer when he or she gets the purchase home. A spouse may question the need for such expenditure. The small business customer may have to defend his or her buying decision to a boss. It's a common fear people have when shopping – *Will anyone think I made a mistake?* This fear makes the buying decision so much harder. Help your customer deal with this by confirming the reasons for his or her decision.

Remind your customer as to why he or she made this decision so the customer can use the same words, if challenged, to demonstrate the real value that he or she purchased. Those words are essentially a brief statement of his or her S.P.I.C.E[3]. Review this with your customer so he or she can repeat this to others.

> "Connie, this will reduce your current costs, give you more and better output for the time spent working, and keep you abreast of the technology curve for five years. This both saves you and makes you money. You made the right choice."

Or with more detail,

> "Bill, you bought these new outfits to impress others and get more chances to win the type of job you want. There is no question that if you wear these suits and accessories the way our photo guide suggests, you'll demonstrate your good taste and look like a man of success. That's what potential employers will be looking for, so you made the right choice."

However you do it, make sure you let your customer know with enthusiasm that you really think he or she made the right decision.

Remind the customer that making this acquisition will significantly contribute to his or her success.

IF THE CUSTOMER DECIDED TO BUY ELSEWHERE

On the other hand, if your customer decided to buy elsewhere, you still need to confirm the wisdom of his or her decision. Perhaps the customer told you he or she would be back but shopped at your competitor and made the decision to buy there. If you ask your customer what he or she bought, and find out the customer bought the right solution, say so. Tell your customer you are pleased he or she found a solution to his or her problem.

If you find out the customer bought something you think may yield less than your solution, bite your tongue and keep your thoughts to yourself. Instead, congratulate your customer for taking action to get his or her problems resolved. Then, emphasize the benefits he or she should experience. If the purchased solution won't yield those benefits, it is best to let your customer discover that outcome on his or her own. Telling your customer of the inadequacy of his or her decision will only alienate you from future opportunities to earn this customer's business.

Just congratulate your customer for getting a solution to his or her problems and restate the benefits you expect your customer to realize by doing so. Reinforcing the decision when the customer has decided to buy elsewhere involves the following steps:

1. Declare the correctness of your customer's decision to buy a new solution.

2. Remind your customer about the benefits and value that should be realized from this solution.

3. Congratulate your customer on making a decision and taking action.

4. Indicate your desire to earn your customer's business and even your disappointment that you did not.

5. Ask for and get feedback about your own performance.

6. Transition to the next step of thanking your customer and arranging follow-up.

For example, the customer may be a student who was looking for a laptop computer to use during his or her years of study. You recommended a solution with particular features, software and accessories that would produce all of the results the student wants to achieve during the three-year program. However, the student bought a computer from a competitor without some of those features and with less capacity than he needs.

> "Justin, I'm glad you made your decision so you can get set up for your studies before the course year starts. As we discussed, it's really important that you start your studies being able do all of your graphic design work, photographic editing, quality printing and storage of the large volume of work you will create during your program. A high performance system will have the power to do these things with speed. I know the software I recommended will allow you to effectively do your design, editing and word processing effectively, and the accessory mouse and design tablet will make all that work easier. I wish you success in your studies. I appreciate that you gave me a chance to win your business. I'm disappointed that I wasn't able to do so this time around and wonder if you could give me feedback about how I could have been more helpful?"

Use the opportunity to get feedback to learn what to do in future situations to prevent losing such business. You might discover you didn't learn a key element of the customer's S.P.I.C.E[3] and your recommendation was not sufficient, where the competitor's was. You might learn the customer bought on price alone. This indicates you need to work both on your relationship building skills and on how you present your recommendations in terms of the total solution and the real benefits the customer wants to achieve. This happens when you fail to show the true extent to which the value of your solution exceeds your price.

It may be that what the customer purchased from your competitor was priced lower because it does not have some of the elements of your solution. You will need to determine in your own mind if those elements of your solution were critical to customer success. If not, recognize that you were trying to oversell to this customer. If so, you may need to apologize to the customer.

> "Jim, I apologize. I was concerned about your need for
> ___X___ and believed you also needed ____Y____ so I
> included a larger XXXXX which added to the cost of our
> solution. I regret that I failed to understand that ___Y___
> was not actually necessary. I want you to be successful
> when you use the XXXXX."

This apology may help the customer to understand your difference in pricing and possibly to even realize that what you proposed was important but without directly denigrating what he or she purchased. This might lead the customer to re-think his or her purchase decision. However, if the extra cost was not justified, you have acknowledged your mistake.

Perhaps the customer will tell you he or she bought because of buyer fatigue. The customer may have parted from his or her meeting with you feeling good about you, even having the intention to come or call back. But after spending time with a competitor, wanting to just get the shopping over with, the customer decided to buy what the competitor had. The customer was comfortable doing so because what the competitor was selling seemed similar.

This might be a clue you didn't ask enough for the customer's business, or you didn't show the customer that the value of buying was much better than the costs of delaying, or you didn't do enough to show the value of you and your organization in the solution you recommended. You didn't differentiate yourself and your solution enough to win the business. Learn from this.

IF YOUR CUSTOMER DECIDED NOT TO BUY AT THIS TIME

In general, the only time it's best for both of you that the customer does not buy is when the proper solution to his or her S.P.I.C.E[3] is not yet available. If this were the case, it would be better for you to convince the customer to wait for the right solution rather than make a recommendation of something less. Instead of making a recommendation, you would suggest,

"Jack, the best XXXXXX to meet your needs is not yet available. I suggest you wait. The current options are not as capable as they should be. I'll watch for any information on the right XXXXXX for your needs and contact you as soon as it's available. It would be better in your situation to wait and get the right solution rather than buy something now that is less than adequate."

It must be true the best solution for your customer's needs is not yet available from you or a competitor. You would have a problem if the customer learns your competitor does have the right solution and you convinced him or her to delay because you did not.

On the other hand, if the customer decides to postpone buying a real and available solution now, he or she probably did not fully realize the Reality Trough of his or her S.P.I.C.E[3]. The customer didn't experience full movement through the drop into the emotional lows and the rise through the emotional highs upon realization that a solution would yield significant benefits. Your solution doesn't seem to have a VALUE exceeding the cost of the solution.

You would still reinforce your customer's decision, indicating your agreement with the wisdom to postpone. You could address this by saying something like,

"Sam, I think your decision is the correct one for you at this time. The solution I'm recommending today doesn't appear to have enough value in your mind to justify making the investment. I think you would be wise to spend more time assessing the problems you have, measuring how much they really cost, and examining the constraints keeping you from making a change today. I believe what I recommended is the right solution, but agree you should postpone until you believe this yourself. So measure your costs now. Then we can determine if the return on your investment will be high enough for you to feel okay deciding to put this solution in place."

or

"Gwen, I get that you don't think buying this vehicle is justifiable right now, and I can support that decision. Waiting longer means that you won't have to take out a loan at this time. I suggest that you keep an eye on your current costs for on-going maintenance and track your costs of operation. I'll check back with you in a few months to see if you're still okay with the way things are. Perhaps at some future date, getting this new XXXXXX will look more attractive to you. It may be that over time you will come to appreciate the lower fuel and maintenance costs, the greater load capacity of this vehicle, and how the better drivability reduces fatigue and accidents. "

Delaying would allow the customer to gather accurate costing of the status quo and to more fully realize how dissatisfied he or she is with the current way of doing what he or she does. Encourage your customer to actively measure the current costs of the problems to confront his or her own reality. Urge your customer to think about whether the constraints are real impediments to taking action now.

Your customer may not be able to afford the purchase at this time and be unable or unwilling to finance the purchase. If you've considered all of the ways available to expedite this purchase, and the customer still decides to delay, reinforce that decision as well.

"Bill, I understand how hard it would be to make this expenditure right now, so delaying the purchase does seem to be the right decision. If the costs of what you're doing now get any greater, then we can revisit financing to reduce those costs, and make more money. That's two ways to pay off the financing. We can revisit this when you're ready. At some point, I think you'll realize the costs are too great to just accept. I'll contact you periodically to see how you're doing. I want to earn your business and help you be more successful."

Reinforce your customer's decision to put off taking action. But be persistent and encourage your customer to build greater awareness of the costs of the status quo so the motivation to do something about his or her problems grows. Tell your customer you will follow up to make sure he or she is still okay with this decision.

And then remember to do that follow-up. You should be committed to your customer's success, so don't just drop this customer from your attention because he or she didn't buy. You need to take on the responsibility of being your customer's change agent, stimulating him or her to make a change that is for his or her own good. Make a note in your day timer for when you should be calling your customer back.

When Reinforcing Won't Work

Reinforcing the benefits of your customer's decision won't work if:

- You haven't really learned the customer's full S.P.I.C.E[3] and have no way to show him or her what the solution will actually do.

- You've persuaded the customer to buy despite his or her initial resistance.

- You've sold your customer up to a price point he or she can't really justify by the limited benefits the products will yield.

- You've totally ignored the recommendations the customer received from his or her influencers, and made a different recommendation of your own without a clear demonstration of the added benefits.

or,

- You've acted less than enthusiastically when you expressed your reinforcement.

Summary

Many customers will buy from you right away. Some of them may leave to shop the competition and then return to buy from you when they see the huge differences between how you treated them and how the competitors dealt with them. Make sure you reinforce their decision to buy from you.

Of those who don't buy from you, some few may buy from a competitor, but this shouldn't break the relationship. Reinforce the customer for taking action. Let your customer know you're glad a solution to his or her problems has been found. Then get feedback. Look for the value your customer got from the competitor and recognize it for what it is. Your competitor prevailed this time. Learn from this.

The adage "Never burn your bridges" truly applies here. There can be many reasons a customer didn't buy from you even when still appreciating you and your interaction together. The customer might recognize your personal value and come back for future purchases plus refer others to you.

This step in the "GET SMARTER" sales process is a brief and very purposeful step. You want this reinforcement to echo through the customer's thoughts. You want your customer to be vividly aware that you have his or her interests in mind and that you are working for your customer's success.

WHEN TO MOVE TO THE NEXT STEP

You know its time to move to the next step when you've said your reinforcing remarks. Presumably, the customer decided to buy and you are both happy with the outcome. If the decision was to not buy from you, then hopefully, you have reinforced the customer's decision with sincerity and your customer will believe you when you move to the next step.

Having reinforced the customer's decision, no matter what it is, your relationship should still be intact. If it isn't, then back up and make repairs. Arrive at an appreciation for the customer's decision and respect the customer for having made it.

In turn, trust the work you did as you followed the "GET SMARTER" sales approach. Even if you didn't get a sale this time, you will in the future. You've built a relationship for life and you are still nurturing it. When you've restored trust and rapport, then you can proceed.

Transition To "Thank You And Follow-Up"

Make a transition statement like one of the following. What you say will depend on the outcome of your sales efforts.

If the customer bought from you,

> "Bill, I envy you for what you just bought. You've got the coolest XXXXXX. I wish I had one myself. I also want to thank you."

or

> "Gwen, congratulations on making this change now. The benefits are too great to delay. Thank you."

If the customer bought from your competitor,

> "Chou, I'm glad you found a solution to solve your problem. It's great you'll be able to reduce your costs and realize those better benefits we talked about. I want to thank you."

or

> "Sue, good choice. It's tough to lose your business this time around but congratulations on making the choice to put a new solution in place. I want to thank you for giving me the opportunity."

If the customer put off buying at this time,

> "Frank, I'm glad we had a chance to talk, and agree it's wise to wait for now. I'll keep my eyes open for the best solution for your needs. I also want to thank you."

or

> "Sandeep, I understand sufficient financial resources to buy this solution aren't available to you right now. I'll keep looking for options and I'll stay in contact to discuss any arrangements I can identify. For now, I'd like to thank you."

Be sincere when making these comments. Believe you're creating customers for life. You enhance the relationship by showing respect. You let your customer know you think he or she has made the best decision for his or her needs, and move to saying a sincere thank-you.

STEP EIGHT – THANK YOU AND FOLLOW-UP

The sale, or even a lost sale, is only the beginning. You have a relationship to manage for the lifetime of the customer. Show appreciation to your customer for the opportunity to earn his or her business. Stay in touch.

Regardless of which outcome you've achieved, thank your customer for giving you an opportunity to earn his or her business and make arrangements to stay in contact.

THE GOALS OF STEP EIGHT

You got the sale, or didn't, and you still aren't done. Again, there are several goals for this step in the "GET SMARTER" sequence:

- Contact your customer to inquire about any problems before he or she calls you (*or your competitor calls if the customer bought elsewhere*).

- Solidify the long-term relationship you started with this first transaction.

- Be defined by your customer as his or her "go to" expert, the person the customer will turn to in all future situations where he or she needs the products and services you sell.

- Maintain ongoing contact with this customer who will buy again and again, and refer family and friends.

- Become your customer's advocate in any future dealings with your organization.

and

- Show you value him or her as a "customer for life".

Your customer should feel like a very important person. The customer should know he or she matters more than as a potential sale.

THANK YOU AND FOLLOW-UP EVERY TIME

Never make a sale without very sincerely thanking your customer for giving you his or her business. This is the easiest time to be grateful. Show gratitude. We're in a very competitive world. Every customer has many potential suppliers. Make sure your customer knows you value his or her business no matter how large (*or small*) the sale.

It's harder to feel grateful when you've lost the sale, but you still need to feel and show gratitude. Never lose a sale without very sincerely thanking the customer for giving you the chance to earn his or her business. The relationship isn't over just because you lost this one sale. This customer is going to have future needs and you want to have a chance to compete for future business.

Although we think few customers will choose not to buy from you when you use the "GET SMARTER" sales approach, you might have a situation where something didn't work out in your favor. If the customer bought from a competitor, show just as much gratitude as if he or she bought from you. You can share your disappointment over losing the sale but you should still express appreciation that the customer gave his or her time to engage in a conversation with you. This must be sincere and you must intend to follow-up with the customer to maintain the relationship.

The sale does not end once your customer has decided to buy. If you did the relationship building properly while doing Steps One to Seven, you're now in a long-term relationship. Think of this customer as your "customer for life" – at the very minimum, as your customer for the life of your career as a salesperson with your current organization. As it is reasonable to expect your employer's organization to survive for a very long time, it's your responsibility to make your customer feel like a valued and long-term customer, and it is in your own best interests to help the customer do so.

Customers should have absolute confidence you will continue to look after them. Always give your customer instructions as to how to reach you. Give your telephone numbers, your work hours, and the name of your back-up person when you aren't around. Give him or her a business card. If your employer doesn't supply retail sales staff with business cards, get your own. Have good custom business cards printed at low cost by any local print supplier. Be seen as a professional.

All of this shouldn't have to be said. Every salesperson should say "thank you" and should follow-up after the customer has the goods and services in place. However, think about your own experiences as a customer. How often have you experienced a genuine and profuse thank you, and a promised follow-up, with the salesperson subsequently honoring that pledge? Unfortunately there aren't many salespeople who achieve this level of proficiency, even though such behavior is just a choice. You can decide to up your level of performance simply by saying "thank you" and following-up effectively.

If the customer bought your solution, this is definitely your responsibility. On the other hand, if the customer bought else where, it is still your opportunity to show gratitude and to call to see if everything is working as expected. The customer might wonder why you're choosing to do this if he or she bought from a competitor. But your customer will appreciate and remember that you did so particularly if he or she encounters future problems with the competitor's solution.

Your request for follow-up contact must be presented in an authentic manner. You want to be the first person your customer calls if anything goes wrong while implementing the solution you recommended. Then you can be the hero and get it fixed. You also want to be the first person your customer calls when he or she has new needs.

SAYING "THANK YOU"

Everyone knows how to say "Thank you" when given something they really value. The problem is two fold:

1. remembering it's the right thing to do, whether you get a sale or not.

and,

2. doing it in such a way your "thank you" stands out as sincere.

Do you have a way to make your "thank you" so distinctive and believable that the customer once again sees you as different from your competition? If so, use that skill as frequently as you can. If not, develop your own way to stand out with a sincere and significant thank-you.

"Thank you for coming in today. I really appreciate this opportunity to earn your business."

or

"I'm very grateful that we had this chance to talk. Our conversation has been very interesting to me and I hope rewarding for you."

or

"I really enjoyed our discussion today. Thank you for giving me this chance to contribute to your success."

or

"Wow. This has been great. I learned a lot and really developed an appreciation for what you do. Thank you."

THE TIMES TO SAY "THANKS"

There are actually five times when you can justifiably say "thank you." You can't express your appreciation too often when it is sincere and offered at different moments.

1. The first happens when you say "Thank You" just after you've reinforced your customer's decision.

2. The second happens while you help your customer through the transaction.

3. The third happens immediately after the transaction as you assist your customer to get the goods into his or her possession, and any services implemented.

4. The fourth happens in follow-up after your customer has installed and is using the new solution.

5. The fifth occurs when your customer turns to you again in the future to buy something else.

Say "thank you" effectively at each of these five moments to insure the health of this relationship and to sustain opportunities for more contact with your customer.

AFTER REINFORCING

Right after reinforcing your customer's decision, show that you value your customer's choice to give you his or her business or to give you a chance to earn that business. Say something like,

"Joan, I really appreciate your coming in today and giving us your business. I really enjoyed our talk and I feel good about what you'll gain when you use this XXXXXX."

or

"Manny, thank you for talking with me today. Your business really matters to us."

or

"Jeff, I'm grateful you gave me a chance to earn your business today. I enjoyed our conversation and hope you did as well."

or

"Rachel, I'm thankful you gave me a chance to earn your business. I know you've decided to buy elsewhere but I would still like to say thank you."

or

"Steve, we know you're very busy and your time is valuable. I appreciate that you shared some of it with me today, and I will do my best to help you with the issues we discussed. I want to earn your business."

Your "Thank You" should follow so closely after giving your reinforcing remarks it seems to be part of that step.

"Fred. You made the right choice, and I sure want to thank you for giving me the chance to contribute to your success like this."

or

"Sandy, by implementing this solution you just reduced your monthly costs by $300, added the ability to do (*what the customer was excited about doing*) and you've made your up-coming job much more pleasurable. I sure want to thank you for letting me help you add to your success."

During The Transaction

Make the transaction easier and faster by ensuring proper invoicing or transaction processes are followed. Customers will appreciate they still have your attention and you aren't running off to find another sale. Whenever possible, chat with the customer while the transaction is being completed by the cashier.

> "Mr. Grantham, I really appreciate your coming in today, and spending time with me as we explored your needs. I'm glad we found a great solution for you that will (*summary of the benefits you just sold*). I expect that your family will be very impressed. Thank you again."

Make every effort to help out at the till, or at least to visit and watch the transaction process. You may have told your customer something that led to his or her decision. Make sure the last person in the purchase chain says nothing to contradict you. If something is said, make sure you address the contradiction and explain your reasons for having said what you said.

Whenever possible, if the items are heavy, carry them to your customer's vehicle and help to load; or supervise those who do so if this is the role of others in your organization. You want your customer's parting impressions to be no less than the positive impressions you created in your pre-sale interactions.

If the goods are to be shipped to your customer, you might want to watch the process of preparing the solution for shipping and make sure the invoice or billing is prepared the way the customer has been led to believe it would be. Perhaps you could play a role in expediting and supervising delivery. Make sure the goods and services are provided on time, and as promised. Call your customer to let him or her know the goods have been invoiced and are about to ship, then say a sincere "thank you" once again.

Immediately After The Transaction

Shake hands and thank your customer. Once again, make a statement to reinforce the wisdom of the customer's decision, and tell him or her you will call in a few days to make sure everything is meeting his or her expectations.

"(*while shaking her hand*) Sally, thank you once again for your business. You've made a great choice and it's really going to pay off. I expect to hear a lot of excitement in your voice when I call in two days to find out how this is working out for you. However, in the event you have any concerns or questions before I call, please call me at (###) ###-#### extension ###. If you don't get me, leave a message or contact Bill at extension ###. He's my back-up and will make sure we take care of you."

MAINTAINING FOLLOW-UP

How do you stay in touch with your current customers, or do you make the mistake made by many? Too many salespeople sell to the next new customer rather than staying in touch with those to which they've already made a sale. You must always be looking for new customers but you mustn't forget your existing clients.

The easiest customer to sell to is the one with which you have already achieved trust and rapport. The second easiest customer is the one who comes to you by referral. Customers who have trust in you will buy again in the future and refer others.

This will work if you've used an insight-oriented sales approach like the "GET SMARTER" sales process, learned all you could about your customer, and built a relationship characterized by trust and rapport. Ideally, you've helped your customer to achieve success using the solutions you've provided. However, follow-up can still add to your effectiveness even if the customer bought elsewhere.

You added some value during your conversation and the customer may have bought what you recommended, even if from your competitor. If you added value, your customer will want to see and hear from you again.

There are several important ways to maintain contact with your customers:

- Complete a scheduled follow-up call within three days of the solution being implemented at your customer's site.

- Call as scheduled to follow-up any quote you gave to your customer.

- Remember your customer's name and use it often when he or she visits your location or calls you.

- Make sure you call the customer to establish if any problems have arisen before he or she calls you.

- Send your customer special notes – "thank you" notes after his or her purchase; new information that you know meets your customer's needs; personalized marketing letters; and updates on the product and services your firm sells, preferably including material which illustrates how these products and services might solve your customer's unique problems.

In other words, you are able to contact your customer in various ways, both verbally and through written communication.

FOLLOW-UP CALLS

Too many salespeople forget about their customers as soon as the customer makes a purchase. Customers know this and often unconsciously resent it. Differentiate yourself and your organization by calling your customer within three days of having dealt with you.

Do this if the customer bought from you, if you gave a quote, if he or she left promising to be back, if the customer declared he or she was going to buy elsewhere, or if you have subsequently discovered a solution to best meet your customer's needs. Professional salespeople see this call as a tremendous opportunity to solidify the relationship, which is even more important in the long run than an immediate sale. Such follow-up calls bring repeat business.

Call after your customer has made a major purchase and advise him or her you're checking to make sure everything is okay. Ask if your customer has any concerns. If so, learn about any problems before your customer feels compelled to complain to others. Generate an effective resolution of the concern. These calls are not made to look for another new sale. These calls are relationship-maintenance calls.

When you regularly make these calls, it's reasonable to expect three possible outcomes:

- Your customer might be quite satisfied.

- Your customer might have realized he or she needs something in addition.

- The customer might be having a problem with the implementation of his or her new purchase.

Because different outcomes are possible, enter into the call with an open mind. You are simply checking in with your customer.

There is no reason to expect the worst. If you do, this will show up as tension in your voice. Similarly, there is no reason to expect a perfectly happy customer. This could seem like arrogance on your part and further frustrate any customer that is already frustrated. Just call to find out how the customer is doing.

WHEN YOU CALL A HAPPY CUSTOMER

Surprise your customer with your caring. Show your customer you remember his or her reasons for buying by asking if the solution meets those specific needs. Deliberately mention the needs and ask if your customer is pleased with the results he or she gets when using your solution. Give your customer an opportunity to tell you about how good he or she feels. Sharing the excitement adds to the quality of the relationship.

"Jacob, good morning. This is Sandra from Qualico. I'm calling as I said I would to see if your new tools work the way they should. Did you speed up your production, and did these tools give you the ability to do new work you couldn't do before? Is everything going according to our plan?"

or

"Jennifer, good afternoon. This is Frank from Broxton Sewing Machines checking in as I promised to see if everything is going well with the XXXXXX that you just purchased? Are the new stitch options giving you all of the results you wanted?"

WHEN YOU CALL A CUSTOMER WHO NEEDS SOMETHING NEW

Remember, you aren't calling to sell your customer something else but to check on the last purchase. Your customer won't feel pressured to buy because you show caring and commitment after the first purchase.

However, if a new need exists at this time, your customer will likely volunteer his or her need for something else. Alternatively, the customer might say something that provides a clue to a new need and you could use the active listening skills to draw out more information. By doing so, you aren't necessarily trying to sell something new. After all, you're just listening for understanding.

Determine what the customer needs. This gives you another chance to impress your customer by getting what is needed in a timely fashion. This will save your customer time. If you find you've called a customer who needs something new, remember to get his or her new S.P.I.C.E[3] and use the insight-oriented process in this new opportunity. As you already know a lot about his or her situation, this will go much faster.

WHEN YOU CALL A CUSTOMER WITH A PROBLEM

If you call a customer who has a problem with the solution you provided, your call rescues your customer from having to deal with the problem on his or her own. Your call gives you a chance to impress the customer by getting the problem resolved. You become your customer's advocate. Get your organization to take care of your customer properly. You deliver on your promise to take care of the customer for the long term. And, lastly, your call prevents the customer from complaining to others about the product he or she purchased, about you, and about your organization.

If the customer bought elsewhere and is encountering a problem, your knowledge might allow you to provide information that facilitates resolution of the problem. Alternatively, you may be able to give suggestions as to how the customer can induce the organization that got the sale to properly fix the issue. Either way, your customer will appreciate that you called, and especially if the competitor hasn't.

THE FOLLOW-UP TELEPHONE CALL

An effective follow-up telephone call should satisfy specific criteria. Your opening comments on such a call would ideally:

- be made within three days of the customer's purchase,

- be made at a reasonable hour or time of day,

- be made when your customer expects your call because you told him or her you would call,

- be opened with an enthusiastic greeting,

- be supported by a clear and positive reason reminding the customer why you're calling,

- contain a reference to the benefits the customer expected to get prior to making the purchase, and

- include a check to see if everything is working properly and the customer is realizing those benefits.

For example,

"Hello Bill, this is Doug, your consultant at Hudsonia Computers."	Enthusiastic Greeting
"As we discussed when you made your purchase the other day, I'm calling to see how the solution is working for you."	Reason for Call
"When we talked about your needs the other day, you mentioned you wanted to use the computer to engage in day trading over the Internet to maximize your return on your investments.	Expected Benefit(s)
Are you able to do what you wanted with this equipment? Is everything operating properly and meeting the needs we discussed?"	Check for Satisfaction

Paraphrase and summarize whatever your customer tells you about his or her experience with the new purchase. If your customer indicates there are problems, make sure you achieve full understanding then respond appropriately to what you learn. If a problem has been identified, offer the solution.

> "You're right. Your XXXXXX isn't working properly. From what you've described, you're using it correctly and it shouldn't be doing that. I think this should be checked out by one of our technicians. Can I send someone out for service within the hour (*or whatever response time your company can meet*)?"

On the other hand, if your customer makes a positive comment, convey your understanding that everything is working to his or her satisfaction and once again, reinforce the decision. Try to learn as much as you can about the specific results.

> "So you're happy with how it's all working. That's great. You've made a fantastic purchase. I wish I had the same XXXXXX myself. I'm glad you're realizing (*the benefits you both expected the solution to deliver*)."

Close with a thank you and an invitation to call if your customer needs anything.

> "Bill, I want to thank you again for the opportunity to earn your business. If you have anything you need to call me about, please don't hesitate. I can be reached at ###-#### extension ####. Just leave a voice message if I'm not in and I'll call you back as soon as I can."

If the call has been very positive in nature, you have the option to close the call with an invitation to refer his or her friends.

> "Bill, it's my job to look after my customers. I want to make sure you're happy with my work, and with (*name of your organization*). If you have any friends or family members you would like to receive the same care and attention, please don't hesitate to call me, or get them to call me themselves. I promise you I'll take good care of them as well."

260

Many salespeople are afraid to make this call, worried something has gone wrong and the customer is upset. The best salespeople aren't afraid. In fact, such salespeople want to call the customer before the customer has to call them.

These same salespeople also welcome a call from an upset customer because the salesperson knows he or she will fix the problem and a fixed problem really solidifies the relationship. More than a sale where everything goes smoothly, this situation proves to the customer you're totally dedicated to meeting his or her needs. If you solve the customer's problem, you truly do win your customer's trust, his or her confidence in making referrals, and future business.

AFTER GIVING A WRITTEN QUOTE

Instead of achieving a sale, you may have given your customer a quotation. If so, it's not enough to just hope the customer will come back. Unfortunately, too many retail salespeople avoid calling after the customer has left. This is probably because the salesperson doesn't want to be rejected. This is somewhat ironic, as the salesperson will be rejected anyway if he or she doesn't call and the customer doesn't return to buy.

Professional salespeople stand out from the pack because they do call to follow-up their quotes. Calls of this type are a continuation of the relationship you started to build during your insight-oriented consultation and your clients should expect these calls. When you give a quote, tell the customer you'll be calling to see how his or her decision-making is going and to see how to be of further help. An expected call is easier to receive, and to make. Arrange the call then make it.

If you've done the first steps properly, reached the recommendation stage after building a relationship and getting to know your customer's needs, you've earned the right to call. You've undertaken the responsibility to help your customer gain success so you must follow-up. Be persistent. By giving of your time in the consultation and assisting your client to achieve new insights, you established a relationship where you have the right to contact your customer and to continue to offer your help.

An effective follow-up call after giving the customer a quote should:

- be made within at most three days of having given the quote,

- have been pre-arranged with your customer,

- be opened with an enthusiastic greeting, and

- clearly state the reason for your call.

A call of this nature might go something like this,

> S: "Hello Mr. Hook, this is Bill Smith, your consultant at (*name of your company*)."

> C: "Oh hi Bill."

> S: "As we discussed the other day, I'm calling to see how things are going in your efforts to find a suitable solution to your needs. Have you made your decision yet, or is there anything I can do to help you?"

Remember this is a helpful call. You're calling to ask if the customer has made a decision or if he or she needs further information and assistance. There are several possible things you could discover:

- The customer could be undecided, confused and trying to sort through the information.

- The customer could be right on the edge of making a decision to buy from you.

- The customer could be right on the edge of making a decision to buy from a competitor.

- The customer might have already purchased from a competitor.

- The customer could be trying to "ditch you" because he or she is unhappy with you.

CALLING THE UNDECIDED CUSTOMER

There are several ways to take care of the undecided customer. You could:

- offer your help to sort through the information so he or she can make an informed decision,

- provide the information the customer needs to overcome his or her confusion,

- check to see if the customer has realized something new about his or her needs, or

- answer the customer's questions.

In this example, the phone rings and the customer answers,

C: "Hello."

S: "Hi Fred. It's Stan here from (*name of your company*). I hope you're having a good day."

C: "Doing fine."

S: "Good. As arranged, I'm calling to follow-up our conversation. How is your decision-making going relative to the quote I gave you?"

C: "Well, I talked with my wife and children and explained the benefits we talked about when you and I met. My wife had a few questions I wasn't able to answer on my own."

S: "I've been expecting her to have questions because she wasn't part of our discussion. Your kids might also have questions. Some of what we talked about they might not have considered yet."

C: "We're wondering if we could set a time when we could all meet with you in the store?"

S: "Oh absolutely."

C: "It will expedite the decision making."

S: "I'm pretty excited about helping your family. I'm quite confident all of them will be happy with the recommendation once all of their questions have been answered, but if they have concerns I hadn't considered, I'll change my recommendation to make sure their needs are addressed. I look forward to talking with all of you. Thanks a lot."

If you call, and your competitors don't, you show you're committed to your relationship with this customer, and to helping the customer make the right decision. You seem both more interested and more eager to win the customer's business than your competitor.

If the customer is undecided and confused, find an opening in the conversation and say something like,

"George, I agree – it can be very confusing figuring out which XXXXX is best for your needs. As a consultant, it's my goal to help my clients make the best possible decision. Do you have any questions I can answer for you?"

Paraphrase any questions to be sure you understand what really confuses your customer, or leaves him or her hesitant to act, and then answer the questions. Once the customer is no longer confused, initiate a call-to-action.

"George, how would you like to proceed from here?"

If, when you call, you discover the customer is just on the edge and getting ready to buy from you, answer any remaining questions, ask for the business, take the order, and indicate when the solution will be delivered. Ratify the correctness of the products and services for your customer's needs. Reinforce the decision. Thank your customer for choosing to do business with you and indicate when you will next make contact.

CALLING THE CUSTOMER WHO IS ABOUT TO PURCHASE ELSEWHERE

If in your follow-up call you sense awkwardness in the customer, it's possible the customer is about to buy from one of your competitors. Handle this call with diplomacy. You would still indicate you are calling to help your customer to make a decision by answering any questions. If the customer hesitates, or anything suggests he or she isn't comfortable, do a feelings check.

264

S: "Janet, it's Bill from (_name of your organization_) calling to follow-up our conversation the other day."

C: "Oh….hi Bill."

S: "Janet. As we agreed, I'm calling to find out how your decision-making is proceeding, and to see if I can be of any assistance."

C: "Well, I… uh…"

S: "Janet, I sense hesitation, that I've called at an inappropriate time, or you've made a decision to buy elsewhere and this feels awkward for you, is this correct?"

C: "Well, I've decided I'm going to buy what they have over at (_name of your competitor_).

S: "I'm glad you're going to take action and get a solution that will (_summarize the benefits this customer was looking to buy_). It will be good to replace what you've been using with something more cost effective, and give you more benefits. I thank you for giving us a chance to earn your business. Do you mind telling me what led you to buy there and not to buy our solution? It's helpful information that will assist me to be a better consultant for all my clients."

It may be the customer will tell you how you came up short in comparison to the competitor. If so, you lost a sale but you gained knowledge that can help you in the future. On the other hand, the respect you show for the customer's decision, and the humility you present as you ask for feedback, might just remind the customer about the quality you brought to this relationship. This customer might be impressed you followed-up and thereby induced to reconsider doing business with you.

Remember, you're calling in follow-up to maintain the relationship you started with this customer. This is your priority during the call. Your conversation might lead to further helping your customer make a decision. You could answer questions he or she has about a recommendation received from the competitor.

If the relationship is your first priority, being asked questions about a competitor's quote might stir up emotions of betrayal – a feeling of being let down by a customer you generously helped to get to this point. However, don't let these feelings distract you from your goal. Retain your integrity and maintain the relationship.

Answer the questions truthfully and without disparaging the competition in any way. The customer has an important decision to make. Demonstrate real value by helping with your customer's decision-making. In exchange, you will learn information about your competition that might prove useful in the future.

> **"Thank you for telling me what our competitor has proposed for your situation. They've put together some products we haven't seen them group together before. However, given what I know about their products, it does appear to me that you will likely gain the benefits we discussed."**

In such a call, be helpful. However, you also want to demonstrate your desire to earn this customer's business.

> **"Sam. I'm both glad you found what you need, and disappointed I wasn't able to win your business. I really wanted to help you achieve even greater success."**

If the customer recognizes the value of the relationship with you, you may still have an opening to earn the business. If the competitor's quote reveals you did not consider one of the customer's needs, apologize for failing to learn about the need earlier. Then if the customer seems to be feeling okay about you, you could ask if you can change your recommendation to meet the need. Ask your customer if this would be helpful.

Alternatively, you may encounter a situation where you see how the competitor's proposal doesn't address some of the customer's needs. You will have to find a diplomatic way to remind the customer about the full set of benefits he or she wants to achieve.

S: "Thank you for telling me what they proposed. Is there anything about their quote that you have concerns or questions about that I could potentially clarify?"

C: "Well, I just wanted to know what you think about the equipment. Does it match up with what you proposed?"

S: "It appears to me that their solution will give you three of the benefits that were critical to you. You wanted to work faster, with fewer errors, with more of the sewing processes fully automated, and it looks to me like you will realize those benefits with their solution."

C: "You mention that it meets three of my criteria, but that implies it doesn't meet all of them."

S: "Samantha, I think it meets your most critical goals. You also wanted a broad variety of stitching patterns, including some old world styles that few of the modern machines have today. Plus, because of the nature of their control system, you will need more time to learn how to use the equipment and you wanted this solution to be up and running quickly."

C: "Those are important concerns as well. The solution you recommended will do more, has the stitching patterns I wanted, is easier to learn to use, is just as fast, will prevent errors, and is highly automated?"

S: "Yes."

C: "But your solution is more expensive."

S: "Yes. The initial investment is higher. You will have to decide which is more important to you – lower initial cost or a wider variety of stitching options and an easier to learn control system."

In such a situation, by showing how your solution adds more value, you will **not** have to match the competitor's price, and may yet win the sale. However, it is critical that you not criticize or disparage the competitor's product.

In some situations you may have to price match if a competitor has offered exactly what you recommended but at a lower price.

> S: "Janet, you've graciously told me our competitor offers the exact same products at a lower price and you can't justify paying more to buy our offer. I agree you shouldn't have to pay more. I'd still like to earn your business. We do have a price matching policy at our firm, so would it be helpful to you if we matched their price? I regret our purchasing department didn't discover this before and alter our price accordingly."

> C: "Thanks for your offer, but I think your company should have given me the best price when it had a chance."

> S: "I agree… and I regret we failed to earn your business this time. I thank you for the feedback. You've been helpful to us by giving us this information. I'm glad you're going to get what you need at a good price, and your success will grow. I enjoyed our conversation. I thank you for giving us this chance and hope we can get another opportunity to earn your future business."

> C: "Maybe next time."

> S: "Janet, I have one more question for you. I want to be the best salesperson I can be. I wanted to make sure that I fully understood your needs and recommended the most appropriate solution for you. Aside from the price issue, is there any advice you can give me about how I could have been more helpful to you?"

Otherwise, you must be able to show how your recommendation includes other elements thereby enhancing the true value of your solution in comparison to the competitor's. Just don't fall into being a persuasion-oriented salesperson, pushing the customer to change his or her mind.

S: "Janet, you've graciously told me our competitor offers the exact same solution at a lower price and you can't justify paying more to buy our offer. I agree you shouldn't have to pay more. However, there is a difference between our two recommendations that is significant and I apologize for not making our recommendation clearer for you."

C: "What is the difference? They look similar to me."

S: "You're correct. The equipment is the same. The difference is that our solution comes with an installer and trainer who will spend two hours in your home, at a time convenient to you, to help you set up the equipment and show you how to use it. This will get you up and running faster so you experience the benefits we talked about. "

C: "I hadn't realized that. I need to see if your competitor offers that service as well within his price."

S: "Can I call you back tomorrow to find out what you learn?"

By being a true insight-oriented consultant for this client, you may yet win her business. You still need to demonstrate you can be trusted and add real value. This won't happen if you give a defensive or attacking response, criticize the customer or criticize the competition. Maintain the attitude reflected in the statement, "I really want this customer to be successful."

CALLING THE CUSTOMER WHO PURCHASED ELSEWHERE

If you call a customer to follow-up your quote, there will be times when you call and discover the customer bought from your competitor. As disappointing as this is, see the goal of this call as maintaining the relationship you've built. Continue the trust and rapport you built in the relationship so the customer will feel comfortable returning to you in the future.

Don't be disheartened as this can turn out to be a very positive call. This can be a real opportunity to learn and to solidify your relationship. Plus, if the customer encounters any problems with what was purchased, and you call first, you have an especially rich opportunity to enhance your relationship by fixing the problem, or providing effective advice for how the customer can get the problem fixed. Remember, you're in the relationship for the long run, not just the first sale.

If you discover there are any difficulties, solve any problems the customer might have and win trust for future purchases. If you call, again and again, and the salesperson that the customer bought from doesn't call once, you truly differentiate yourself.

C: "Hello, John here."

S: "Hi John. It's Ray calling from (*name of your organization*)

C: "Oh hi Ray." (*interrupting with a grimace on his face*)

S: "How's it going?"

C: "It's going okay."

S: "As I indicated on Friday, I'm following up just to see if you've made your decision yet."

C: "Well, I bought a computer over the weekend."

S: "Oh, you did. You made the purchase already." (*surprised but controlling his disappointment*)

C: "Yeah. I did. I told you I was going to shop around. By the end of the day, I got to a place and what he had to recommend was pretty close, not exactly what you recommended but pretty close to what you were talking about. I was tired and eager to get going on this thing so I went ahead and did it. "

S: "Okay, I understand. It's great you managed to get a solution. It's sounds like I should have discovered it was important for you to get a system before the weekend, and I apologize."

C: "Actually, I just didn't realize how tiring the process was going to be."

S: "It is. I know."

C: "I wanted to get it over with."

S: "Well, buying a computer and especially one at that level of investment is tough. I'm glad to hear you got something similar. At least, you got what you need and that's important to me."

C: "Well, when I got home, I realized the guy I bought from, he and I hadn't talked about the scanner. You and I had talked about that and..."

S: "Scanning all of the slide pictures that you've taken over the years."

C: "Yeah. So I still need a scanner."

S: "Oh great. Hopefully I was some help in getting you an idea about the right solution."

C: "Definitely. You were a great help actually. I felt guilty buying it from the other guy, but I was just so tired of shopping by then. I do want to get a scanner from you."

S: "Thank you. I'm pretty sure I understand correctly but let me check. You have a lot of old slides you wish to get into your computer to put into a website. You said you also wanted to save these images on another media so a DVD burner made sense. That would give you another way to safeguard the images. So you're telling me you intend to go ahead and buy the scanner, scanning software, the website development software, the DVD burner and software, and the supply of discs – all the other stuff I had on my quote. Correct?"

C: "That's what I really appreciated about our talk. You really listened and understood what it was I was trying to accomplish. Get it all ready for me. I'll pick it up later today. As I said, I feel bad about buying the computer from the other guy."

S: "Don't worry about it. You had to make a decision that worked for you. I'm glad to hear you got the equipment and I appreciate I have this chance to supply the scanner and related supplies. It will all be ready for you when you drop in later. With the complete solution you'll be able to realize all of the benefits we talked about. Thanks a lot for giving me this business."

So is this an example of a salesperson's failure, or an example of how to win a customer for life? The latter applies if the customer now realizes he made a mistake in buying elsewhere, and also realizes his life will be made easier by just turning to this salesperson in the future, whenever new needs emerge.

Learn from the customer. Ask for feedback about what the customer decided to buy. Maybe that solution is a better choice than what you recommended. Ask for feedback about how the competitor won the customer's business and ask for feedback about what you could have done more effectively. Show humility and impress the customer with your desire to improve.

S: "I'm disappointed that we didn't win your business this time, but I congratulate you for taking action and getting a new solution in place. The benefits will fully justify the investment. I'm curious to know what our competitor proposed."

C: "They suggested a jet boat with full overhead ski towing rig and rear platform for both wave surfing and fishing so we can do both from this boat. The lower draft of this boat will allow us to cruise both the lake and up the relatively shallow river that feeds the lake."

S: "That's an interesting solution to your situation. Because of our concern about cost, we hadn't considered that option so our competitor truly did out-perform us in this instance. Craig, you know I want to improve my skills as a consultant. Looking at our conversations in hindsight, is there anything you can see that I could have done to better understand your needs?

CALLING THE CUSTOMER WHO WANTS TO "DITCH" YOU

If you call and get the sense the customer is uncomfortable talking with you, listen closely. If it seems he or she wants to ditch you, be sensitive to any clues of irritation, avoidance, or rejection. Use the paraphrase and feelings check skills to reach for understanding. If the customer is unhappy about something, he or she generally wants to tell someone. So be the "someone" the customer talks to. Ask for feedback and listen for understanding.

If a correctable problem surfaces, offer to fix it. If you're the problem, ask the customer how you let him or her down, and learn from the feedback. Thank the customer for his or her honesty and the feedback you've been given, as it will help you to be a better insight-oriented salesperson.

Many people will reverse their first impressions of you when you do this. It's surprising when you care enough to want to learn. Many people will give you a second chance. If you're sincere, your sincerity will show.

If during your follow-up call, you discover the customer wants to ditch you, find an opening in the conversation to ask something like the following,

"Susan, it's my goal to be a professional consultant for customers like yourself. Even though I sense you aren't very happy with me right now, will you please do me a favor? Something happened this time where I was not successful in winning your business. I apologize for letting you down. I would appreciate it if you would help me to

273

learn by giving me feedback about how I failed to meet your needs in this situation, and how I could have been more effective?"

Most people will respect a sincere desire to be better next time. The customer will likely give you some feedback from which you're able to learn. In turn, the customer might re-examine his or her opinion of you and turn to you when he or she next has a need.

It's critical you use the active listening skills to understand what the customer tells you. Don't get defensive, argue or contradict. Respect the information and show respect for the customer. Do your best to put yourself in the customer's shoes. Once you learn how you let the customer down, apologize with sincerity and assure him or her you've learned from the feedback.

You must want to truly learn from this situation so your sincerity is visible to the customer. In this example, the phone rings and the customer answers,

C: "Hello Kate.

S: "Ah the advantage of caller ID. Rafa, as we agreed, I'm calling to follow-up to see how your decision-making is going."

C: "Kate, I'm going to buy elsewhere."

S: "(*pause in shock*) Rafa. It sounds like I let you down somehow, failed to properly address your needs and concerns. Is that correct."

C: "Yeah, after I left the store, I felt unsettled. Then I visited a couple of your competitors. I think you fell short."

S: "Sounds like I really failed to perform as I should have. Rafa, I want to learn to be as effective a salesperson as I can and would really appreciate hearing how I failed on this one. Would you mind taking a few minutes now to give me feedback?"

C: "Your competitors showed much more enthusiasm about winning my business. I felt much more excited about what they were proposing after hearing what they had to say about the features and benefits. I wasn't sure you had the expertise to give me accurate information. In particular, your solution doesn't seem to have (*specific feature*)."

S: "It sounds like there were several ways I underperformed relative to your expectations. First I didn't convey enough of my excitement for the solution I recommended and you felt underwhelmed by both the presentation and the solution. The second was not presenting a solution that clearly has a feature you wanted. I missed that in our conversation about your needs. Have I understood correctly?"

C: "Yes I think you have."

S: "I appreciate your frankness and that you gave me your reasons for not doing business with me at this time. I assure you I'll use your feedback to improve my performance with all of my clients. Thank you.

C: "I hope you're able to do better next time."

S: "If any situation arises in the future where my company may have the solutions you're looking for, I ask you to give my company another opportunity to earn your business. It doesn't have to involve me. I can put you in touch with another of our salespeople who would be glad to help."

C: "Actually Kate – I haven't completely made my decision on this one yet. Because I found our original conversation to be so productive, I was hesitating to buy elsewhere. Can you change your recommendation to include the need for (*specific need*) and be able to show me how it does what I need."

S: "If I understand correctly, you need a solution that also does *(salesperson's interpretation of the specific need)*, is this correct?"

C: "Yes. That's critical to being able to *(desired benefit)*."

S: "I can't say enough how much I appreciate this second opportunity to win your business. The solution I proposed does have the feature you are excited about and I didn't emphasize that because I didn't fully appreciate your need for that ability. With this complete solution you'll be able to do all you want, and at a lower cost than you are paying now."

C: "That's excellent. So to verify, you're telling me that your XXXXXX will do (*desired benefit*)?"

S: "Yes, it definitely does all of that plus it gives you all of the other benefits we talked about."

This salesperson heard rejection by the client but sought feedback. She didn't seek the sale by arguing why the customer should still consider her recommendation. She asked the client to help her to learn to do better. She then paraphrased for full understanding and the customer agreed she understood. Following her demonstration of understanding, she assured the customer this feedback was helpful and she would use the knowledge to improve her work with all of her clients.

The customer recognized the sincerity of her request and re-evaluated his stance. He then offered her a second opportunity to sell him what he needed. Remember, she likely earned this second chance by how she treated the customer during the rest of the "Get SMARTER" process.

Even if he had not revived his interest in her solution, the salesperson gained valuable feedback to increase her future success. She learned that she wasn't being effective in communicating her enthusiasm about the solution she recommended. She also learned that she failed to learn a key element of the customer's needs, which the competitor touched on when he or she emphasized a particular feature. Even if a sale is lost, the call has real value.

Written Follow-Up

The "GET SMARTER" sales approach also includes effective written communication as a follow-up to any sale or interaction with a potential client. Written follow-up can occur in two different forms:

- personalized "thank you" cards, notes or letters, and

- marketing letters and notes.

Differentiate yourself by using both. You have a quality relationship with this client and such communications keep that relationship healthy.

Personalized "Thank You" Notes

Stay in contact with your customer with a mailed "thank you" card, note, or letter. Show your commitment to this relationship, and let your customer know you appreciate his or her business. We think this is a basic requisite for effective relationship maintenance and insight-oriented selling.

Send a personalized "thank you" card to every customer who makes a major purchase. The threshold might be a purchase involving tens of dollars, five hundred dollars, or thousands of dollars depending on what you sell. At the very least, contact those who spent a significant amount of money to buy what you recommended. Show your gratitude. In addition, consider sending a "Thank You" card to any customer with whom you were able to learn the customer's S.P.I.C.E[3].

Send a handwritten, personalized card. Make it obvious this is not a form letter but a personal note of appreciation specifically for your customer. In your note, comment on at least one significant piece of information you learned about your customer in your needs assessment. This will show you paid attention and subsequently remember what you learned.

Effective written communication can also include sending personalized "Thank You" letters. This could be a letter of its own, or something longer and typed that you slip into your "Thank You" card. Such a personalized letter can be sent after any sales conversation, after you've given your customer a quote, or after your customer made a decision to buy from you.

If you send such a letter after a purchase, the letter would summarize the S.P.I.C.E^3 you discovered and the benefits your solution should provide. Express your expectation that the customer is actually realizing those benefits. Let your customer know you want to be the first person he or she will call if any problems arise. Say "Thank You" for his or her business, and promise you will work just as hard to help any referred friends, family and colleagues.

To add efficiencies to your work, parts of the letter might be a form letter you use over and over again with different clients, but each letter should be personalized with regard to your customer's S.P.I.C.E^3 and clearly look like a personalized note to each customer. If you're using a template for these "thank you" letters, we suggest using several different templates so repeat customers get different letters.

If the letter is typed, handwrite some comment near your signature, as if you added an additional thought. This could be something like,

> "I'm really looking forward to having a conversation where you brag to me about all that you've achieved with this new solution."

or

> "Thank you again. I really enjoyed working with you."

or

> "I want to look after you if any problems arise. Please don't hesitate to call."

or where a very large purchase has been made and you've created what feels like a friendship relationship,

> "If you're up for it, I've got tickets for the game next week so we can go, have a beer, and talk about how things are going with your new (*whatever the new solution is*)."

If additional benefits could be realized through a different use of the products you sold, describe them. These could possibly be ways to use the solution that haven't yet been discussed between you and this customer. You could add a handwritten comment to this effect.

"Frank. I just learned that another of my customers who purchased the same XXXXXX that you did, has been using his in a new way by (*describe the alternate way to use the product*) to realize (*a result achieved by using the product*). That might be something that you could try. "

When the note or letter is well written, customers often tell their friends and colleagues a salesperson sent them such a "Thank You" and this acts as a referral leading to new business. Most of us are getting less meaningful mail through the post. Your letter of " thank you" will really stand out.

Unfortunately, few salespeople ever send such a card or note acknowledging that a relationship continues to exist well after the sale. Some salespeople do manage to send something after the purchase but they don't personalize their note. Such non-personalized communications are typically perceived as sales techniques and customers just discard them. We know customers are very impressed if they receive a personalized note of thanks. This happens to us so seldom it's truly notable.

In some cases, companies have adopted the practice of sending a form "thank you" card from the president of the company. When this is received and nothing comes from the salesperson, it is easy to see this as a message that the president doesn't trust his or her sales staff to effectively thank the customer on their own. This can cause a customer to question the quality of the relationship he or she thought existed with the salesperson.

In such situations, the customer should get separate personalized letters of appreciation from both the president and the salesperson. Because the salesperson has had more personal contact with the customer, learning the customer's S.P.I.C.E[3] in the process, the salesperson should be able to write a more personal "thank you" to his or her client.

If you make the commitment to send such "thank you" cards or letters, there are tips the best-of-the-best use to do this task the right way.

TIMING

Mail out the "thank you" letter or card so your customer receives it within three to five days. This is your signal that you thought of your customer after the sale, and it lets the customer know he or she still matters to you. It will also make it easier for the customer to receive your follow-up call. Even if your customer hasn't yet made a purchase, mail a "thank you" card the customer will receive within three days following your sales conversation.

This keeps you at the top of your customer's mind. You will be remembered as someone to turn to whenever he or she has needs related to the products and services you sell, or when he or she encounters someone else who is seeking your products and services. You definitely benefit from having top of mind presence.

We suggest you write the personalized "thank you" card or letter immediately after the sale or encounter. Place it in the post to go out later the same day, and you won't have to worry about getting it done at a later date. By writing it immediately, you won't forget material you could use to personalize your comments. It only takes a minute or two, but will generate significant results.

Learn how to use the dictation function of your smartphone and record your thoughts right after the meeting or sales encounter. Save them as text to be included in a letter you will prepare when you are able to sit at a computer later in the day. You can draw this text into a template and produce a letter in minutes.

If you aren't able to prepare your card or letter immediately following your conversation with your customer, do so at the end of your workday, and take your letters to the mailbox on your way home. Get it done so delivery can arrive within three to five days. If you delay, you will likely forget to write one, or forget the information you need to personalize what you write.

INGREDIENTS OF A QUALITY "THANK YOU" CARD OR LETTER

Although just sending something is better than not sending a "thank you" card or letter at all, there are particular ingredients to an effective card or letter of appreciation used by the best salespeople:

- If your handwriting is decent, the note should be hand written. A letter would be typed with a possible hand written postscript.

- The card or letter should be included in a distinguishing envelope preferably showing your company's logo.

- The card itself should be unique and appealing to your customer.

- Remind your customer about the benefits he or she hoped to achieve.

- Confirm your enthusiasm for the solution your customer purchased, the solution you recommended, or for the opportunity to earn your customer's business.

- Say "thank you."

- Reaffirm your commitment to look after your customer, now and in the future.

- Invite him or her to contact you if any questions, concerns or other needs emerge.

- Invite referrals.

- Promise to look after any person your customer refers with the same commitment.

- Declare a sincere thank you for giving you the opportunity to take care of your customer and earn his or her business.

- Include your business card.

By including information you learned about your customer's S.P.I.C.E[3], it becomes very clear to the customer you listened, value his or her needs, and want the solution to work. This personalized approach far exceeds a simple "Thank you." Consider the following example:

"Bill, when you came to SystemsCo shopping for your computer, you were excited about starting your new program at CAIT and getting equipment and software you could use over the next two years of your graphics design studies. I'm hoping you've had time to set everything up, and you've found it's all you need for your artistic expression, page layout, photo editing and web design courses. Personally, I'd love to have a system like this myself.

I'm still committed to looking after you now that you've made your purchase. If you have any concerns, questions or other needs, please call me at XXX-XXXX extension XXX. Your satisfaction really matters to me. In fact, if you ever refer a friend or family member to me, I promise you I will treat them with the same respect and care I have shown to you. I'll do the best I can to make sure they get what they need.

Good luck with your studies. Please keep me informed about your progress."

The preceding personalized sample contains the essential ingredients for an effective note of appreciation. It could be hand written on a card for the most impact, or typed and personally signed on a piece of paper inserted into a "thank you" card. Adding a short handwritten note such as "Go (_the name of the school athletic team_)!" would also help.

Make sure you sign this letter in ink, preferably a different color from the printed ink, and don't use a computerized or rubber stamp signature. You do want to find efficiencies so you can do such notes and letters to every customer, but not in any way that depersonalizes the "Thank you."

Make the notes your own. Write in a style fitting your personality. Make sure your handwriting is legible. If not, choose the typed note approach with some sort of following comment such as a "P.S. I want to look after you if any problems arise. Please don't hesitate to call". Your note must clearly show your customer this isn't a form note you send to everyone. Your customer needs to experience this as making him or her feel special.

In this digital world, there are various alternatives to sending a note in the mail. Some digital services allow you to send a personalized e-card (*see jacquielawson.com for an example*). Many of these options are very creative and can be pleasing to receive so investigate to see what works for you (*a word of caution – these e-mail cards take a few moments to play which might be frustrating for a very busy client*). Alternatively, you could use your e-mail to send your "thank you" note. This is better than not sending a "thank you" note at all. However, it will not stand out as dramatically as receiving a "thank you" card in the mail.

Remember this card or letter contains a set of promises you must live up to – when your customer tries to contact you, when he or she consults you again, or if your customer makes a referral. Do these notes on a regular basis. Don't be lazy. They're easy to do and will bring you more business.

MARKETING LETTERS AND NOTES

If you totally adopt the role of being a professional salesperson, you have the opportunity to show extra initiative and send out marketing letters or e-mails to those clients with which you've built relationships. Done right, and not too frequently, this feels like a personal service to your customer and furthers your reputation as an insight-oriented consultant.

The easiest customer to sell to is the one who has already bought from you. Few salespeople ever take the initiative to send a subsequent letter to customers telling them about other things the customer might be interested in. Some do, but too many tend to send form advertisements that wind up in the wastebasket.

However, in our experience, customers are very impressed if they receive a personalized marketing letter informing them about products that meet their particular needs. Sending such personalized marketing letters says, "I'm always on the look out for what will help you be even more successful."

An effective marketing letter is typed on original corporate letterhead paper. Each customer should receive what looks like a personalized letter specifically tailored for him or her. The letter should be targeted to people with a highly relevant interest and should make a compelling offer or announcement that will motivate action on the part of the customer.

Never send a photocopied document. Even if you're sending the same letter out to many people, each recipient should receive what appears to be a unique letter. Use your mail merge function in your word processor. In the merge, include the name, address, and a first paragraph specifically explaining why you think this product or solution has value for your customer. This should relate to what you learned in the discovery of the customer's S.P.I.C.E[3].

A personalized marketing letter should contain the following elements:

- the customer's specific name and address,

- a personal and friendly greeting,

- a description of the interest you remember being expressed to you by the customer,

- a description of a great new product, service or complete solution that fits the customer's particular interest,

- the benefits the customer would experience in using the product, service or complete solution,

- your reasons for sending this information,

- an indication you could show the customer more about the product, service or complete solution,

- a notice you will be calling at a certain day and time to speak with the customer about this opportunity, or at least an invitation to call you, or to speak with you when the customer next visits the store, and

- a "thank you" for taking the time to read your letter.

Optionally, the letter could include a special pricing offer if the customer chooses to act on the letter to buy the items from you. This would likely need a manager's approval so work with your people to create opportunities to make such compelling offers to your existing client base.

Typically, you won't need to offer a discount if the customer is likely to appreciate the benefit of being the first to get the product, service or complete solution. In addition, you definitely won't need to discount the price if the value clearly exceeds the cost of the item or solution.

Many years ago, we were taught the power of personalized marketing letters in our own retail setting by one of our young salespeople. He asked permission to contact customers who had previously purchased statistical analysis software packages. We were operating in a university town and he had many researchers as his customers.

He composed a letter describing a brand new product he had discovered. This software allowed the user to visually see the data within his or her statistical samples in three dimensions. This 3D modeling software worked with the statistical analysis software the customer had already purchased and improved the ability to analyze data. He described what the new software could do and the benefits the user would gain. Essentially, he shared his enthusiasm for the product. Ninety percent (90%) of the recipients of his letter elected to buy the new package and many of them referred others who also bought the software.

The cost of preparing and sending these letters was minimal compared to the sales results. In this case, his letter was very much the same for each customer, lacking a great deal of personalization, but it still worked very well because he only sent it to customers who shared the same interest. It also worked well because he had a strong relationship with his clients based on his consultative interactions with them in the past.

One of our best retail salespeople would greet a first-visit client and take the time to learn about the customer's interests, business, goals, lifestyles, etc. He would enter this information in a coil-ringed pocket notebook. Before the Internet was available to him, he would review his notes just prior to sitting down in his evenings and reading trade journals and industry magazines.

If he found an advertisement or an article matching any of his customers' needs, he would stick a Post-It note on the magazine page and later photocopy the article or ad. He would place it in an envelope and put the customer's name, interest and phone number on the envelope. He then phoned the customer and would say something like,

> "Joe. When we met last week, you mentioned you needed something that could do (*desired use and benefit*). I've just found an article describing a brand new product that does exactly what you want. I've copied the article for you. It's here for you to get when you next visit the store. This product looked so good I got our purchasers to bring some in. They'll be in stock within a few weeks."

Customers really appreciated this gesture. They always came in to get the copy of the article. While in our store, they bought something to make the visit worthwhile. Later, the customers typically called to order the product covered in the article. This salesperson strengthened his relationships with his customers by doing this and consistently won new business from his existing client base.

The impact of this strategy was vividly revealed one day after he had been selling in our store for nine months. In the August doldrums when retail was notoriously slow, seven customers were in the store, as were he and six other salespeople each eager to help. All seven customers chose to wait for this one salesperson. The last customer waited almost two hours. These customers waited because they knew he gave them this type of service. No one else ever had.

Following the advent of the Internet, he would review the notes he had in his personal organizer about customer interests then surf looking for information of value to his customers. Once again, if he came across any articles of interest, he would e-mail the information or links to his customers, along with notes indicating he remembered their interests and had discovered information he thought they might like to see.

Another young retail salesperson, who specialized in selling entertainment software, built up a steady clientele by sending marketing letters to people he knew had an interest in certain types of gaming software. For his avid gamers, he would look for items he knew would be of interest and ask our purchasers to order these items. He made sure a demonstration unit was put out on display in the store, and then sent a letter to the avid gamers in his database inviting them to come and take a look. He was always successful in getting sales of the new items to those customers.

In addition, he built a reputation as the "go-to" gaming software expert in the city. He was typically a high producer just by selling game software, joysticks, other gaming input devices and Internet subscriptions for those interested in multi-player on-line gaming. Other salespeople were chasing those customers who were looking at computer systems while this young fellow outsold many of them by taking this initiative to sell lower priced items.

There is very little marketing more powerful than a personalized recommendation from a trusted expert. We know this process works. The only impediments to success will come from you. If you fail to get to know your customer's interests and needs, you won't be able to personalize such communications. If you fail to do the homework to look for products and services meeting special interests, you'll have nothing to offer. Or if you fail to make the extra effort to write and send a letter, you won't initiate this type of repeat business.

Our observations of the behavior of the best salespeople have shown us how you can be highly effective when using such follow-up techniques. We suggest you:

- keep records about your customers and their specific interests,

- build a template to use for other marketing letters for other customers to make the process easier and more efficient,

- within your template, leave room for you to add a description of the customer's specific problems or opportunities that have led you to send this letter,

- describe the problems that are solved by the new products, services and solutions,

- clearly explain the benefits of the products, services and solutions,

- if possible, provide some sort of offer motivating action, or clearly show how the value achieved by using the products significantly exceeds the price,

- have someone else read your marketing letter before you submit it,

- get your manager's prior approval before sending out the letter (*get the manager to proof read your letter to make sure it satisfies corporate standards*),

- tell the customer you welcome feedback on the information you've provided, and

- if you already have a very strong relationship with the client, you could send such marketing letters by e-mail.

Think about the number of times you've received "junk" mail targeted at the masses and what you've done with such material. Then compare your behavior after receiving a personalized letter. If you have ever received a personalized marketing letter, we're willing to bet, given your own response to the targeted letter, you have proof the recipient appreciates this form of communication.

Doing this type of comparison might be tough for you, because like most people, you may have never received a personalized marketing letter from a salesperson you know and trust. You may not be able to compare your reaction to such a letter with the receipt of junk mail, but you do know "junk" mail looks like junk, and personalized mail gets opened and read.

When it's a personalized communication, the relationship glue gets reinforced and the customer values what he or she receives. The customer, even if he or she doesn't take advantage of this particular offer, remembers who thought enough to send the useful information. This is personally relevant and valued.

Clinique and Elizabeth Arden representatives call past customers once or twice per year to advise of specials on the customer's particular cosmetic preferences. A "gift" is included with any purchase. Their customers appreciate these activities. However, these examples stand out because they are rare.

In a world where many other salespeople fail to take such initiative, you immediately differentiate yourself (*you as a brand*) from the competition. Your reputation grows, becoming something your customers talk about with others. Instead of chasing around trying to find and sell to new customers, you get to spend more of your time selling more to your existing clients and to those they refer.

You will still want to seek out new business, but your livelihood can be more secure by selling to the easiest customers, those who already have a positive and trusting relationship with you. In a nutshell, you have this opportunity to turn more customers into easy customers.

Once you've said your repetitive "thank you" and done your follow-up communication with your customer, you've completed the "GET SMART" portion of this sales process. If you do this with every customer, it is highly likely you are now experiencing increased sales success. But you still aren't done. There are two more significant steps in this sales model.

EVALUATE AND REPEAT

Assess your prior performance, fix any deficiencies, and look for additional opportunities with new and existing customers.

You've made a sale and built a relationship positive enough to allow future opportunities. Having done so, you've ensured your most efficient future work as a salesperson, and your most profitable results. You've improved your sales results by using the eight steps of "GET SMART" and this has been rewarding.

G	Greet	A greeting and approach to begin a conversation.
E	Engage	A level of engagement in conversation allowing trust and relationship building to occur.
T	Learn the customer's needs (Get The customer's S.P.I.C.E^3)	An open discussion to get the customer's S.P.I.C.E^3 and create customer insights.
	Half Time	*Determine a solution for the customer's S.P.I.C.E^3, prepare to make your recommendation, and if necessary, rehearse your summary of the customer's S.P.I.C.E^3.*
S	Show Full Understanding	Show understanding by summarizing the customer's S.P.I.C.E^3, and asking if you have fully understood.
M	Make Your Recommendation	Make your recommendation in terms of the benefits the customer is hoping to achieve.
A	Ask How To Proceed	Ask for a decision and initiate a call-to-action. Ask for the business.
R	Reinforce The Customer's Decision	Assure the customer he or she has made the right decision.
T	Thank The Customer And Follow-Up	Thank the customer and stay in contact with the customer as part of the on-going relationship. Give after-sale support and service.

As a salesperson using the "GET SMARTER" approach, you recognize you have two more steps to complete. Do them with vigor. Pursue improvement just as you pursue your sales. During these two steps, you enhance your learning and further increase your proficiency.

E	Evaluation	Assess your performance as a salesperson in three ways – through measurement of the results your clients have realized with the solutions you provided; customer feedback; and self-analysis.
R	Repeat	Return to the beginning, and repeat the insight-oriented selling process with both new and existing clients.

Some people don't see these additional steps as part of the sales process because they see the customer's purchase as the end of the sales transaction. Having gotten the sale, they tend to focus on the next customer. If each customer is new, then such salespeople have to work from the very beginning of the sales process to try to win a new sale. Instead, you have the opportunity to make your life as a salesperson easier as you stand out by taking on the two additional steps of the "GET SMARTER" sales process.

STEP NINE – EVALUATION

You only improve if you assess your own performance. Measure the results your clients are achieving using your solutions. Are you contributing to their increased success? Ask for feedback from others, and engage in self-assessment – during your sales conversations, immediately after an interaction, and later by looking at how you've been interacting with all of your customers. Challenge yourself to reduce your mistakes and enhance what you do well.

It's now time to evaluate your performance, to check on how well you're doing in your sales activities.

GOALS OF THE EVALUATION STEP

Even after completing sales to many customers, you still have several goals in this evaluation step:

- to learn from your experiences,
- to make sure your customers are happy with your solutions,
- to collect anecdotes of customer success,
- to show your customers that you want to improve,
- to be the best salesperson that you can be, and
- to improve your overall results.

Even if you are a high performance salesperson, you're still able to improve your sales performance by adding the step of evaluating yourself. Self-assessment is a key element of growing and learning.

Professional athletes evaluate their performance all the time. Lawyers, doctors, teachers all engage in on-going learning to improve their skills. As a professional salesperson, adopt the same attitude. Engage in life-long learning stimulated by continual assessment of your skills and performance.

Assess your performance as a salesperson in three ways. Firstly, find out how well your customers are doing using the solutions you've provided. Discover if you made a significant contribution to their success. Secondly, obtain feedback from your customers about what you do effectively as a salesperson and what you could improve. And thirdly, engage in self-analysis to review the sales processes you use with your clients and compare your results against your goals.

OBTAIN CUSTOMER FEEDBACK

After a period of time has elapsed, two weeks, perhaps a month, several months or longer, depending on the products you sell, find out how your customer thinks and feels things have turned out since the solution was put in place. Find out if you truly did satisfy the customer's S.P.I.C.E[3]. Then learn what the client thinks and feels about your sales interaction. This is an evaluation to assist your own learning.

FOLLOW-UP VISITS JUST FOR FEEDBACK

Not intended as a sales interaction, this engagement should specifically be for the purpose of getting feedback from your customer. Solicit his or her thoughts about how well your prior solutions are working, and discover his or her thoughts about how well you did as a salesperson in your prior encounters.

As a retail salesperson, most of your follow-up evaluation sessions would happen when you next encounter the customer on the sales floor; or you could deliberately call to discuss his or her feedback on the telephone. When a purchase has been particularly large, you might want to schedule an appointment to do this face-to-face.

Make sure your customer knows the agenda for this meeting is to discuss both the performance of the solution and your performance as a salesperson. Tell your customer you would like an opportunity to meet for an appraisal of your performance. Expect the customer to be pleasantly surprised.

You know the person you're meeting, so make eye contact, offer a handshake and greet him or her by name. Engage as you would for any sales interaction by referring to something you know matters to this person then get down to the business at hand.

"Bill, I wanted to meet with you for two reasons – to find out how the solution I sold you is working to determine if the benefits you now experience match what I promised, and secondly, to find out how you feel about the way I dealt with you when we last met. First, I want to make sure the solution is working to your satisfaction?"

IF THE CUSTOMER HAS PROBLEMS

If there are any problems with the implementation of the solution you sold, then your customer will want to focus on the problems first. There are several possible causes for delivering a product or service that doesn't fully satisfy the customer's S.P.I.C.E[3]:

- You didn't fully understand some significant aspects of the customer's situation, problem, implications, constraints or expectations.

- You didn't deliver the right product or service given your customer's needs.

or

- There are defects or product quality issues.

The product quality issue requires that you become a customer advocate to cause your company to fix the problem. The first two issues relate to your behavior as a salesperson. You will need to both fix the problem and to alter your behavior to improve.

Paraphrase and clarify what those problems might be. If your solution doesn't deliver the benefits you promised, you have a responsibility to fix the issue. Work together to figure out how this can be done. You may need to involve your boss if you over-promised and under-delivered. To preserve this client relationship, fix this situation.

You may need to end this meeting so that you can pursue a solution. If so, re-schedule the personal feedback session for sometime after you expect the problem to be resolved.

"Marsha, thank you for bringing this to my attention. Neither of us wants this to be happening so I think I need to end this meeting now to expedite the process of getting this fixed. Are you okay with that? It will take me three days to have that done. Could we meet again next Friday?"

or,

Stan, thank you for bringing this to my attention. I'm very concerned about this problem and want to get it resolved right away. If you have the XXXXXX with you, lets take it to our specialists and get them to look at it. If not, can we arrange to get a technician to work on it? We can talk about my performance after the XXXXXX is working properly if that feels more comfortable to you?

There may be occasions where you could promise to get the problems fixed and continue this feedback meeting. If there are any problems with the results the customer is getting, there will likely be perceived problems with you.

Once you've identified the product problems and made arrangements to have them fixed, you will need to shift focus to a discussion of your performance. Even though you know this will be critical feedback because the solution isn't delivering what was expected, you still need to reach for feedback about your performance.

> "Joe, I realize the solution isn't yet satisfactory, and this is probably because I missed something important in our sales discussions. I will get this fixed. As soon as we finish here, I will expedite our problem resolution process. Meanwhile, I want to improve my performance as a salesperson, so I need your evaluation of how I did. I was trying very hard to understand your needs. I tried to listen so I could understand your situation, problems and goals. I thought I understood and recommended what I considered to be the best solution to meet your expectations. Can you help me to understand how I failed to accomplish this? Where did I go wrong?"

If the customer gives you critical feedback, stop any impulse to defend yourself. Use the active listening skills to achieve full understanding. Learn from this. Find out what you did, or didn't do, that interfered with successfully understanding the client's needs. Discover what you could have done to better understand.

IF THERE ARE NO PROBLEMS

Hopefully, your follow-up contact three days after the purchase would have immediately discovered any problems with your solution and the problems would already be fixed. This subsequent evaluation meeting would have a more positive focus. Or, everything may have worked fine from the beginning and you may just find your customer was and still is very pleased with the results achieved with your solution. Before you proceed to a discussion of your performance, try to learn concrete information about the results the customer is now achieving.

Find out, as specifically as possible, if your customer's costs have been reduced, if your client is now getting increased payoffs, and whether or not he or she experiences any unexpected benefits. Find out if the customer has been making creative uses of your solution as this may give you new insights to be helpful to other clients. Try to get a measure of the real savings or real gains.

Invite your customer to measure his or her results as specifically as possible.

"Jorge, when we discussed what you wanted to achieve, we identified several costs of concern when you used your old XXXXXX, and we identified how getting something new in place could improve your revenues. Can you tell me how much you've saved in the past two months? And if you've realized any new revenue, how big was the gain?"

or

"Bill, you wanted a new wardrobe because you felt your appearance was underwhelming employers when you were looking for a new job. Since we got you into those new outfits, have you been getting better results? Any increase in second interviews, job offers, or better feedback from the interviewers?"

or

"Shandra, you came to me because you were experiencing significant skin irritation and dryness on your back and your shins, so badly that it was disrupting your sleep. How has your skin been since you've been using that vitamin E moisturizing cream? Are you sleeping better? On a 1 to 10 scale, how would you rate the improvement? "

or

"Maya, when we discussed what you wanted to achieve, you told me the frequent failure of your old XXXXXX cost you about $30 per month in repairs. You also lost an average of $500 in revenue because you couldn't do your work when this happened. How much have you saved since we put the new XXXXXX in place?"

Continue to build rapport and use the active listening skills to draw out the customer's assessment of results. Let your customer do the evaluating. Learn all about the results achieved with your solution and listen for any clues pointing to where the solution could have been improved.

Even from contented customers, you may learn things to take back to your employer leading to product and service improvements. You could ask your customer to think about how the solution could have been even better.

"Sally, I love hearing that you've experienced some wonderful benefits from using your new XXXXXX. But as you think back, is there anything that could have made the solution even better, easier to implement, easier to use, more productive?"

For your customer, measuring results reinforces the value of working with you. For you, you gain anecdotal information to share with future clients. This increases your credibility. Quantify the gains as much as possible.

Once you've learned about the results delivered by your solution, shift to a focus on your own performance. Tell your customer you want to continue to improve how you work with your clients. Explain the sales approach you're using and why you're doing this. Ask specific questions about how your customer experienced what you were doing when you worked with him or her.

"Janet, I'm working to develop my skills as an insight-oriented salesperson. It's my goal to help my client's achieve new insights that allow them to improve their results. I want to work with each of my customers to identify problems that hold them back from achieving greater success, and then determine how critical it is to find a solution to reduce costs and yield greater benefits. I want to be able to deliver solutions that really make a positive difference. To do this, I spent considerable time with you trying to understand your needs. I tried to listen effectively so I fully understood your situation, problems, implications, constraints and expectations. How well do you think I listened to you, and did I really understand your needs? Did our conversation open up new insights about what you could achieve?"

By asking for such feedback, your client will be impressed for several reasons:

- You seek his or her evaluation of your performance, and few other salespeople ever do this.

- You demonstrate respect for your customer's evaluation of your performance.

- You indicate you really do intend to improve your ability to take care of him or her in the future.

- You articulate what you've been doing and he or she will better understand the difference in your approach versus your competitor's behavior.

and

- At this moment in time, you aren't there trying to sell something else.

Your relationship with your client at this meeting has equal priority to learning information that will help you to improve your skills. By asking for feedback, you add glue to the relationship.

Reach for a frank and open assessment of your sales conversations with your client. Ask any of these specific questions to keep the conversation rolling:

- Do you think I listened well enough to fully understand your needs?

- It's my goal to help you understand your needs even better than you did before we met. Did I help you to clarify your needs and goals?

- As a result of talking with me, did you have a larger expectation for what you could achieve if we put the right solution in place?

- Did I frustrate you in any way when I was first meeting with you to discuss your problems and needs?

- How effective do you think I was at learning your needs?

- Do you think I wasted your time in any way as we were discussing what you were looking for?

- Is there anything you wish I had asked you, or talked with you about before I made my recommendation?

Once your customer answers your question, use the active listening skills to work toward full understanding of the feedback. Paraphrase what the customer says. Do a Feelings Check in response to any non-verbal behaviors that suggest underlying feelings. Check any inferences you're making. Identify with the customer. Consider how you would have felt in response to dealing with someone like you.

Draw out your customer's honest impressions of you as a salesperson. Learn how this other person experienced any prior interactions with you. Use this feedback to improve. Be the best you can be.

You might be tempted to ask these questions of your customers via e-mail or in a telephone conversation. However, if you do so, you will likely lose many of the benefits achieved when you sit or stand in front of your customer. You conduct this face-to-face interview with your customer so he or she fully sees that you hold yourself accountable for his or her success and satisfaction.

In addition, as you listen, you clarify what your customer tells you and reach for deeper understanding. Your customer has the opportunity to clearly express what he or she needs from you in future interactions, further building a relationship for life. This can't happen via e-mail and is not as effective by telephone.

Asking for feedback is an implied promise you will use what you receive from your customers to modify your behavior. Now that you've asked and been given feedback, they should see changes in your behavior. These changes should be in the direction of what your customers have collectively suggested you need to change. Asking and not using the information your customers give you will disappoint them and reduce your credibility.

If you find you are struggling to make the changes, don't be afraid to let your customer's know you are working on the change, but finding it harder to accomplish. Your customers will support you in this struggle, becoming your agents for change, and this will further add glue to your relationship with them.

CUSTOMER SURVEYS

As well as holding face-to-face feedback sessions, you can also periodically send out surveys to all or a sample set of your clients. We suggest that you do this once a year.

Such surveys give you information about how your collection of customers sees you – a bigger picture view than you get in one-to-one interviews. Because you're getting this information from multiple people, similar answers will give you key information about how you come across.

Give your customers an opportunity to complete the survey anonymously. This will provide a way to tell you something the customer might not have felt comfortable telling you in a face-to-face interaction. You could use a third party survey source to provide even more assurance to your clients that their responses are anonymous. For example, you could use the online service provided at surveymonkey.com or other similar survey services.

Again, you might be tempted to conduct such a survey through e-mail. However, this is not an anonymous method of communication. For surveys of many customers, you really want to provide anonymity to your clients so you obtain more truthful responses.

The quality of the relationships you've built with your customers will be reflected in the rate of returned surveys you receive. Customers who see a great deal of value in working with you will respond. Those who do not yet trust your ability to help them will be less likely to respond. Although you won't know why some do not respond, consider the possibility that their non-response is feedback that you have work to do on your relationship-building skills. In addition, if you were not authentic in your use of the "GET SMARTER" approach, expect a low percentage of survey returns.

In the introduction to the survey, tell your customers it is your aim to continuously improve as an insight-oriented salesperson. Indicate you wish to deliver the best results for your clients. Tell each of them you are seeking feedback from a sample of your clients, and ask each person to take a few minutes to complete a survey. Make it clear the survey is anonymous so your customer can feel comfortable being completely frank with you about what he or she would like you to improve.

If conducting the survey by mail, indicate you've enclosed an addressed envelope complete with postage. Indicate to your customers that filling out the survey and putting it in the envelope will take approximately eight minutes of their time. Although an arbitrary number, we think eight minutes is the maximum amount of time that it should take to fill out such a questionnaire.

Your survey should fit on one side of an 8½" by 11" page and should contain no more than ten questions. Explain how the questions in the survey work. You could try a mix of different types of questions or just use one question type. Use questions you think will get you information that is useful to you.

For example, you might have ten questions where you ask your customer to rate your performance on a five point scale from 1 = poor to 5 = great. Or you might have ten statements where you ask the customer to indicate his or her agreement with each statement on a ten point scale from 1 = strongly disagree to 10 = strongly agree. You could use open-ended questions that require the respondent to write his or her feedback on the survey form. This requires more work on the customer's part and will cause your response rate to drop, but you might get useful feedback from the hand-written additions. If using open-ended questions, have fewer of them.

To truly invest in this process, it would be best if you could invent some of your own questions. However, we offer some suggestions to give you a sense of what we would ask. For rating scale questions, you could use some of the following:

- How well do I listen to you when we discuss your needs?

- How well do I understand your needs?

- How well do I make you feel comfortable when we talk about your problems and the implications of those problems?

- How well do I use your time when we discuss your needs?

- How well do I explain my recommendations?

- How well do I do at thanking you for your business?

- How well do I do at follow-up to make sure everything works the way it should?

- How well do I contribute to your increased success?

Alternatively, you could ask questions seeking a simple Yes/No/Maybe response plus customer-handwritten responses on two blank lines under each rating. For example, you could ask:

Do I make you feel uncomfortable in anyway?

Yes No Maybe – Please explain:

_____

_____

Using this format, you could ask other questions such as:

- Do you come to understand your needs better in our conversations?

- Do our conversations lead you to new insights about your problems, implications, constraints and potential opportunities?

- Do you feel any discomfort when I ask for your business

- Do I act professionally at all times in our interactions?

- Do I have enough knowledge and expertise to instil confidence in my ability to help you gain greater success?

- Do you feel comfortable referring your colleagues, family and friends to me?

It's your survey questionnaire, so design it so it works for you. Prepare a survey with questions that fit your need to evaluate how you're doing in the eyes of your clients. (*See Appendix 4 for a sample letter and survey form*).

Test the questionnaire in advance. Ask people who know you well to fill it out. They might not be customers, but they can tell you whether the questions worked for them or caused some difficulty. Ask for comments from your sales manager. Get his or her advice as to what you should ask.

If you have a large number of clients, you could send this to only a sample of them. The sample size should be large enough to represent the total population of your customers. If you know you have a subset of less than happy clients, make sure you include some of them in your sample. You don't just want "I love you" feedback. You will learn most from critical comments and evaluations.

If you can afford to do so, give each customer a reward for filling out the survey. For example, you might include a crisp $5 or $10 bill. This will improve your response rate. It is safest to invest that money when you know you've established significant relationships with your customers, but it can be useful when still working to build a client base. It will show how serious you are about improving your skills. Think of this as an investment in your professional learning.

Make sure the survey page finishes with a sincere "thank you" for the time the customer gave you in filling out and mailing the completed survey form back to you. You want to continue to convey that the relationship with your clients is critically important to you.

Once the surveys are returned, sit down and transfer the results to an analysis sheet. If the results come in the form of ratings, use a spreadsheet. Use the statistics functions of the spreadsheet to analyze the data. Take a community education course at your local college if you're not sure how to do this.

If the feedback is written, don't just read the replies – analyze them. Transfer all replies to each section of the survey into a word processor. Look at each question and all the responses given to that question. Look at all of the answers and then group them into categories. Put like responses with like responses. The frequency of similar responses will give you an idea as to how common this feedback is.

Manage the data and draw general conclusions from the information. Get a sense of where your customers think your performance is okay, and where they have concerns. Know what your customers want you to do more of, and what should change. This will give you fuel for your self-analysis.

EARN CUSTOMER FEEDBACK

You only gain permission to obtain effective and constructive feedback by doing the full "GET SMART" sequence. It is critical that you worked to establish an open and trusting relationship. It is imperative that you made your best effort to learn and take the customer through his or her S.P.I.C.E[3], working to help your customer to open up new insights. Fundamentally, you had to be striving to identify then solve real problems with complete solutions.

If you did anything less, why should the customer give of his or her time and effort to help you learn? If you just sold the products the customer asked about, or flogged your products using persuasion and information sales processes, or if you just attempted to become the customer's buddy using a relationship sales approach, you haven't earned the right to ask for feedback about the value you contributed. You didn't extend yourself to contribute extra value to the customer so he or she will see no reason to extend him or herself to give something you want.

Do what it takes to earn the right to ask your customers for feedback. By building an ongoing relationship with each customer, and making your best effort to help your customer be more successful, you should be able to ask, and will likely receive useful information that will help you to grow in your profession.

SELF-ANALYSIS

By this time in the book, you're either experimenting with a few aspects of this model; deliberately trying to implement it whole-heartedly; or, you've concluded you already know better what works for you, and you're going to stick with what you know. Hopefully as an adult performer, you're the expert on yourself so it's tough to challenge whatever conclusions you've made about your level of proficiency.

However, we offer words of caution. Your own judgement might be questioned if your results disappoint your employer or your customers. If others within your organization or industry do better than you do, selling the same solutions you are, then there is evidence you could do better.

Even if you are at the top of the heap, are you at the top of the mountain? Do you still have room to improve your results? If your customers are only lukewarm in their ratings on one or two areas, then you still could enhance your performance.

On the other hand, if you're a corporate hero because of high sales achievement, then you might be right. If your customers rave about you in their survey responses, again you might be correct. If your sales manager constantly tells you he or she is very impressed by your work, then you might be the best you can be. However, we still argue that you should take moments to think about how well you are doing, and where you could improve.

PERIODIC SELF-ASSESSMENT

There is usually room for improvement. Assess the feedback you get from your customers, and do your own assessment of your performance. Are you getting the results you intend to achieve? Are your customers getting the results they want to achieve? Is there a steady stream of repeat and referral business? Are there particular aspects of your sales process where you stumble or feel you have to work harder than necessary? The answers to these and other questions will point to areas for future growth.

Use your own desire to be successful. Motivate yourself to perform such self-analysis. Self-analysis is important to your overall success. People are seldom successful by accident. Accomplishment is an act of will. This entails:

- identifying what we want to achieve,
- determining how we have to act in order to accomplish our goals,
- forming a plan for change,

- making a deliberate decision to act on our plan, and then
- executing our plan.

We typically experience roadblocks and difficulties that impede and slow down progress. We have to analyze what we're doing, what we're encountering, and figure out how we can modify our behavior to get better results.

One definition for insanity, attributed to Albert Einstein, is doing the same thing over and over again while expecting different results. Persisting with the same behaviors while wanting better results is self-defeating. Ask yourself what behaviors you need to change.

As you look at how you spend your time, are there holes where you lose or miss out on business? Do you find you're less successful with certain types of clients? For example, you may succeed well with clients already eager for change but have trouble getting less eager customers to understand their problems, implications, constraints and new opportunities. If so, what can you do to fill in these holes and raise your performance bar?

Use the feedback you receive from customers as a stimulus for your own self-analysis. What do your clients describe as your strong points, your weaknesses, and areas where you could improve? Does their feedback match your own impressions of your performance – if not, why not?

Use feedback from your sales manager. Your manager may have concerns about the results you achieve and may be pointing at deficiencies in your sales approach. Does his or her feedback match your own sense of how well you're doing – if not, why not? Seek and welcome his or her feedback. Listen to your sales manager's advice for how to improve. We predict that making efforts to implement what your manager suggests will increase your results and your own rewards will improve.

Ask for feedback from those salespeople who achieve greater success than you experience. Look to them as coaches and listen to their advice. Ask how they achieve their results and experiment with the skills and approaches they describe.

However, your sales manager and the other salespeople may be using traditional sales approaches that we have challenged as no longer appropriate for our current economic world. You will need to sort out what is useful in what they tell you and determine how that fits within the "GET SMARTER" approach if you want to make this transition. It may be useful to have discussions with them where you ask them to react to the ideas in the "GET SMARTER" approach. You might find you're offering new possibilities for their learning.

Just thinking about the concepts, ideas and tips presented in this book should have encouraged you to move a little bit from your comfort zone to try something new. If not, self-analysis should lead you to consider what your resistance is all about.

Get in the habit of frequently examining your own S.P.I.C.E^3 as it relates to your own sales success. This means asking yourself the following questions:

- How much am I actually using the "GET SMARTER" approach, and the requisite sales skills in my daily sales activity?

- What results am I getting from my sales encounters with customers?

- What problems am I having being as effective as I could be, as effective as others expect?

- What does it cost me when I have an ineffective encounter?

- What's keeping me from getting better results and from getting better at using the "GET SMARTER" approach?

- What would I gain if I could:

  o get conversational with more customers,

  o learn each customer's complete S.P.I.C.E^3,

  o help more customers achieve new insights about problems, implications, constraints, and potential benefits,

  o recommend complete solutions with confidence,

o present the solution in terms of the benefits the customer will achieve,

o give and demonstrate better reasons to buy from my firm and myself,

o get fewer concerns and objections in response to my recommendations,

o win each customer's business,

o build long term relationships, and

o earn more referrals?

Ask yourself, "How motivated am I to get better?" and, "Am I my own biggest impediment to success because I don't have enough drive?"

The best athletes all describe their own ability to self-analyze as an important attribute helping them to get over slumps. They deal with their own poor performance through a calm and confident examination of their behavior and their own thinking. Getting into a tense funk does not improve their performance. The same is true for you.

Even if you achieve great success as a salesperson, you still need the skill of self-analysis. Develop the ability to calmly consider what you think, what you do, how you do it, the results you're getting, and what to improve to get better outcomes.

You will always encounter new challenges – customers who present new opportunities, competition getting better at what they do, new solutions needing new ways of presentation to customers, and changes in programs and promotions. To adjust your skills in the face of change, self-analyze then adapt. If you don't, you wind up clinging to a hope the old ways will return. And they never do.

Self-analysis is important to mastery in any endeavor. The best salespeople demonstrate:

- a commitment to the welfare of the company they sell for,

- a passionate commitment to doing well and winning, and

- continuous self-analysis.

You can choose to be one of the best. Are you doing the self-assessment that will allow you to improve?

As a salesperson, what should you analyze? First off, assess your use of the ten-step "GET SMARTER" model. Do you do all steps with every client, or are you taking short cuts and only doing some of them?

Are you guilty of spending less of your time in the first half of the selling process? Are you jumping into "selling" your products and services before you get full understanding of your customer's situation, problems, implications, constraints and expectations? Do you talk too much about product and not the complete solution? Do you fail to ask for the business? How well do you do each step? Are you careful to make sure you follow all of the elements of each step?

Look at your use of specific skills. How well do you engage your customers in conversations? If you fail to get into conversations, you won't get sales. How well do you use the active listening skills to listen to your customers for full understanding? Are you able to lead your customer to new insights by reflecting back what you understand?

How well do you draw out your customer's S.P.I.C.E[3], taking him or her through the Reality Trough to the point of excited anticipation of the solution you will recommend? How enthusiastically and confidently do you make your recommendation? Do you always invite your customers to buy from you?

How frequently do you thank your customers for the gift of their time and attention, for their business, for their feedback? Are you effectively showing your appreciation? Are you sustaining the relationships that you build? Too many people don't do the follow-up step and fail to stay in contact with their customers in lasting relationships. This failure inhibits their overall results. Do you follow-up?

In easy economies, you might get by with only moderate sales skills, just because people buy more readily in hot market conditions. However, in this complex world the market place is very competitive. The strong will survive. Continue to grow and develop so you're one of the strong.

ANALYSIS AFTER EVERY SALE

Minimally, do the periodic self analysis, but it would be even better if you could take a moment after every sales conversation to analyze how the interaction with the customer went. Did the customer accept your recommendation and purchase your solution? If he or she did, ask yourself why. Ask yourself "What did I do right to earn the business?"

Even if the customer bought from you, use the experience to learn how to improve by asking your self, "Was there anything I could have done better?" Perhaps your solution was not as complete as it could have been. Maybe you did win the sale but not a comfortable trusting client who will come back and refer others. Where could your performance have been even more successful?

If the customer did not buy, you also need to think about why you were unsuccessful. Ask yourself, "In hindsight, what could I have done better? How effectively did I follow the "GET SMARTER" process with this customer? What did I do well? Where did I fail? Can I still recover and win his or her business? What were some of the cues from the customer suggesting I wasn't being effective? What was I doing when these cues were present? What feedback did the customer give me and how can I adapt my way of selling to incorporate what I've learned?"

If the customer does not buy from you and buys from a competitor, you can't blame anyone else.

- Don't blame the customer.

- Don't blame the lost sale on price.

- Don't blame your company for not providing you with products the customer wants to buy.

- Don't blame your competitor for scooping you out of the sale.

Blaming others is self-defeating. Take responsibility for the result and look to see how you could have done better so you have improved performance with your next customer.

It's fair to say this model was built from an examination of many highly effective salespeople and no single salesperson had a complete mastery of the whole "GET SMARTER" approach. In the observations we've made, no one has yet demonstrated 100% implementation of the "GET SMARTER" sales approach with all of their customers. This is true even for those exceptional few that far out-performed their peers and helped us learn what it takes to be a high performance salesperson. Every salesperson has problems to overcome. Everyone could improve his or her performance and his or her results.

However, if you aren't improving, if your results remain similar from day to day, week to week, month to month, ask yourself, "What's stopping me from changing my bad habits?" If you aren't getting better, you certainly have a skill problem, an attitude problem, a motivation problem, a bad habit problem, or a resistance problem.

You won't get better until you work on your own problems. These problems are solvable – if you apply yourself to improvement. You can make a difference by changing your behavior in the right ways. If you make a deliberate effort to adopt the "GET SMARTER" approach, your sales will be easier to achieve.

STEP TEN – REPEAT

Be consistent. Use the "GET SMARTER" sales approach all of the time, and make sure you consistently get your customer's S.P.I.C.E^3.

The last step in the model is somewhat obvious. Repeat your use of this insight-oriented "GET SMARTER" sales approach with every client or potential client you encounter.

Goals Of This Step

There are good reasons to have this last step in the "GET SMARTER" sales model. Your goals for repeating all of the steps with each client are:

- to build your proficiency and unconscious competence through repetition so that you are freer to listen to your customers without having to worry about following the steps,

- to meet and satisfy the expectations of customers who have come to you because of the reputation you've earned for how you sell, and

- to achieve the best possible sales results.

Customers always have a S.P.I.C.E[3] for you to discover, and this presents new opportunities to find ways to sell them complete solutions to further increase their success.

With Existing Clients

Once you have this relationship, you have a customer for life – if you continue to work in the "GET SMARTER" way. This is not a time to switch to the Relationship Selling approach or to the Information Selling process. Most certainly, don't suddenly become a Persuasion-oriented salesperson. Continue with an insight-oriented process, always looking for new problems for which you have solutions. Don't rest on your laurels because you achieved a few big sales.

You would turn success into a failure if you use a few big sales to become a friendly salesperson that just visits with your past buyers. You have to see yourself as the person who continuously works to help each client achieve new insights and greater success.

Whether you're selling clothing, cosmetics, cars, cell phones, furniture, home electronics, houses, jewelry, fitness equipment, or tractor trailer units, you're there to help the client assess his or her status quo, determine what new problems have arisen, look at the costs of those problems, evaluate any constraints, and figure out what could be achieved if the new problems are solved. It's always about the customer's S.P.I.C.E^3.

WITH NEW CUSTOMERS

When you encounter potential clients, stay with this process. Use the "GET SMARTER" approach with every person you encounter in your sales role, and even with those you meet socially. Learn this sales process so completely it feels like breathing – a natural set of behaviors you absolutely must do for survival and success.

We believe success with some clients doesn't give you permission to just do triage looking for those customers similar to those with which you've had previous success. Give every customer a chance to tell you about his or her S.P.I.C.E^3. Do this with the discouraged, disinterested and resistant customers just as much as you do with the eager and curious customers. As your skills improve, you'll find you do this more quickly than when you first started out. You'll accrue efficiencies as you improve.

Some of your new customers will come as a result of referrals from other satisfied customers. It's critical you use the same sales approach with the referred customers because this is what they expect. People who have been referred are already prepared to buy from you. Use the same approach and be an effective insight-oriented salesperson to ensure this new customer buys the right solution. Anything less would be failing on a promise you made, either explicitly or implicitly, to the customer who did the referring.

No sales situation should be thought of as a small sale. We think what might first appear to be a small sales opportunity can involve solutions to help those clients achieve greater success and more growth. In turn, such growth means these larger customers will eventually bring larger opportunities.

Some of our customers, novices who were afraid of the technologies we sold, would go and hang-out in the cable section of our computer store. While there, they would observe, trying to learn by watching and listening to other customers talking with our sales staff about the computers they were buying. An approaching salesperson might be told by the shy customer that he or she was just looking for a cable.

For those who used the "GET SMARTER" approach, such larger conversations often turned into sales of full computer systems, complete with software, peripherals, accessories, supplies, and specialty add-ons solving the customer's particular problems. And the customers were very happy. Instead of just a cable, these customers bought complete solutions because they needed them.

However, you may work in an organization where your job is to pursue larger sales in a particular department selling high-ticket items. You may be in a situation where you encounter a smaller client and your organization might want you to refer this to a junior salesperson so you're free to find larger opportunities. If this is the case, learn the customer's S.P.I.C.E^3, or as much of it as possible in a short interval. Determine which salesperson would best fit the customer's needs, and then make the referral.

Do this in person. Meet with the new salesperson and the client together. In front of the client, introduce the salesperson while affirming for the customer this salesperson has the needed expertise. Tell the salesperson what you know about the customer's S.P.I.C.E^3. If there are elements you haven't yet discussed, say this to the salesperson. Thank the customer for having given you an opportunity to earn his or her business, explain that the new salesperson has the necessary time and expertise to provide better service and excuse yourself.

The same approach can be used if you meet someone in a social situation. Learn about his or her S.P.I.C.E^3 and then refer this person to someone in your organization with more experience in the area of the customer's particular need.

Any time you're dealing with potential customers, use the "GET SMARTER" approach – but force yourself to use more of it than you've done before. Deliberately apply skills you haven't yet implemented. Use the tips you haven't yet tried. Keep yourself in a learning mode.

There is a built-in humility to learning, which is exactly the attitude and demeanor that will make you a better insight-oriented salesperson. Customers will be much more comfortable talking with a person that sincerely wants to learn from them.

You're caught in a paradox. You're an expert that sells solutions in which you likely have more expertise than most customers but you have to accept that you're only a student when learning each customer's S.P.I.C.E.³. As such a student, you will be much more humble, much easier for the customer to relate to, and much more likely to really listen.

WITH EVERY CUSTOMER

If you follow the "GET SMARTER" steps with every client on every visit (*our recommendation*), you will likely experience:

- increased sales both in size and frequency,

- more efficient use of your time,

- customers who achieve greater success and growth leading to larger sales opportunities in the future,

- more customers who will simply choose to do business with you, as well as more customers through repeat and referral business,

- easier and easier customers to deal with because your reputation will precede you,

- higher evaluations for performance from your employer resulting in increased compensation,

- an improved reputation in the market place meaning more opportunities for career development,

- more confidence and peace of mind,

- more professional satisfaction,

- increased funds to support the lifestyle you wish to have, both now and in retirement, and

- a happier family life.

We think achieving these outcomes would likely satisfy your own S.P.I.C.E.³. So, we ask, "How would you like to proceed?"

IT'S YOUR CHOICE

(DECIDE TO "GET SMARTER")

> If others can achieve elite results, then you can as well. Such salespeople have already proved it's possible. You just have to make the commitment to learn how to do what they do and then act on your commitment.

TIME TO MAKE YOUR DECISION

You could resist adopting the "GET SMARTER" model. You could resist doing all or some of the elements of this approach. You may have some success using other approaches such as persuasion, information, relationship or basic consultative selling – any of these approaches will get you some sales. However, we contest that you will not get all you could accomplish. We think you will have costs in your current status quo associated with lost opportunities.

There are benefits to making the changes we've proposed. We've consistently seen higher performance from those who undertake to learn, use, and master the "GET SMARTER" sales approach. The "GET SMARTER" model has been built from the success of others.

We urge you to give this approach your full commitment. Learn it. Practice it. Achieve proficiency. Use it in each encounter with any potential client. Repetition facilitates competence. However, development of mastery will take time, much repetition, and continuous self-analysis.

We think for most salespeople it takes a full year to absolutely learn and move toward mastery of the "GET SMARTER" approach. Disciplined and organized use of the techniques and skills described in this book will lead to greater success as you learn, but full mastery will come from enough experience dealing with different customer types, and different customer problems.

If you make this commitment and dedicate yourself to this learning process, it's highly likely your sales results will be exceptional, seriously distinguishing you from others doing the same work. Of course, as this happens, your income will grow, and you'll be increasingly indispensable to the organization with which you work.

Your value to other sales organizations will grow possibly leading to new job offers. Your own confidence will increase and this will make you a much more effective negotiator in such situations.

We believe this success will only come when you fully commit to using the "GET SMARTER" sales approach. We had a young salesperson give us a testimonial to the benefits of making such a commitment.

"When I first started working as a salesperson, I was very nervous and it was an overwhelming experience. In the first three months, I was told by experienced salespeople to just find my own way. Because I saw their decent sales results I thought, "Well, I guess I've got to have my own approach.""

"Not having worked in a sales role before, I tried numerous things. I particularly tried giving as much information to my customers as I could. I was being helpful. However, what I was doing didn't work so well in terms of sales results."

"I was aware that the new salespeople hired after me were getting training in the "GET SMARTER" approach and I was curious. However, my peers kept telling me to stick to my own way, saying it would be better in the long run. Unfortunately, my numbers left something to be desired and my paycheck was less than I wanted."

"Finally, I took the training in the "GET SMARTER" approach. I worked really hard at implementing it into my sales. But again, for the first little bit, I still struggled. I struggled until I made a personal decision, in my mind, in my heart, to really do this 100%."

"Then I started to see results. I started seeing a lot of sales to repeat customers. And the paycheck has been great. That's probably the best part about it. That's probably the main reason why I do "GET SMARTER" selling – because of the paycheck. And it makes me a lot happier. My customers are a lot happier. I have relationships with my customers now. Nothing better than having a customer call me up to meet new needs. It makes me happy, they're happy and my employer is happy. That's why I do "GET SMARTER" selling."

This isn't about working harder. It's about working smarter, making selling easier. Be amongst the best salespeople by disciplining yourself to use the materials in the "GET SMARTER" approach. Continually analyze what you're doing. Keep looking for ways to get even better. Learn from your victories and your defeats, and achieve greater success.

Selling experience, disciplined self-analysis, and using the "GET SMARTER" framework leads to success. You will gain experience with each customer you engage. This will be meaningful experience if you analyze your behavior using the structure of the "GET SMARTER" approach. Determine how you might have done better in order to improve next time. Improvement in your selling behavior will lead to better sales results. You too could be a member of the elite by mastering the insight-oriented sales approach.

OUR ADVICE

As we've said before, we all have an enormous capacity to resist change. We're able to live with a status quo that could be, and probably should be changed. We have the ability to do this because we can subconsciously deny our pain or discomfort. Our first challenge is to force ourselves to be aware of the discomfort, frustration, dissatisfaction we have within our status quo, and then to recognize the real costs of not making a change.

As you think about your own sales results and sales approach, consider your own problems and implications and then look for ways to make things better. Experience your own S.P.I.C.E[3], realize you have solutions available to reduce costs, achieve better results, and increase your excitement about being the salesperson you are.

Mastery does not come by chance or simply from thinking you understand. Like the athlete who practices all of the basics of his or her sport, practice the basics of your own work. To gain mastery, step outside of your own comfort zone. Some of the skills we address in this book you already have and use. However, we're also willing to bet we have introduced other skills where you do not yet have proficiency. Work at these skills to gain mastery.

You may have to make a personal paradigm shift to abandon a current sales approach (*such as Persuasion, Information, Relationship or basic Consultative Selling*) in order to even accept these skills as relevant. You will have to challenge yourself to step outside of your box, and try something new. Consider the specific skills that are outside of your comfort zone, consider the steps in the "GET SMARTER" sequence that you don't usually include in your everyday sales behavior, and experiment.

PARADIGM SHIFTING

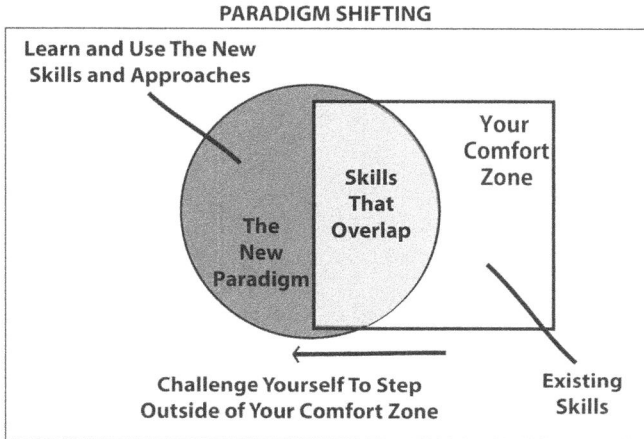

We encourage you to use this approach and succeed as an insight-oriented salesperson such that:

- your customers buy,

- your customers buy again and again,

- they refer family, friends and colleagues,

- your customers are comfortable making purchases that are profitable to you and your organization, because their own profitability is increased, and

- your employer sees you as an invaluable member of the sales team.

We sincerely thank you for purchasing this book and taking the time to read it. We wish you the best of success in your sales activities, and trust that you will work to make sure your customers also achieve greater success.

APPENDICES

APPENDIX 1: "GET SMARTER" SALES

G	Greet	Greet and approach showing interest in the customer and beginning a conversation.
E	Engage	Engage in conversation allowing trust and relationship building to occur.
T	Take Time to Learn the Customer's Needs (Get His or Her S.P.I.C.E^3)	Get the S.P.I.C.E^3 in an open discussion of the customer's needs, taking time to actively listen to the customer such that the customer does most of the talking while you clarify for understanding; thereby leading your customer to new insights.
	Half Time	*Identify the best solution, prepare to recommend a complete solution, and if necessary, rehearse doing the S.P.I.C.E^3 summary.*
S	Show Full Understanding	Before trying to sell anything, show understanding by summarizing what you've learned about the customer's needs and expectations, and ask if you fully understand. Take the customer through his or her S.P.I.C.E^3 in an organized sequence, stimulating the Reality Trough, arriving at eagerness to hear/see the solution.
M	Make Your Recommendation	Make the recommendation of a complete solution in terms of the benefits the customer is hoping to achieve.
A	Ask How To Proceed	Ask for a decision and initiate a call-to-action.
R	Reinforce Your Customer's Decision	Reinforce the benefits of the customer's decision and let your customer know he or she made a wise choice for specific reasons (*re-iterating the specific benefits that matter to the customer*).
T	Thank You and Follow-Up (*After-sale support and service*)	Thank your customer for the opportunity to earn his or her business, help the customer through the purchase transaction, and stay in contact with the customer as part of the on-going relationship.
E	Evaluate	Assess your performance as a salesperson in three ways – through measurement of the results your clients have realized with the solutions you provided; customer feedback; and self-analysis.
R	Repeat	Return to the beginning and repeat the insight-oriented consultative selling process.

APPENDIX 2: READINESS AND THE S.P.I.C.E³ SEQUENCE

Readiness For Change

	State	Common Emotions	Intentions
GO Zone (GREEN)	**Ready for Change**	Eagerness, Excitement, Expectations,	We know what we can do, so let's do it.
WAIT Zone (YELLOW)	Accepting Status Quo	Calm, Comfortable, Accepting	Let's just stay the same.
STOP Zone (RED)	**Stuck and Pained**	Loss, Frustration, Irritation, Anxiousness	We really need to do something but can't.

Readiness To Change Plus The The S.P.I.C.E³ Sequence

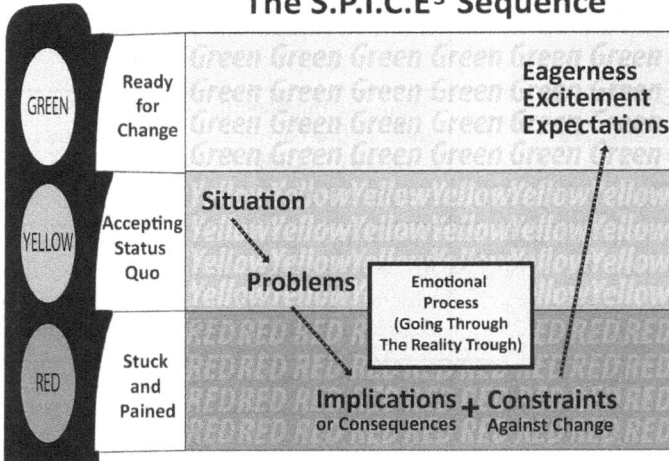

GREEN — Ready for Change — **Eagerness Excitement Expectations**

YELLOW — Accepting Status Quo — **Situation** → **Problems**

RED — Stuck and Pained — **Implications** or Consequences **+ Constraints** Against Change

Emotional Process (Going Through The Reality Trough)

Appendix 3: The S.P.I.C.E³ Sheet

Customer: _____ Tel. No. _____

Company Name: _____

SITUATION

_____

_____

_____

_____

PROBLEMS

_____

_____

_____

_____

IMPLICATIONS/COSTS

_____

_____

_____

_____

CONSTRAINTS

_____

_____

_____

EXPECTATIONS, EXCITING BENEFITS, EAGERNESS

_____

_____

_____

APPENDIX 4: SAMPLE CUSTOMER SURVEY

Dear (*Customer Name*)

I've sent this to you as one of my customers at (*name of your organization*). I'm working very hard to improve my skills as an insight-oriented salesperson. An Insight Salesperson is someone who helps his or her customers to achieve a deeper understanding of:

- his or her current situation,

- current problems and opportunities

- the implications and costs of problems and missed opportunities,

- the constraints that prevent change,

- the minimum expectations for what a solution must deliver, plus those exciting benefits that would be ideally achieved if an optimum solution could be found.

In addition, an Insight Salesperson works to deliver complete solutions that fully satisfy customer expectations and desired benefits. My goal is to increase your success. In our previous interactions when you visited our store, I focussed on doing this with you.

I'm asking you to take just eight minutes or less to complete the survey on the following page. This survey is anonymous. Once you complete it, please place it in the enclosed stamped and addressed envelope and mail it to me at your earliest convenience.

To thank you in advance for taking the time to give me this feedback, I have enclosed a $5 bill. However, I'm hoping the best way I will be able to show my appreciation is to use the feedback you provide to improve my proficiency as an Insight Salesperson.

Cordially;

Please rate my performance in response to each of these questions on a 1 to 5 scale where 1 is low and 5 is high. Please circle the appropriate number.   Lo   Hi

How comfortable do you feel talking with me?	1 2 3 4 5
How well do I listen to you when we discuss your needs?	1 2 3 4 5
How well do I understand your needs?	1 2 3 4 5
To what degree do you come to understand your needs better in our conversations?	1 2 3 4 5
How effectively do our conversations lead you to new insights about your problems, implications, constraints and potential opportunities?	1 2 3 4 5
How comfortable are you when I ask for your business?	1 2 3 4 5
How effective are the solutions that I recommend?	1 2 3 4 5
How comfortable do you feel referring other fiends and colleagues to me?	1 2 3 4 5

In this section of questions, please circle either Yes, No or Maybe, then explain your answer in the two following lines:

Do you think I have enough knowledge and expertise to instill confidence in my ability to help you gain greater success?

Yes No   Maybe – Please explain:

_____

_____

Do I act professionally at all times in our interactions?

Yes No   Maybe – Please explain:

_____

_____

Thank you for the gift of time spent completing this survey.

APPENDIX 5: THE SMART MANTRAS

A mantra is a word, phrase or sentence that can be silently repeated in one's mind, or said out loud in a private setting, to focus one's energy and to cement an underlying belief. You're invited to try some of the following sales mantras as you embed the underlying beliefs of the "GET SMARTER" insight sales approach.

THIS CUSTOMER, AGAIN AND AGAIN, WITH REFERRALS

Your goal is to get to know your customer so well, and to be of so much value to him or her as a "go to" salesperson, he or she gives you all of his or her repeat business, and trusts you enough to make referrals.

MEET THE CUSTOMER IN HIS OR HER MOMENT.

When you first approach a customer, set aside any agenda you might have to achieve an immediate sale. Instead, make it your purpose to connect with this person, however he or she wants to connect. Begin a relationship by learning about this person, and what goals led to his or her shopping and buying activity.

LEARN THE CUSTOMER'S S.P.I.C.E³.

Before you ever recommend (*or pitch*) a product or service, know the customer's situation, his or her problems, the implications of those problems, the constraints preventing problem resolution, and the customer's expectations, excitement and eagerness to experience what he or she could achieve once the problems are solved. Learn your customer's S.P.I.C.E³. Otherwise, you could be selling the wrong solutions.

LEAD THE CUSTOMER TO NEW INSIGHTS.

In turn, help your client to better understand his or her own needs. Lead your customer to new insights about real problems, the true cost of not taking action, the actual constraints as opposed to imagined constraints, and the new opportunities about which the customer can feel excitement. Otherwise, you'll just be selling commodities and your customers will likely look elsewhere for the best price.

THE FIRST HALF OF SELLING IS ABOUT GETTING INFORMATION.

The first half of the selling process is <u>not</u> pitching your product, services, your company, or yourself. Spend this first half of your selling time getting information about your customer's S.P.I.C.E³. Use a process that causes your customer to understand his or her situation, problems, implications, constraints and opportunities in an entirely new way, and more deeply than he or she did before.

THE CUSTOMER SHOULD WIN.

The best selling is about helping your client to be more successful, not just about selling your products or services. The customer's success matters most. Your own success will naturally emerge as you help your customers with theirs.

THE MOST RESISTANT PERSON TO THE SALE SHOULD BE THE SALESPERSON.

Suspend your selling efforts if you detect any client resistance or objection. Back up and learn about the underlying needs that are triggering the resistance. Only let your customers buy when you both know it's the right thing for them to do. Be the most resistant person to the "sell" and your customer won't have any reason to resist.

PRICE DOESN'T MATTER.

What matters is how you solve your customer's problems, reduce costs, and increase gains. What matters is the customer's S.P.I.C.E³ and providing solutions that improve results. The value of those results should exceed any price the customer would have to pay.

DON'T TALK PRODUCT.

As a salesperson you don't need to talk about your product or its features, and probably shouldn't unless answering a specific customer question. The products or services themselves don't matter. What matters is what your product or services, combined as a complete solution, will do for the customer. Focus on solving problems, reducing costs, and increasing your customer's gains. Talk about the benefits the customer wants to achieve and show how your complete solution will yield those benefits.

SELL TO EASY CUSTOMERS.

The easiest customers are those who previously purchased from you and those referred to you by customers who previously bought from you. Don't disappoint them. Keep them happy by delivering new insights and effective solutions. Stay in regular contact with them. The next easiest are those new customers you help to have an epiphany about their problems, implications, constraints and new opportunities.

MAKE ALL CUSTOMERS EASY CUSTOMERS.

Use a sales approach where your customers become eager customers wanting the solutions you have to sell. Use the "GET SMARTER" sales approach.

APPENDIX 6: SMART TIPS FOR SALES MANAGERS

An insight-oriented salesperson needs a different form of management. Gone are the days of the harangue and motivational speeches. Certainly, we should never see another scene like the one in which Alex Baldwin in *Glengarry, Glenross* attacks his sales group for underperforming.

Insight-oriented salespeople need help in understanding the "GET SMARTER" sales process, the particular skills the salesperson can use to help his or her customers achieve deeper insights about the customer's needs, and how the products and services to be sold can be combined as complete solutions to those needs. It is the Sales Manager's responsibility to assist each salesperson in his or her learning.

Apply these tips and we expect you will have more than a few exceptional salespeople within your team.

TIP ONE: DISCOVER EACH SALESPERSON'S S.P.I.C.E³

Sit down and have one-on-one sessions with each member of your sales team. Have a S.P.I.C.E³ conversation. Ask some of the following questions and use the active listening skills covered in this book as your salesperson answers each question. Draw out the salesperson's S.P.I.C.E³.

- As a salesperson, how do you work, how do you get the results you achieve?

  o How do you greet, approach, and engage your customers?

  o How many of the customers that you approach actually engage in conversations with you?

  o How do you discover your customer's needs?

- What problems do you encounter as a salesperson?

  o How many of the customers that you approach decline to enter into a conversation with you?

- Are you able to turn your conversations with potential customers into sales – some, most, all of the time?
- How many customers that know they need what you have to sell, choose to buy from you?
- How many customers who are only curious about what you have to sell, choose to buy from you?
- How many of those customers who are disinterested in what you have to sell, even when you know they have a need, choose to buy from you?
- How many customers who are initially resistant to buying from you, even though they know they need what you have to sell, choose to buy from you?
- Are you encountering much in the way of customer rejection, time spent with customers that decide to buy elsewhere, sales based primarily on best price, constant competition for the same client's business, any dissatisfaction with your work?
- What percentage of your customers are brand new customers and what percentage of those are referrals?
- Are you working too many hours during evenings and weekends to organize yourself for your sales activity?

- What do you think it costs you as a salesperson when customers don't talk with you or don't choose to buy from you?
  - Out of ten people you approach, how many choose not to buy from you?
  - How much business do you lose when customers don't buy from you, being as specific in your estimation as you can about the dollar amount?
  - What percentage of your time do you feel is wasted on sales efforts that don't lead to sales?
  - How many of your sales fall short of selling a complete and complex solution?

- o Are you making as much income as you would like?
- What constraints do you encounter that prevent you from achieving greater success?
  - o What stops you from selling to those customers who choose not to buy from you?
  - o What roadblocks get in your way of selling to more customers, or selling more to your existing customers?
  - o What do you think inhibits greater sales success?
  - o Which of those roadblocks you think block your success are possibly imagined or self-imposed constraints and not real limiting factors at all?
  - o Which roadblocks, if any, are internal – limiting beliefs about your abilities, attitudes about selling, or resistance to change?
- What benefits would you experience if you could make larger sales to more customers?
  - o What do you think you would gain in personal income if you could sell more stuff to your existing customers?
  - o What do you think you would gain in personal income if you could sell to more new customers?
  - o If you don't win them all, what would you gain if you could improve your percentage of success, approach closer to 100%?
  - o What do you think you would gain if you could have more people approaching you because of referral from your existing customers?
  - o How would you feel about your work if your sales were easier to make?
  - o How would you feel about your work if you were able to help more of your clients succeed because of the solutions you sell?

o How would your family benefit if you could accomplish greater sales while having more time to spend with your family?

o Are you interested in improving and developing your already successful skills as a salesperson?

o Would you be interested in improving your sales skills such that you could achieve larger sales in less time with even the most difficult customers?

o How eager are you to learn what it takes to achieve greater results with a new sales process?

Once you know a salesperson's S.P.I.C.E[3] then help the salesperson to solve his or her problems.

TIP TWO: EXPLORE TYPICAL CUSTOMER S.P.I.C.E[3] ELEMENTS WITH YOUR SALES TEAM

Schedule and hold serious conversations with your total sales team in which you discuss any of the following:

- resources within client situations that integrate well with the solutions offered by your organization,

- the symptoms that point to problems for which your organization has solutions, with a particular search for those significant symptoms that your customers may not typically consider,

- the different problems that your company's products are capable of solving when bundled from within the full range of products and services that your company manufactures or resells, and the products and services available through alliance with other companies,

- the full range of costs that your customers experience, including both tangible and intangible costs, related to the problems that your solutions resolve,

- the constraints that might prevent a client from implementing a new solution and how these can be turned from real constraints into imagined constraints, or otherwise overcome by your solution,

- the minimal expectations that customers typically have about what the solutions to their problems must deliver,

- the much higher and more desirable benefits that could be achieved using your complete solutions,

- the new opportunities that your company's solutions can release for your customers, and

- the different elements that are of value to different client types (*i.e. what do each of individual consumers, couples, families, and small businesses see as most important, etc.*) so your sales team gains sophistication at talking with each client type.

TIP THREE: PROVIDE BUSINESS EDUCATION TO YOUR SALES TEAM

If your retail salespeople sell to business customers in their retail sales environment, arrange for different members of your own corporate management team to sit with your sales team and present what each of these managers sees as his or her main goals, main business concerns, main priorities, and main measures of business success. Issues of importance are different for presidents, financial officers, production managers, and marketing and sales managers.

Have each senior manager postulate what his or her equivalent in customer organizations would see as key aspects of successful implementation of the solutions your own company sells. Have each senior manager teach your sales team the appropriate business language to discuss with each respective manager type. Discuss what business concerns are common across all managers and which concerns are unique to each manager type.

If your retail salespeople do not sell to any small business customers, you might still hold such meetings so your salespeople gain a better appreciation for the significance of their role to corporate success. Make sure your salespeople see how your company is dependent on each salesperson's sales results.

Emphasize how the income derived from all sales covers all of the expenses incurred by the business. Show how the salaries of all other organization members depend on sales success. We suggest breaking this down to show each salesperson what his or her

337

respective share of those expenses looks like to explain why you have certain sales targets in place.

TIP FOUR: HELP YOUR SALES TEAM IDENTIFY POTENTIAL CLIENT INSIGHTS

Assist your sales team to identify the possible insights they could help their customers achieve. Hold a discussion in which everyone attempts to identify the symptoms of problems to which customers might not be attending. Hold another discussion and bring to awareness all of the implications of the problems that might be ignored by customers. In a third, identify possible constraints, both real and imagined that might be immobilizing customers. Then have your team share ideas with each other about the benefits that might most excite your customers if they could believe an ideal solution was possible.

TIP FIVE: HELP YOUR SALES TEAM IDENTIFY THE SOLUTIONS IT SELLS

With your complete sales team, brainstorm the many different ways your company's products and services, and the products and services available through alliance with other suppliers, can be bundled into different solutions for different client problems.

TIP SIX: HOLD REGULAR S.P.I.C.E^3 REVIEWS

Have weekly sessions in which each member of your sales team shares the S.P.I.C.E^3 of one of his or her clients. This will reinforce the requirement that each team member is to have a S.P.I.C.E^3 conversation with at least one client per week. This will also allow some discussion of what could be bundled together as a complete solution for each S.P.I.C.E^3, thereby reinforcing the notion of selling complete solutions, and thereby expanding both the team's awareness of the range of problems that can be solved and the range of solutions they can sell.

If your sales team is too large to have each person present in every meeting, there is an alternative method. At the end of each meeting, designate one salesperson to be the presenter of a customer's S.P.I.C.E^3 at the next meeting. This will cause that salesperson to be very focussed on collecting at least one example. However, to keep the others focussed, tell them that you will also select one person randomly. In this way, two people will present at each meeting.

TIP SEVEN: TEACH YOUR SALESPEOPLE THE "GET SMARTER" APPROACH

Before you send your new salesperson out on the sales floor to sell to consumers, teach your salesperson how you want him or her to sell. Too many organizations ask their new salespeople to learn by trial and error or from only brief shadowing of existing team members. Both approaches result in lost sales, disappointed customers, and more opportunities for your competitors. Teach your salespeople how you want them to sell before you ask them to do so. Teach the "GET SMARTER" sales approach for the best results. Your customer's will appreciate that you did.

APPENDIX 7: RECOMMENDED READING

We recommend these additional books. They also address the requirements of selling in this competitive world. Although terms and principles may differ in some ways, they each address some of the elements of effective insight-oriented selling that can lead to greater success for you, your employer, and your customers.

Bleeke, Nancy. *Conversations That Sell: Collaborate With Buyers And Make Every Conversation Count.* 2013, AMACOM, a Division of American Management Association, ISBN 978-0-8144-3180-1

Dixon, Matthew and Adamson, Brent. *The Challenger Sale: Taking Control of the Customer Conversation.* 2011, Penguin, New York. ISBN 978-1-59184-435-8

Lawhon, John. *Retail Selling (Book One and Two).* Reprint Edition, 1986, J. Franklin Publisher. ISBN 0961673605

Rackham, Neil. *SPIN Selling.* 1988, McGraw Hill, New York, ISBN 0-07-051113-6

Thull, Jeff. *Exceptional Selling: How The Best Connect and Win in High Stakes Sales.* 2006, John Wiley & Sons, Hoboken, New Jersey, ISBN-13: 978-0-470-03728-7

Thull, Jeff. *Mastering the Complex Sale: How To Compete and Win When The Stakes Are High! 2nd Ed.* 2010 John Wiley & Sons, Hoboken, New Jersey, ISBN 0-4-70-53311-0

Acknowledgements

First, I give thanks to those high performance salespeople that showed me how the most effective salespeople tend to work. There are many but I would like to specifically acknowledge the three salespeople who first opened my eyes to a higher order of selling – Ray Kebbi, Harold Lazaro and Todd Bush. When I asked them, they each had a hard time telling me what they were doing that others weren't doing, but their customers knew and kept coming back.

There were specific people who worked with me to develop training videos originally used to train retail sales personnel at our computer superstores and I specifically thank Bernie Spak, Ray Rozicki and Jason Robideau for their willingness to be video taped as salespeople in sales role-plays. Others such as Derek Anson, Mike Stevenson, Tamara Sigrist and Crystal McKee participated with enthusiasm as customers. That act of capturing on tape what I believed the higher performers were doing helped me to better understand key sales behaviors.

I appreciate the many conversations I had with the sales personnel working within our organization. They would challenge my thinking, argue when they didn't think something would work, and tried out the ideas at my requirement. Some did with enthusiasm and proved the concepts worked and were learnable. Some resisted, explaining their reasons for doing so, thereby causing me to find better ways to both explain the concepts and to build bridges between their reluctance and my wish for them to use the "GET SMARTER" approach. I also thank Ryan Watson for reminding me many years later that what I was teaching, even if only in a brief role play in a recruitment interview, made an everyday difference to his work as a salesperson.

The initial work on understanding then mapping out the original GET SMART" sales approach was funded by Softwarehouse (West) Inc., which was co-owned at the time by Hartco Enterprises Inc. and myself. I acknowledge that the funding was significant to the project. This allowed me to formulate my initial thinking and gave me a foundation upon which I was able to expand my understanding of high performance selling.

Deep appreciation is felt for the work done by Katherine Caine and Roberta Carey who each read several versions of this manuscript and gave me their feedback and helpful suggestions. A hearty "thank you" is extended to Kelly Vanderbeek and David Ford, Olympians, Corporate Speakers, and Trainers, who kindly served as models for the cover images. I very gratefully thank Ray Rasmussen for helping me through the relatively painful print-on-demand and eBook publishing processes. I thank Gary Linford, owner and operator of Blackbird Business Owner Support Service for his insightful feedback as a reader of an earlier version of the book.

Lastly, I wish to acknowledge the contribution of Bernie Spak who consulted with me at different intervals during the development of this book. He contributed ideas to the content, made important suggestions as to how the book should be structured, and most importantly provided significant encouragement urging me to complete this project. We both felt the need but he saw it more dynamically in his work. When I would suffer any loss of motivation, he urged me to keep on working. However, any weaknesses or faults with this book are entirely my own.

ABOUT THE AUTHOR

GARY R. FORD, MBA, PHD

After achieving undergraduate and master's degrees in business administration plus a PhD in Educational Psychology, Gary has had a varied career with all work experience leading to his development of sales training programs based on the new Insight Sales approach. He worked as a lecturer in a business program at the University of Alberta. He practiced as a registered psychologist doing counseling with individuals, couples, and families, as well as organizational development work with health, social service, legal and educational institutions. Through this work he developed his listening skills and expanded his understanding of change processes and systems theory.

Seeking practical experience in effective development of his own organization, he then made a radical career choice and operated a retail and corporate sales organization for 20 years, after which he entered his first retirement. Unable to sit still for long, he then worked as a Dean of Business with a start-up Canadian university for five years. Following the death of his spouse of 43 years, he retired again; and used his time to write and develop training materials on Insight Sales and Getting The S.P.I.C.E[3].

Gary knew that the work done to observe then define the practices of the best salespeople was important. However, once he retired from his business, it bothered him that the ideas were not available to the public. He has spent considerable time working to write this book so that more salespeople can learn the Insight Sales approach. Our customers deserve nothing less.

Gary is currently spending his time engaged in writing and amateur photography. You can see his work at www.garyrford.ca.

ABOUT THE CONSULTANT

BERNIE SPAK

Bernie's career as a salesperson began as an eighteen-year-old working in the customer service center of a large furniture retailer. He saw salespeople making a far greater income and begged to be given a chance to sell.

This organization held a once-a-year mega-sale, and offered Bernie his first opportunity to work on the retail floor during that sale. Intuitively understanding the sales process and being innovative in his approach, he out-sold his peers on that day, and thereby earned his first full-time appointment to a sales role. He became an avid student of selling, reading everything he could and taking courses from various sales guru's. He ultimately built his own sales approach with a personal commitment to selling with integrity.

From this position, Bernie migrated to selling services with an extended warranty organization; moved into the role of Director of Sales and National Programs for an organization operating a national chain of computer superstores, a national chain of retail locations in malls, and a chain of corporate sales offices selling technology solutions; worked as Vice President for a company that manufactured merchandising products for retail stores where he introduced their solutions to large retail chains; and after taking time off in the role of "Mister Mom", returned to sales activity in a role as Senior Account Executive for a large warranty provider selling products to the communications industry.

Bernie worked on our initial project to identify the skills and behavior of the most effective performers in our sales organizations. He played an instrumental role in creating and developing the sales training program that we rolled out to a national chain of retail stores.

In his work, he encounters many salespeople who want to improve, need to learn a more effective sales process, and wish to acquire more effective skills. He urged completion of this book to better equip these motivated salespeople and to facilitate their learning of the sales approach and skills used by the best of the best.

INSIGHT
PUBLISHERS

Box 2 Site 3 RR #1 South
Thorsby, Alberta, Canada
T0C 2P0
www.garyrford.ca/insight

Other Insight Books Published By This Author

Insight Sales (Corporate)

Insight Sales (Corporate and Retail)

A Quick Guide To Insight Sales

Other Insight Books Pending By This Author

Insight Solutions: Creative Problem Solving

Insight Peer Counseling

Other Published Books

intimate moments: A Haibun Collection